On the Principles of Social Gravity
How Human Systems Work, From the Family to the United Nations

Tobore Tobore

Revised Paperback Edition

Critical Perspectives on Social Science

VERNON PRESS

www.vernonpress.com

In the Americas:
Vernon Press
1000 N West Street,
Suite 1200, Wilmington,
Delaware 19801
United States

In the rest of the world:
Vernon Press
C/Sancti Espiritu 17,
Malaga, 29006
Spain

Critical Perspectives on Social Science

Library of Congress Control Number: 2017948825

ISBN: 978-1-62273-334-7

Cover design by Vernon Press, using elements selected by freepik

Table of Contents

Preface

Everywhere I go, I see the same problems; From marriages, health care systems, to the economy, everything seems to fail. I have never stopped wondering why.

I remember my first exposure to the political system of Nigeria, when I was a little boy, because of the riots and mass strikes that engulfed my hometown of Warri in 1989. Soon after, a coup d'état brought in the military junta of General Sani Abacha. The end of military rule changed little, as corruption and nepotism still dominated the political system. As much as I detested the political system in Nigeria, I learned firsthand from my travels around the world that political systems are about the same everywhere.

In 1997, my dad, my little brother and I fled our house to escape the ethnic war that was engulfing Warri. We had driven only a mile before we met the first roadblock mounted by armed militias who demanded to know our tribe. My little brother and I were too scared to speak. My dad, unsure whether the militias were from our tribe, shouted, "Urhobo! Urhobo!" Luckily the militias were Urhobo, and they allowed our car to pass. We made it the through several other militia roadblocks and finally arrived safely at our house on the outskirts of town. Even today, the ethnic divisions that caused the crisis in Warri still exist and can easily erupt at any time. Across Nigeria, where I spent most of my childhood, ethnic and religious conflicts are common. From conflict between Ile-Ife and Modakeke in the southwest to religious conflicts in the north of the country, many people have lost their lives and property.

During my medical studies in Russia, my classmates were mostly from Sri-Lanka where there was an ongoing civil war between the Tamil Tigers and the government. The tensions between the Tamils and Sinhalese members of my group reminded me of the same problems I experienced in Nigeria. A few weeks after my arrival in Russia, I was the victim of a xenophobic attack that almost caused me my life. I have received unwelcome treatment in many other parts of the world I have lived in and visited and observed racial and ethnic divisions in America. These experiences have taught me that human hostility towards the "other" is not unique to Nigeria, Russia, Sri-Lanka or America; it is the same everywhere.

Over the years, I have met young people with crushing student debt and meager salaries, inadequate to repay their loans. This touched me deeply. Over the course of my travels, I have seen the dramatic effects of different types of immigration policy. My travels around the world have also given me a unique insight into the strengths and weaknesses of different healthcare systems. I have seen people die in Nigeria because of their inability to come up with a mere $150 to pay for an operation. I have seen the positive and negative effects of free healthcare in the United Kingdom, Russia, and Malaysia. In America, I have seen sick people delay medical treatment because of the cost of care.

In Nigeria, the criminal justice is broken. Police and military officers act with impunity. The rich can buy their way while the poor languish behind bars for the same crime. In the United States, I see the same problems with the justice system.

From these experiences and much more, I started to see certain patterns in the way human or social systems work. I realized that just like everything in the universe, some fundamental principles governed all such systems, and these principles determine their success or failure, from the family to the United Nations. My purpose in writing this book is to explain these principles and provide a fresh way for people to look at the different systems we have created. My application of these principles to select systems in America is intended to demonstrate their effect and show that human systems can only thrive if we adhere to them.

Chapter 1

Introduction to Social Gravity

The family, healthcare system, Social Security, schools, the military, community, nation-state, criminal justice system, and the United Nations all have one common denominator; they are institutions created of and for human beings. So, although they may look very different because of their tremendous range in size and purpose, the factors that influence their success and failure are the same. These systems can all be categorized as human or social systems.

In the United States, many social systems appear broken. The political, economic, higher education, criminal justice, and higher education, healthcare systems all seem to be showing signs of strain.

On the political front, politicians from both sides of the aisle seeking office shout the same slogans of change and promise of reforms, only to maintain the status quo once elected. The Citizens United ruling, released in January 2010, which eliminated the corporate and union ban on making independent expenditures and financing electioneering communications, only helped reinforce the idea that the political system is rigged in favor of the rich and powerful (Liptak, 2010). The rise of populist politicians in the 2016 election cycle, like candidate Senator Bernie Sanders and the electoral victory of Donald Trump, is a testament to the deep sense of frustration many Americans feel towards Washington's elites and the entire political system.

On the economic front, ordinary Americans are struggling with stagnant wages and debts. The middle class is shrinking, and inequality is on the rise (Pew Research Center, 2016). According to the Organization for Economic Cooperation and Development (OECD), in the United States, the average income of the richest 10% is almost 20 times as large as for the poorest 10% while the OECD average is 9.6. The United States is now the most unequal of all Western nations, with significantly less social mobility than Japan, Australia, New Zealand, Canada and Switzerland (Förster and Levy 2004). Globalization and trade agreements have changed the job market perhaps forever, with mixed results. The Occupy movement that began on September 17, 2011, is evidence that the current economic paradigm is not working well for everyone.

In the higher education sector, many college graduates are drowning in massive debt with no idea how they can repay their loans. The total outstanding student loan debt in the US is well above $1.4 trillion, and over 44 million

Americans hold student loans (Student Loan Hero, 2017). According to the Consumer Financial Protection Bureau, one in four student loan borrowers is either in delinquency or default on their student loans. For many college graduates, the future appears difficult, and the decision to go college increasingly looks like a mistake.

The criminal justice system is facing its own problems. According to the center of prison studies, the US has less than 5% of the world population, but about 25% of the world's prisoners. Mandatory minimum sentencing laws have caused the prison population to balloon (James, 2016). The recent deaths of unarmed citizens at the hands of law enforcement officers, as well as the killing of law enforcement officers, is evidence of considerable distrust and legitimacy issues in the system. Also, the rise of protest movements, like Black Lives Matter and other activist groups due to criminal justice concerns, is a sign that the system isn't working optimally for all Americans.

In the healthcare sector, there are serious issues of affordability and universal access. The US spends more on healthcare than most developed countries, yet affordable quality care remains elusive for many Americans. Health spending accounted for 17.8% of the nation's economy in 2015: that's $3.2 trillion, or an average of nearly $10,000 per person (Center for Medicare and Medicaid Services, 2017). This is the highest in the world. A survey conducted by The New York Times and the Kaiser Family Foundation found that many Americans face financial hardship from medical bills and having health insurance does not buffer against this hardship (Sanger-Katz, 2016). The Affordable Care Act (ACA), or Obamacare as it is popularly called, was supposed to reduce costs and give more Americans access to healthcare services. Although it succeeded in covering more Americans, it is showing signs of buckling under its own weight. Premiums and deductibles have skyrocketed for most healthcare plans, and many insurance companies are pulling out of its exchanges. A Kaiser Family Foundation analysis estimated that 31% of US counties would have only one insurer in 2017 (Cox and Semanskee, 2016). The future of the ACA looks increasingly uncertain, and quality care for all Americans remains a distant dream.

On the international stage, the threat of a major escalation or war looms. The United Nations (UN), the organization entrusted with managing global affairs, is failing to live up to its duties. Russia's annexation of Crimea, the inability of the UN to resolve the territorial disputes in the South China Sea, and the failure of the UN to act decisively to stop the loss of lives in Syria have clearly revealed the organization is stuck in the past, unable to meet the challenges of the 21st century.

Over time, social systems have a natural tendency to move towards greater disorder, decay, and breakdown. This explains the disorder and decay with social systems in America. This tendency to increased disorder and decay has been described as social entropy (Klaus 1986; Bailey, 1990).

Entropy is always present in a social system. It could be low or high. In a state of high entropy, a social system is characterized by such vices as fraud, waste, inefficiency, corruption, dissatisfaction, crime, financial distress, ethnic and racial tensions, moral breakdown, conflict, discrimination, and all those factors that hamper its ability to thrive. On the other hand, in a state of low social entropy, the system is free of most of the vices or problems that could hamper its success. It might exhibit small or insignificant levels of decay or stress, but overall it functions and operates well.

Every member of a social system can be described as a contributor to the system. The contribution of a contributor to the system entails their input in the system, their burden, competence, expertise, skill, or qualification. There are two types of contributors: primary and secondary contributors. Primary contributors are those at the foundation of the system without which the system cannot exist, and secondary contributors (or third parties) are those who augment the system. For example, considering the healthcare system, primary contributors would be patients and healthcare professionals, and secondary contributors would be private insurance companies.

Also, every social system is characterized by both positive and negative traits. Positive traits such as honesty, integrity, moral uprightness, responsibility, selflessness, judicious spending, literacy, good health, and wealth are beneficial to the system and contribute to lower entropy. Negative traits are deleterious to the system and increase entropy, pushing the system towards failure; examples include quarrelsomeness, dishonesty, violence, drug use, reckless spending, irresponsible behavior, prejudice, selfishness, greed, corruption, poverty, sickness, and illiteracy.

Furthermore, every contributor in a social system has an entropic energy associated with the type of traits they carry. Contributors with negative traits have high entropic energy while those positive traits have low entropic energy. The actions, behavior, and condition of people with high entropic energy tend to drive the system towards greater entropy compared to those with low entropic energy. In the healthcare system, for example, the old and sick and those contributors who engage in fraudulent and illegal activities are considered high entropic. They put more strain on the system's resources than the rest of the population. If a healthcare system becomes dominated by such people, its long-term sustainability is threatened. In a neighborhood or community, criminals are high entropic people because their actions and behavior are detrimental to the proper working of the system. In a workplace or family, a quarrelsome and abusive person is high entropic to the system.

Entropy in social systems is driven by;

1. The dynamism of things and human interests;

   A. From the climate to people's interest, things tend to change over time. People's interests, goals, ambition, dreams, plans, taste, etc. tends to change over time, and this constant change has an entropic effect on all social systems.

   B. Random unforeseen and unexpected circumstances often outside the control and by no fault of any contributor of the system e.g. accidents, natural disasters, death of an important contributor, economic downturn, misfortune, etc.

2. Human Imperfection.

   A. Human negative traits which continuously creates challenges for the system.

   B. Human errors and mistakes in dealing with these challenges.

No social system is devoid of entropy because of the dynamism of things/human interests and human imperfection, and this is why entropy in a social system is never at a point of zero. The best it can be is low.

Change is a fact of life, and it presents a constant challenge for all social systems. Social systems that can compete, overcome the effects of change or spearhead it continue to thrive while those unable to respond to it effectively or overcome the challenge it poses, fail. As the interest, goals, and ambitions of a contributor change, they move on to join other systems that satisfy their interest or goals. For example, people in elementary school, move onto high school and then to college. People move from job to job, move in search of greener pastures, to escape persecution or war, etc. This constant change creates a huge challenge for all social systems.

Also, random unplanned and unforeseen events outside the control of the system arise from time to time, and this has an entropic effect on all social systems. Events such as food scarcity because of drought, epidemic or pandemic, accidents, natural disasters, etc. increases entropy and threaten the existence of social systems.

Human imperfection also poses a significant problem. Contributors are usually born low entropic and tend to acquire negative traits over time. This essentially means that contributors tend to move from low to high entropic states over time. This tendency is influenced by;

1. A person's environment and the company they keep.
2. Negative events and experiences in the course of their lives.
3. Human nature, the need to survive and the pursuit of status.

A person's environment and the company they keep influences their tendency to acquire negative traits. Being in an environment with people with negative traits increases a person's likelihood of acquiring negative traits over time. Negative events in life can influence people adversely causing them to acquire negative traits. Also, due to human nature, people get old and sick over time. In addition, because of the need to survive, and the pursuit of status and glory, people sometimes act at the expense of the system in pursuit of their interest or at the expense of a competing system or group in favor of their own.

Therefore, for any social system to thrive, it must counteract this force of human entropy by adhering to certain vital principles or rules. These principles act as the force of social gravity or anti-entropy that pushes back on entropy, allowing the system to thrive. A social system that fails to adhere to these principles marches faster towards its demise. Even if it does adhere to these principles, emerging challenges and human imperfection presents a constant battle between the forces of social entropy and social gravity. The point where entropy is highest is called the point of maximum entropy: characterized by persistent and severe dysfunction such as anarchy, conflict, anomie, severe financial distress, stagnation, massive corruption, irreconcilable differences, dearth of communication for a long period of time, etc. Once a system reaches this point, it can be described as failed or collapsed and it is irreversible. Only systemic reforms that overcome the causes of the dysfunction can return it to a state of low entropy, and the reformed system is considered a new system.

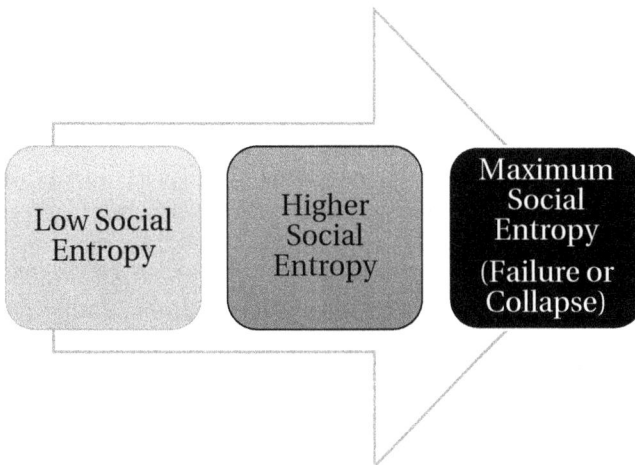

Figure 1-1: Entropy tends to increase in a social system, pushing it towards failure or collapse.

As entropy starts to increase in the system, which of course is a sign the forces of social gravity have been overpowered, it can only be returned to a state of low entropy by restructuring it to adhere to the violated principles. This process is called **De-entropification.**

Below are the nine principles that counteract the force of entropy and act as the forces of social gravity in every social system:

1. the principle of general homogeneity;

2. power or authority of any contributor in the system should never exceed their contribution;

3. benefits of any contributor in the system should never exceed their contribution;

4. all contributors must act within the established rules or laws, and everyone must be equal before them (The rule of law);

5. the law or rules in the system must be clear, simple, and consistent

6. deterrents, or negative consequences, must always be equal to the severity of wrongdoing;

7. negative consequences or punishment in all forms must be confined or limited to the wrongdoer, and not applied to the group;

8. primary contributors must communicate with one another directly and frequently; and

9. secondary contributors (third parties and middlemen) should be avoided if possible.

1. The Principle of General Homogeneity.

General homogeneity encompasses all forms of homogeneity. Homogeneity is one of the most important counteracting forces of social entropy and can be best described as an attractive force that binds contributors together. Homogeneity strengthens the system through the bonds of social capital, social trust and solidarity (Alesina & La Ferrara 2000; Charles & Kline 2006; Knack & Keefer, 1997). Furthermore, it increases group cohesion, loyalty, and overall performance (Costa & Kahn 2003).

There are two dimensions of homogeneity, and one or both apply to all social systems. These two dimensions are commonality (or similarities), and equality. Commonality or similarities imply that contributors share characteristics which allow them to be able to co-exist harmoniously or without problems or conflict. The greater the shared characteristics or similarities between contributors in a social system, the lower the social entropy tends to be in the system. Conversely, in social systems characterized by lower levels of commonality or similarities, there is a greater tendency toward higher social entropy.

Equality, the second dimension of homogeneity, simply means that all contributors in the system enjoy equal rights, access to services, and opportunities. Greater levels of equality result in lower social entropy, and greater levels of inequality lead to higher social entropy.

Commonality, or similarities, goes arm in arm with equality of rights and opportunities in any social system. High levels of commonality or shared characteristics are associated with a greater degree of equality of rights and access to services and opportunities, and the reverse is true. Minorities often face discrimination in social systems.

Furthermore, a social system is either in a state of positive or negative homogeneity. Positive homogeneity enhances cohesion, social trust, social capital and reduces entropy in the system. Negative homogeneity is associated with heterogeneity or diversity which lowers group cohesion (Cohen & Bailey 1997; Webber & Donahue 2001). Also, diversity is associated with lower social trust and social capital (Eisenberg 2007; Newton & Delhey 2005; Coffe and Geys 2006; Anderson & Paskeviciute 2006; Poterba 1997; Vigdor 2004; Alesina, Baqir and Easterly, 1999; Leigh 2006; Glaeser & Alesina 2004; Pennant 2005; Jordahl & Gustavsson 2008; Soroka, Helliwell & Johnston, 2007; Charles & Kline 2006).

The table below lists the traits and characteristics of both states of homogeneity.

Figure 1-2: Differences Between Positive and Negative Homogeneity.

Positive Homogeneity	Negative Homogeneity
Always characterized by positive traits.	Always characterized by negative traits.
Often characterized by contributors who are similar in many respects. (Identity, culture, language, race, ethnicity, wealth, interest, intelligence, skill, income, socio-economics, religion, etc.)	Often characterized by significant dissimilarities or heterogeneity between contributors.
Most or all contributors enjoy equal rights and opportunities. In other words, discrimination and inequality is low or absent.	Significant disparities in rights and access to services and opportunities. In other words, discrimination and inequality are significant.

In larger social systems like a community or nation-state, there tends to be a division of the system into a positive and a negative homogenous group. The positive homogenous group is dominated by low entropic contributors or those with positive traits. In contrast, the negative homogenous group is dominated by high entropic contributors or those with negative traits. Contributors in negative homogenous groups are called odd ones.

In the healthcare system, the old and sick, all contributors without health coverage and those that engage in unethical, illegal and fraudulent activities make up the negative homogenous group. In contrast, the young and healthy with health coverage and all contributors that do not engage in unethical, fraudulent and illegal activities in the system make up the positive homogenous group. In the criminal justice system, impartial or non-biased judges, prosecutors, and jurors; low-level offenders; law enforcement, correctional officers and parole board commissioners with positive traits, make up the positive homogenous group. In contrast, recidivist criminals, felons, and prisoners serving long sentences; prejudicial or biased jurors, prosecutors, and judges; law enforcement, correctional officers and parole board commissioners with negative traits, make up the negative homogenous group.

In the road transport system, contributors that are driving with the right papers or documentation and obeying traffic laws make up the positive homogenous group while those that violate traffic laws and drive without the necessary documentation make up the negative homogenous group. In a nation-state, the poor, unemployed, uneducated, those with criminal convictions, that cannot speak the lingua franca, and those that are discriminated against for one reason or the other make up the negative homogenous group. In contrast, those that are rich or middle class, educated, gainfully employed, free of criminal conviction and not discriminated against in any form make up the positive homogenous group. In the international arena, nations that act outside established norms and behavior make up the negative homogenous group while those that adhere to established rules make up the positive homogenous group.

This phenomenon of positive and negative homogenous group is more often seen in larger social systems than in much smaller ones like a nuclear family of three or four. It can therefore by hypothesized that as the number of contributors increases in a social system, odd ones tend to increase causing a positive and negative homogenous group to inevitably emerge.

In a state of complete positive homogeneity, a social system is characterized by a full positive homogenous group and no odds ones. In a good state, it is characterized by a large positive homogenous group and a small group of odd ones. In a state of negative homogeneity, it is characterized by a large negative homogenous group and a small positive homogenous group.

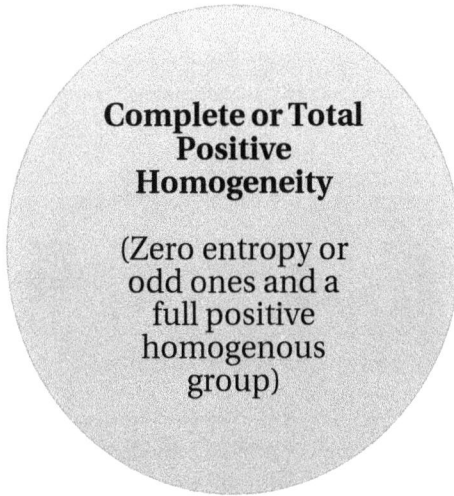

Figure 1-3: A Perfect Social System (Impossible to achieve because entropy is always present.)

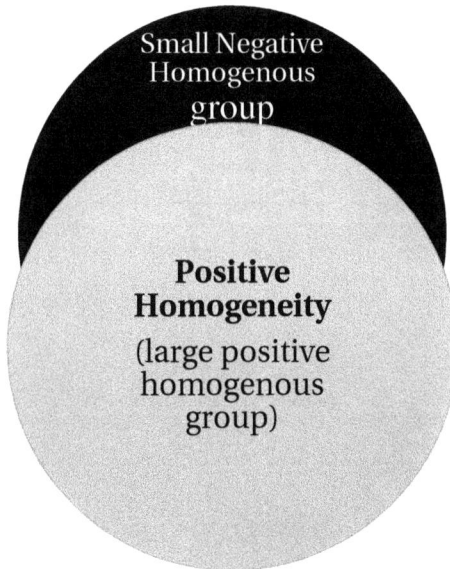

Figure 1-4: A Good Social System

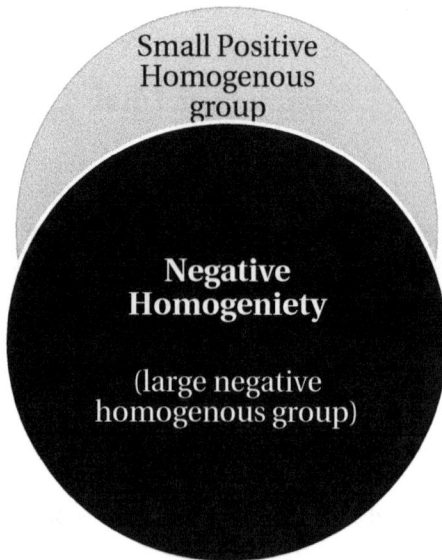

Figure 1-5: A Bad System

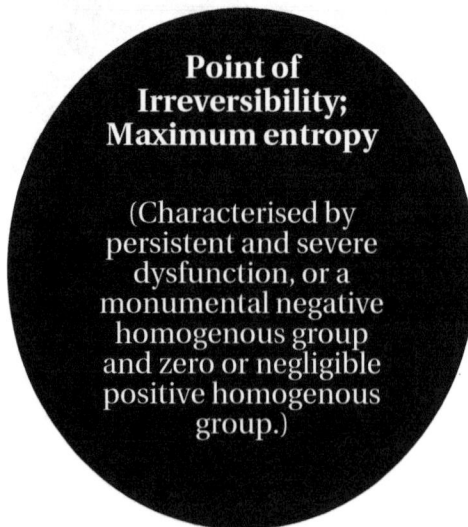

Figure 1-6: Point of Maximum Entropy. At this point, the system is considered failed or collapsed.

Although homogeneity enhances trust and cohesion in social systems, negative traits and differences or dissimilarities between contributors tends to increase over time because of the dynamism of things/human interests and human imperfection. This means there is a tendency for systems to move from positive to negative homogeneity. Therefore, to continue to thrive, a social system must expend a lot of energy and resources to maintain positive homogeneity. This means maintaining the shared characteristics of the group, fighting discriminatory tendencies, and ridding itself of or reforming the odd ones.

As an example, authorities in a nation-state expends a lot of energy to make sure that all citizens speak a lingua franca, and to promote an educational system that ensures the sustenance and continuation of shared values, heritage, or identity. Laws are enacted against discrimination to promote equality, and immigration control to prevent undesirables from coming in.

Organizations counteract this tendency towards negative homogeneity by excluding people who do not share their common goal, interest, values, etc. Admitting people who do not share the goals and interest of the group, threatens its harmony, prosperity, and existence. Many organizations expend a lot of energy in their recruitment or admissions process to get the most suitable employees or members who can fit in with the culture and goals of the organization. They fire or expel members who violate acceptable behavior. All this effort is to maintain positive homogeneity and push back on the force of social entropy.

In a family, to counteract this tendency towards negative homogeneity, all members esp. the parents must expend a lot of energy to maintain positive homogeneity. From reluctance to do their homework, tendency to hang out with the wrong friends, or consume the wrong media content, children are always trying to get out of line or learn values and behavior alien to those of the family. Parents must expend a lot of energy to keep the children in line with family culture, behavior, ethics and standards. This battle of children going out of line and the parents counteracting it by teaching and training them in the culture and values of the family is one the family must win to keep it thriving.

In a marriage or friendship, to counteract this tendency towards negative homogeneity people expend a lot of energy to look for a partner with shared values, ideals, culture, interests, goals, etc. Differences and negative traits tend to increase in every relationship over time. From changes in financial fortunes, interests, and health status, every relationship must be able to withstand this constant negative force of entropy if it is to thrive. If differences become unbridgeable, the relationship gradually slides into negative homogeneity, and then failure.

In a neighborhood or community, to counteract the tendency towards negative homogeneity people tend to segregate themselves along the lines of race, ethnicity, culture, religion, tribe, national origin, and so on. New arrivals are treated with suspicion and even hostility if they do not fit. As a neighborhood becomes more associated with negative traits, or more dissimilar, people tend to move out to other neighborhoods dominated by similar others, in part to counteract the force of social entropy.

There are two prevailing theories about heterogeneity or diversity; contact and conflict theory. Contact hypothesis argues that as people encounter those who are unlike themselves, they overcome their initial concerns and ignorance and trust between them grow over time. It suggests that heterogeneity dissolves in-group/out-group differences, and lowers ethnocentrism (Stouffer 1949; Allport 1954). On the other hand, conflict theory argues that when people are brought in physical proximity with people of another race or ethnic background, they tend to stick to those who are like themselves and distrust the "other". It suggests that heterogeneity makes the in-group/out-group differences more pronounced, strengthens in-group bonding and increases ethnocentrism (Quillian 1995, 1996; Brewer & Brown 1998; Blumer 1958; Giles & Evans 1986; Blalock 1967; Taylor 1998; Bobo & Tuan 2006).

Although they seem diametrically opposed to each other, they are essentially saying the same thing. At the center of both arguments are differences or dissimilarities. Contact theory argues that contact can make people see past their perceived differences while conflict theory argues that it makes them self-segregate. Self-segregation results in isolation or lack of regular and positive contacts, and this makes the differences between groups to remain or even grow. However, if efforts are made to reduce the differences or dissimilarities between contributors, then trust and social capital can grow and become established. So, in a nutshell, by reducing the differences between contributors in a system, it can gradually be made to achieve positive homogeneity over time. The process of reducing the differences between contributors in any social system is called homogenization.

Homogenization can be achieved by promoting contacts between groups, equality, inclusion, fair representation, and integration. Efforts to move people from the negative to the positive homogenous group through programs like affirmative action can help in this direction. Laws against discrimination, the introduction of a lingua franca, single educational curricula, promotion of interethnic or interracial marriage and other integration efforts can also help to homogenize a system.

In ethnically diverse Nigeria, in efforts to homogenize the system, the federal government introduced the federal character principle and the national youth service corps (NYSC). The NYSC scheme is to ensure that youths are exposed to the culture of people in different parts of the country outside their ethnic group. Its goal is to build a trans-ethnic consciousness and help unify the country. The scheme is not without problems, but it has been helpful in creating a more unified Nigeria (Udende and Salau, 2012).

In ethnically and racially diverse Malaysia, the One Malaysia policy is an effort to homogenize the country by creating an integrated society in which all citizens regardless of race, religion or creed share a feeling of unity and solidarity (Wan Norhasniah, 2011). India's "reservation policy" which is designed to help members of disadvantaged groups by using a quota system for public jobs, places in publicly funded colleges and in most elected assemblies is an effort to homogenize the country. In the United States, desegregation, decriminalization of interracial marriages and other integration efforts are efforts at homogenizing the country. These policies have helped to create a richer American identity and helped liberalize white Americans opinions about many racial issues (Schuman, Steeh, Bobo, & Krysan, 1997). Also, it has reduced racial prejudice and discrimination from virulent to subtle (Sears, 1988). In Myanmar, failure to homogenize the country has seen the rise of violence in the state of Rakhine. Discrimination and exclusion of Rohingya minorities has increased the entropy in the country, and unless efforts are made at homogenization, the country cannot reach its full potential (Kipgen, 2013).

For a marriage or relationship in negative homogeneity, homogenization can be applied to find common ground between contributors. Efforts at bridging differences, finding ways for all contributors to tailor their behavior and actions appropriately can help homogenize a relationship and hold it together. In a health care system, training healthcare professionals' to be culturally competent and provision of subsidies or tax credits to help the poor and needy purchase health coverage are efforts to homogenize the system. Restructuring the police force so that its officers are representative of the community they serve is an effort to homogenize it. Homogenization can he applied to any social system in negative homogeneity to reduce the entropy in it.

The principle of homogeneity holds true for all social systems. No social group can survive when the differences or dissimilarities between contributors become too great or when negative traits become pervasive.

2. The Power or Authority of any Contributor in the System Should Never Exceed Their Contribution.

Power and contribution must always be equal or matched. In other words, a person's input, burden, experience, competence, or qualification must be the only basis by which power or authority is entrusted to them in the system.

This principle is very important to maintain the stability and optimal functioning of any system.

There is a tendency for power and contribution to be unequal or mismatched, and many social systems expend a lot of energy and resources to counteract this tendency. For example, parents only earn the authority or power to oversee their child's affairs if they are competent to do so. Child protection services remove children from homes where the parents are incompetent to care for them. Entrusting authority to unqualified or incompetent parents could lead to serious negative consequences for such children that could reverberate negatively to other social systems in which they would become contributors in the future. Child protection services help counteract the increased entropy that emanates when competence and power are unequal.

In a political system, the use of free and fair democratic elections is an effort to choose the most qualified or competent person for political office. The vetting and interviewing of candidates for a position is an effort to match qualification with power. The accreditation of universities to earn the power to issue certificates and diplomas to students is an effort to match competence or qualification with authority or power. If colleges can issue certificates and diplomas without a strong accreditation process, quality will drop with significant negative consequences.

Furthermore, in an effort to match the burden or input with power or authority, every individual is given the rights or power to ownership of what they have worked for or acquired through certain acceptable means. For instance, a person who purchases a car from a dealership assumes authority over the car. No one, regardless of authority or place, can take it away from them or assume power over it. A property owner does not pay rent to someone who leases their property, and a business owner cannot be fired by his or her employees. A person who toils to invent a machine must have rights or power over the invention. Parents must have authority over their children, albeit for a period of time. Also, owners or rights holders have the power or right to sell what belongs to them, or give it away to anyone of their choosing.

Matching contribution to power is crucial to holding any social system together. The further away from the point where contribution and power meet, the greater will be the social entropy in the system.

3. Benefits of Any Contributor in the System Should Never Exceed Their Contribution.

Benefits and contributions must always be equal. In other words, a person should never get a benefit or reward that exceeds their input, burden, value, competence, skill, or qualification. This principle is very important to maintain the financial stability and optimal functioning of any system. The further away the point where contribution meets benefit, the greater will be the social entropy in the system. There is a tendency for benefit and contribution to be unequal or mismatched, and for any social system to thrive, it must counteract this tendency.

A customer of a bank cannot withdraw more than what they have deposited into their account or what they have deposited plus interest (depending on the type of account). If they do so, the bank would be in the red in no time and go out of business. To stay in business, banks match benefits to contribution by investing in technologies to ensure a customer's withdrawal does not exceed what they are entitled to. Furthermore, in efforts to match benefits and contribution, the United Kingdom's National Health Service recently introduced identity checks and payment to overseas patients to claw back 500 million pounds it loses annually from treating overseas patients (Ross, 2017). In the realm of higher education, the use of examinations or testing to determine who is admitted, rejected, and allowed to pass or fail, represent efforts to ensure that benefits and contribution are matched. Students are not allowed to graduate from a course unless they have fulfilled all requirements and demonstrated sufficient knowledge of the course. If people with insufficient knowledge are allowed graduate, then mediocrity triumphs, with significant negative consequences.

Anti-doping efforts and anti-doping agencies in sports represent efforts to make sure that the hard working, or most qualified, are rewarded accordingly. Without such efforts, the entire system would collapse. In the workforce, periodic evaluations of employees to increase pay based on performance, while cutting the pay, demoting or firing those with poor records, are efforts to match benefit with contribution. The use of credit scores and history to determine who qualifies for a loan or credit card, and how much they should receive, is an effort to match contribution and benefit. The 2008 Wall Street crash happened in part because of irresponsible mortgage lending to "subprime" borrowers with bad credit histories who couldn't repay them (The Economist, 2013). This was a failure to match benefit and contribution

A person who invents or creates a product should enjoy the benefits of their hard work and sacrifice. The use of trademark, property rights, intellectual rights protection, etc. represent efforts to ensure that benefits and contribution are matched. Also, valuation companies are created to determine the actual price of a product or property, wine authentication experts to determine true value or worth of fine and rare wine, stock markets and exchanges where market forces of demand and supply determine price are created, to ensure that benefits and contribution are matched. All these are all efforts to counteract the force of entropy.

4. All Contributors Must Act Within the Established Rules or Laws, and Everyone Must Be Equal before Them (Rule of Law).

The action and behavior of all contributors in any social system must be guided by rules or laws, and no one should act outside of them. In other words, no contributor should act without or outside the imprimatur of the established and agreed rules or laws, and all contributors must be equal before them regardless of authority, race, religion, ethnicity, socioeconomic status, etc. The principle of the rule of law is crucial in holding any social system together, for when the rule of law is not upheld, dissatisfaction reigns and people work to undermine the system.

In every social system, contributors tend to want to break or subvert the rules to gain an advantage. To counteract this tendency, a government or some form of authority to uphold and enforce the laws or rules is necessary for every social system. Negative consequences like shunning, banishment, expulsion, shaming, imprisonment, etc. are also necessary to make people act within the law or rules of the group. In addition, culture, value systems, ethics, and education are invented to make people act within the law or rules. Religion flourishes for the same reason.

Culture inculcates certain values to the individual that influences how they behave in the system. By emphasizing the honor or dishonor of acting in a certain way, it eventually defines the cultural standard. A proper indoctrination for the young, through religion, education, and culture is extremely important in shaping their worldview, ethics, morality, and perspective in order to conform to the needs of the social group. From the family to the nation, social systems expend a lot of energy to educate, train and instill the right values to all their members in order to counteract the force of social entropy and hold the system together.

Furthermore, there is a tendency for the rules and laws to be applied unequally, resulting in a two-tier system that unevenly punishes minorities, the weak, the poor, the vulnerable, and the uneducated. To counteract this tendency, many social systems give each contributor inalienable rights to challenge the law or rules such as freedom of speech, freedom of expression, freedom of religion, etc. These rights are crucial in ensuring that everyone is equal before the law and able to challenge wrongdoing against their person by anyone in authority acting outside the law. Free press, due process, regulatory bodies, legal institutions, checks and balances in the system, a free and active civil society, means of redress, accountability, and transparency are all means to counteract this tendency of the laws or rules towards greater inequality.

So, for a social system to flourish, it must have a center of authority and create rules or laws that all must follow. Further, it must develop a culture and value system that encourages people to stay within the rules or law. Also, it must enact negative consequences or deterrents so that the law is respected. Finally, it must create mechanisms to ensure that the law or rules are supreme, and applicable to every contributor, regardless of authority or creed.

5. Law or Rules in the System Must Be Clear, Simple, and Consistent.

Although rules and laws are important, for them to effectively counteract the force of social entropy they must be simple, clear or well defined, and consistent. The more complex, ambiguous, and arbitrary the rules, the higher the level of entropy in the system. When rules or laws are not simple, they become unnecessarily deleterious to contributors not sophisticated enough to fully understand their implications.

Also, when the rules or laws are vague, or not written with sufficient precision, they become susceptible to abuse or misuse. Ill-defined or poorly worded laws or rules confer too much discretion upon those in authority, and the more decisions are reached by personal discretion, the greater the tendency for unfairness. If the law is ill-defined or has broad applicability, those in authority can use it at their discretion to punish or prosecute those they don't like personally.

Moreover, the more complex the rules or law, the more it tends to contradict itself, opening it to misinterpretation. If the rule or law is simple and clear, it eliminates many vices from the system, from waste to corruption. As laws become increasingly complex, these vices begin to appear, and adding more layers of rules or laws to close one loophole or misinterpretation introduces another

In addition, when the rules or law are changed arbitrarily, the system cannot flourish. Consistency of the rules means they are stable and not arbitrary. Consistency brings prosperity, progress, and stability, while arbitrariness of the rules keeps the system on edge, increasing dissatisfaction, confusion, volatility, and chaos.

Unfortunately, over time the rules or laws in social systems tend to move towards arbitrariness, ambiguity, and greater complexity. To counteract this tendency, many social systems have a redress or appeals system, law- or rule-making body that constantly reforms the rules or laws, civil society to challenge the rules for their fairness and constitutionality, debate, transparency on the law-making process, etc. The battle for clarity, consistency, and simplicity of the rules or law is ongoing in every social system. Any social system that fails to provide a mechanism to address this problem is likely to be mired in corruption, inefficiency, tension, dissatisfaction, etc.

6. Deterrents, or Negative Consequences, Must Always be Equal to the Severity of Wrongdoing.

Deterrents or negative consequences for violating the laws and rules are cru-cial in holding a social system together. However, for them to effectively coun-teract the force of social entropy, they must be equal to the severity of wrong-doing. In other words, punishment or negative consequences must be com-mensurate to the harm the wrongdoing does to the system or threat it poses to it.

In every social system, there is a tendency for negative consequences to go beyond the severity of wrongdoing because finding the point of equality is quite hard. Increased incarceration and harsh punishments are a natural tendency to fight crime or bad behavior. Unfortunately, such an approach may turn out to be ineffective at combating certain crimes or rehabilitating contributors that act outside the law or rules. Harsh or disproportionate pun-ishment could damage a contributor psychologically and cause personality problems such as anxiety and helplessness (Engfer and Schneewind, 1982). Harsh punishment that does not recognize and consider the underlying fac-tors of bad behavior results in the waste of system resources both human and financial. Also, it results in apathy, dissatisfaction, resentment, fear and flight or desertion, threatening group cohesion. On the other hand, light punish-ment for certain crimes fails to serve as an adequate deterrent and emboldens bad actors. The need, therefore, to match the severity of wrongdoing to nega-tive consequences is essential to create a stable and thriving system.

7. Negative Consequences or Punishment in any form Must Always be Confined or Limited to the Wrongdoer, and Not Applied to the Group.

Although negative consequences or punishment are necessary to hold a social system together, for them to effectively counteract the force of social entropy, they must be applied only and strictly to the wrongdoer. The extension of negative consequences (hate, violence, animosity, discrimination, rejection, arrests, profiling, etc.) to contributors associated or related to the wrongdoer, is a natural tendency in social systems. Such actions are extremely counter-productive, divisive and are likely to result in alienation, feelings of marginali-zation, anger, distrust, and could even lead to violence. To counteract this tendency, most social systems promote the integration of different groups, a culture of zero tolerance towards all forms of discrimination, bigotry or hate speech, law enforcement accountability, education through the media and schools, and antidiscrimination laws.

Moreover, to ensure a stable system, efforts must be expended to promptly identify and punish an erring contributor. For example, to simply punish all the students in a classroom or those at a particular area of the class because an unidentified student threw a stone at the teacher is counterproductive and destabilizing. In the same vein, a military campaign that indiscriminately kills people who are not enemy combatants because of their tribe, race, religion or other forms of association to the rebellion results in hatred, anger, and alienation. Such actions end up swelling the ranks of the rebellion, thus, worsening the situation. So, to achieve and maintain a stable system, the extension of punishment in any form to a contributor or group of contributors because of an association with the wrongdoer must be vigorously counteracted and avoided regardless of the magnitude or severity of the wrongdoing.

8. Primary Contributors Must Communicate or Interact with One Another Directly, and Frequently.

Although it is important for all contributors to communicate frequently, it is particularly important that primary contributors communicate regularly and directly with each other. Without direct and frequent communication between primary contributors, the system falls apart. Lack of frequent and direct communication weakens any sense of togetherness and reduces collaboration and quick resolution of misunderstandings. Also, it heightens tension and pushes primary contributors further apart. This threatens the viability and stability of the system.

Importantly, events tend to push primary contributors apart and hinder their direct and regular interaction. In a family, for example, everything from stress on the job to travel pushes spouses apart. For children, from moving to another town for college, marrying, and having arguments about one thing or the other, events are always pushing them from direct communication with their parents and siblings. In an organization, employee or interdepartmental competition for resources and glory tends to push contributors apart, restricting direct and frequent communication. Even in the international arena, competition and rivalry between nations tend to push them apart from communicating frequently and directly.

To counteract this tendency, organizations require regular contacts and meetings. Families do the same through regular vacations, dinner together, etc. In the international arena, nations open embassies and send envoys or ambassadors to keep channels of communication open. Furthermore, the use of post mail, electronic media, and other means of communication are efforts to counteract the force of entropy that could easily overwhelm a system in the absence of direct and frequent communication. Social systems that neglect to create an effective means to achieve this or expend the necessary energy and resources to ensure it will eventually fail.

9. Secondary Contributors (Third Parties and Middlemen) Should Always Be Avoided if Possible.

Primary contributors should always interact directly, without any secondary contributor or third-party interference. Many years ago, healthcare was strictly a doctor-and-patient affair. Today, the government and private insurance companies play a huge role in healthcare. The same trend can be seen in the higher education sector.

When third parties are avoided or when things are done in-house, the system tends to work better overall. Cases of overutilization, waste, abuse or fraud are reduced (Buff and Terrell, 2014), conflicts are resolved quickly, image and quality control issues are absent, loss of sensitive materials is avoided, mistakes or errors are quickly noted and corrected, the interests of primary contributors are better served, and so much more. The benefits of avoiding third parties are too numerous to mention. However, there are times when they are necessary for a system. They may be employed in a system if:

- doing it in-house will be at a disadvantage or if one or more primary contributors is or will be at a disadvantage that cannot be overcome;

- there is insurmountable tension between one or more primary contributors;

- it will ensure the stability, security, safety, and optimal operation of the system;

- it will strengthen the rule of law in the system; or

- it will increase or enhance accountability, transparency, quality control and promote fairness in the system.

If a primary contributor would be at a disadvantage in a direct interaction with another primary contributor in a social system, a third party or secondary contributor could be introduced. For example, health insurance companies are third parties in the healthcare system. Due to the high cost of care, they are introduced into the system to help most patients overcome this disadvantage. Similarly, instead of doing it in-house, a small company could outsource payroll processing, accounting, distribution, and many other important functions to an independent third-party firm because they are at a cost disadvantage. Larger companies outsource some things to third parties, especially information technology (IT) needs, to cut costs and to focus on their core competencies.

Also, a third party or secondary contributor could be introduced in a social system when there is insurmountable tension between primary contributors. In this case, a third party could be in the form of an arbitrator to help resolve differences between them. Law enforcement officers, religious authorities, and extended family members are all third parties in a nuclear family unit that could help resolve differences. The Equal Employment Opportunity Commission (EEOC) is a necessary third party in a dispute between an employer and an employee. Direct communication between both parties would most likely resolve the problem more quickly and inexpensively, but the tension and bad blood between them may make such arrangement impossible.

A third party or secondary contributor could also be introduced if one or more contributors have become too powerful such that the stability and progress of the system could be undermined. Anti-monopoly regulatory bodies are examples of third parties that could stop a company from becoming too powerful and prohibiting fair competition. They keep competition and innovation alive and remove the system from the danger of being subject to the whims and dictates of a powerful contributor. Also, a third party could be necessary to maintain the rule of law. The Securities and Exchange Commission (SEC), a third-party organization, oversees the financial industry and makes sure that all contributors are working within the law. They are necessary for the financial industry to keep the system from falling apart. Third parties could also be introduced to increase accountability and fairness in a system. This point is particularly important in the investigation of allegations of wrongdoing against a person. Independent investigators could be introduced in an internal investigation to remove any sense of partiality, lack of objectivity, and unfairness.

However, if the system can find a way to keep direct interaction between primary contributors without any disadvantage to any of them, it would work better overall. For this reason, all efforts must be exhausted to see if third parties can be avoided, with a focus on introducing them only if and when it is necessary to do so.

Exceptions

Although these nine principles are vital to every social system, there are rare occasions when a violation of one or more of these principles may result in lower instead of higher social entropy in the system. Affirmative action in university admissions violates the principle that benefit and contribution should be matched, because it gives preference to qualified minorities in favor of more qualified people from groups considered to be better off educationally. This program represents an effort to homogenize the system since its intention is to increase the number of minorities who are mostly in the negative homogenous group into the positive homogenous group and it is good for the system in the long term.

The rule of law can be violated on rare occasions. Post-Apartheid South Africa and post-war Rwanda violated the rule of law by choosing not to prosecute all the wrongdoers in order to promote national healing. This strategy was helpful for the system overall after many years of war and turmoil. Allowing illegal immigrants to apply for drivers' license violates the rule of law but it could help to homogenize the system by pulling them from the negative to the positive homogenous group. This effort also helps to equalize power or authorization to drive on the road and contribution (competence) and could go a long way in reducing the number of high entropic drivers on the road. Nevertheless, it is ultimately the best-case scenario for a social system to adhere to these principles.

These nine principles can be used to understand the flaws in any social system and applied to fix entropic events in the system. De-entropification which is the process of employing these principles to achieve that can be used to correct small and major flaws in any social system, regardless of its size or purpose, from the family to the criminal justice system. The healthcare industry, which is facing problems of high cost, quality, and access, can be "de-entropified" for the better. The criminal justice system, currently characterized by racial disparities and mass incarceration, can be understood and de-entropified to become a better system. The higher education system, which is now characterized by huge student debt, can be de-entropified to work better for all contributors. Social Security and pension funds, and even the United Nations, can all be de-entropified for the better. De-entropification allows for very smart and creative solutions to both simple and complex problems in social systems.

Figure 1-7: De-entropification Application Framework

Principles of Social Gravity	General Application	Exact situations for application.	Possible ways to achieve this
Principle of General Homogeneity.	1.Homogenization.	1. When there are significant differences or disparities between contributors in a system and eliminating these differences will improve its performance, functioning, effectiveness, efficiency, quality or standard.	1. Promoting integration of the different groups through intermingling, intermarriage, integrated schooling, integrated neighborhoods, etc. 2. Mandatory national service or alternative civilian service to increase contact between the different groups. 3. Create a new and more encompassing identity that integrates the identity of all contributors to unify them e.g. general recognition and celebration of the religious or ethnic festivals of the different groups. 4. Affirmative action, subsidies, and welfare to help people from the negative homogenous group move into the positive homogenous group. 5. Prohibit contributors from being members of competing organizations or groups to ensure an undivided loyalty and strengthen group identity. For a nation-state, this means the abolition of dual citizenship. 6. Create or introduce a lingua Franca. 7. Introduce a uniform clothing to all contributors to promote a sense of oneness or togetherness. 8. Strengthen group identity by introducing hand gestures, greetings, signs, symbols etc. that are unique to the group. 9. Ban speech or conduct that promotes division, hate or may incite violence. 10. Ensure a fair and balanced media or information that contributors consume. 11. Cultural competency training. 12. Create and celebrate heroes and heroines whose deeds and actions promote and strengthens the values shared by all contributors.

1

			2. When there is a lack of uniformity in decision making, method of operation etc. between contributors or group of contributors in the same system and uniformity would significantly optimize or improve the performance of the system.	1. Standardizing the methods of operation, or processes etc. to achieve uniformity across the board. 2. Centralize the system to increase cohesion, efficiency and improve decision making.
		2. Positive homogeneity.	1. To maintain positive homogeneity.	1. Maintain a lingua Franca. 2. Maintain a standard educational system and curricula. 3. Restriction of admission to only those that share the values, interest, goals, etc. of the group and are able and willing to contribute to its advancement or are qualified to join the positive homogenous group. 4. Maintain a group culture and expel or punish those that violate the norms, code, and values.
		3. To achieve system effectiveness, efficiency, and harmony.	1. When there are significant differences in need, skill, goals, condition, culture, capacity, interest, etc. amongst the contributors in the system and splitting it will increase efficiency and performance. 2. When uniformity of operation, decision making etc. is a hindrance to the harmony, effectiveness and maximum development of the different groups or entities that makeup the system.	By decentralizing or splitting the system into homogenous subgroups. In a nation-state, this can be achieved by creating a federation of states. For a corporation or business, this can be achieved by splitting it into separate independent entities under a parent company.
2	Power should never exceed or go beyond contribution.	To fix a system where power is wrongly or poorly assigned.	1. When power or authority of one or more contributors is unequal to their input or burden. 2. When power or authority is given to the unqualified or, incompetent.	1. Restructuring the power structure to ensure that the power and contribution of all contributors are equal. 2. Put mechanisms in place to ensure that each contributor's power is equal to their contribution.
3	Benefits should never exceed or go beyond contribution.	To fix a system where benefit is haphazardly or poorly distributed.	1. When benefit or reward is unequal to the input or burden of a contributor. 2. When benefits or reward is unequal to the skill, competence or qualification of a contributor.	1. Restructuring the benefits system to ensure that the benefit of all contributors is equal to their contribution. 2. Put or create mechanisms to ensure that each contributor's benefit or reward is equal to their input/burden.

4	All contributors must act within the established rules or laws, and everyone must be equal before them (The rule of law).	1. To ensure equality of all contributors before the law.	1. When the rules or laws fails to ensure that all contributors regardless of authority are equal before the law or rules.	1. Restructuring the system to ensure that the equality of all contributors before the law or rules.
		2. To ensure order and stability of the system.	1. When the system is in a state of disorder or when existing laws or rules are not adequately enforced.	1. Enforce existing laws or come up with new ones and enforce them to ensure that order returns to the system. 2. Introduce or create a positive values system or culture that imbibes in all contributors the need to act within the law or rules, and that attaches honor to following the rules and dishonor to disobeying them. 3. Create a form of authority or strengthen the powers of the existing one so that it can maintain law and order. 4. Install equipment or recording devices to monitor contributors in real time and make them aware of this so that they act within the law or rules. 5. Create heroes and villains or enemies for the group. Teach contributors to hold the hero in high esteem and model their behavior like them but should never associate or followed the footsteps of the villain or enemy.
			2. When there is a cultural, socioeconomic, sociocultural or health problem etc. that causes a contributor or large number of contributors to act outside the law or rules and negative consequences are unable to remedy the situation.	1. Create or introduce an intervention program to address the health, social, economic, socioeconomic, cultural or sociocultural issues. 2. Address the grievances of the group if their behavior is due to systemic marginalization or other forms of unfair treatment. 3. Install equipment or recording devices to monitor contributors in real time and make them aware of this so that they act within the law or rules. 4. Increase training and education to achieve greater compliance with the rules or laws.
		3. To ensure consistency in application of the law.	When there is inconsistency in application of the laws or rules.	1. Introduce more competent and impartial contributors to enforce the rules or laws. 2. Ensure that the training of those contributors enforcing the rules/laws are same or the same contributors enforcing the rules/laws are present in all occasions in which the rules or laws are being enforced.

5	Negative consequences must be equal to the severity of wrongdoing.	To ensure the stability of the system.	1. The negative consequence fails to sufficiently deter high entropic contributors.	1. Raise or increase the consequences to match the harm caused by the wrongdoing to the system such it can deter high entropic contributors and stabilize the system.
			2. The negative consequence is excessive for the wrong doing such that it creates more problems in the system or it excessively punishes a low entropic contributor for a wrongdoing committed by mistake.	2. Refine the negative consequences to be more effective, and proportionate to the wrongdoing so that its purpose is not defeated.
			3. To correct a situation where the negative consequences unfairly affect some contributors more than others for the same wrongdoing.	3. Refine the situation to ensure that the negative consequence for a wrongdoing is the same for all contributors regardless of socioeconomic status or place, race, ethnicity, etc.
6	Rules or laws should be simple, clear and consistent.	To adjust or refine the rules or laws to ensure their effectiveness.	1. When the rules of laws are ill-defined or too broad such that they have become susceptible to misuse or misinterpretation. 2. When there are inconsistencies in the rules or laws. 3. When the rules or laws are unclear or ambiguous such that their meaning and implications are comprehensible to all contributors.	1. Simplify the rules to become more well-defined. 2. Refine the rules or laws so that all loopholes and inconsistencies are eliminated. 3. Refine the rules of laws to become clearer or unambiguous and takes steps to ensure that all contributors understand their meaning and implications.
7	Negative consequences or punishment on all forms should be limited to the wrongdoer and not the group.	To maintain peace and harmony between the different contributors or groups in the system.	When one or more contributors are unfairly treated or punished because of their association with a wrongdoer.	1. Introduce laws and penalty against such practices. 2. Proper training and education of all contributors especially those in authority or law enforcement to ensure that every contributor is treated fairly and equally without any regard to their race, ethnicity, national origin, sexual orientation, etc. 3. Introduce laws against racial, ethnic and religious nationalistic or inflammatory rhetoric that can increase tensions or incite violence.

8	Primary contributors must always communicate or interact directly, and frequently.	To create, maintain and promote trust, cooperation, togetherness and collaboration.	1. When there is misunderstanding or the potential for misunderstanding. 2. When there is poor or dearth of communication between contributors in a system.	1. Create forums for contributors to come together regularly to meet and discuss. 2. Improve the means and frequency of communication between contributors.
9	Secondary contributors or third parties should always be avoided and only employed when necessary.	1. To protect the system from external threats and errors. 2. To ensure system efficiency and stability.	1. When doing in-house will be at a clear and demonstrable disadvantage that cannot be overcome. 2. When a primary contributor will clearly be at a disadvantage by dealing or interacting directly with another contributor.	Introduce expert third party or secondary contributor to help overcome this disadvantage.
			2. When there is insurmountable tension between one or more primary contributors.	Introduce an impartial third party or secondary contributor to mediate and resolve their differences.
			3. When oversight or proper regulation is essential to the optimal functioning of the system.	Introduce a competent and an impartial third party or secondary contributor to supervise or oversee the system.
			4 When there is need to ensure the fairness, equality, objectivity or impartiality and transparency of a process in the system. 5 When the system is unable to ensure that the rule of law is upheld or equality of all contributors before the law.	Introduce a third party or secondary contributor to oversee the process and empower them with the necessary authority to do their job.

Chapter 2

The Healthcare System

The US healthcare system is in a state of crisis. For decades, it has been plagued by two tremendous problems: lack of coverage for all Americans, and extremely high costs to both the government and patients.

The Affordable Care Act (ACA), also called Obamacare, which was signed into law in 2010 by President Barack Obama was hailed as a step towards solving these two problems. Since its inception, the ACA has been a controversial law; however, it has helped to close the access gap. The number of uninsured people, particularly in the states that operated their own exchanges and chose to expand Medicaid coverage, has reduced drastically. In 2010, the year that the Affordable Care Act became law, about 49 million Americans (16% of the population) lacked insurance. A 2016 report from the National Center for Health Statistics shows that, in the first 3 months of 2016, 27.3 million or 8.6% of persons of all ages were uninsured; a staggering 21.3 million fewer persons than in 2010 (Cohen, Martinez and Zammitti, 2016). This means that only about nine percent of the country remains uninsured. This is a milestone in healthcare coverage for Americans.

The ACA also appears to have helped reduce overall expenditures on healthcare. According to the Congressional Budget Office (CBO), the ACA made numerous changes to payment rates and rules and repealing it would cause spending for Medicare to increase by an estimated $716 billion over the 2013–2022 period (Elmendorf 2012). Using the 2015 forecast, Researchers at the Urban Institute found that cumulative projected national health spending for 2014 to 2019 had fallen by about $2.6 trillion lower than original 2010 adjusted ACA baseline forecast of $23.7 trillion (McMorrow and Holahan, 2016). However, the law faces several serious challenges that make its future uncertain.

Health spending accounted for 17.8% of the nation's economy in 2015, up from 17.4% in 2014; that comes to $3.2 trillion, or an average of nearly $10,000 per person (Center for Medicare and Medicaid Services, 2017). According to the Department of Health and Human Services, the ACA increased federal spending on healthcare and this was driven mainly by the ACA's expansion of Medicaid eligibility and enrollment. Under the ACA, the federal government has been paying nearly all the cost of Medicaid coverage for newly eligible beneficiaries, and 31 states have so far chosen to expand eligibility. Although, this growth is a 5.8% increase from 2014 which is below the rates of most years prior to passage of the ACA, the cost is still too high and unsustainable (Martin, Hartman, Washington and Catlin 2016).

Furthermore, many people who signed up for 2016 health policies under the ACA face higher premiums, and this is expected to rise in 2017. Across the country, insurers have raised premiums steeply for the most popular plans. Out-of-pocket costs such as deductibles, copays, and coinsurance have also risen significantly in many of their offerings. Some plans have deductibles as high as $5,000, with patients expected to pay their share of $2,500 upfront before any treatment is covered. The increases are often dramatic:

- In Alabama, individual plan premiums will increase an average of 36% in 2017.

- For Nebraskans, the individual health insurance rate is expected to increase 35% on average, with a range of 12% to 50% in the marketplace in 2017.

- For Oklahomans, individual premiums are expected to increase 76% in 2017.

- Pennsylvanians purchasing health insurance through the marketplace in 2017 will pay 33% higher premiums, on average, for 2017.

- In Tennessee, for 2017, state regulators have already approved the highest annual increase in the nation, according to data at ACASignups.net. The state-approved individual plan increases of 44%, 46%, and 62% from Humana, Cigna, and Blue Cross Blue Shield, yield a weighted average increase of nearly 56%.

- In Illinois, the price of healthcare premiums will increase 40% to 50%, on average, for plans purchased through the individual marketplace.

- In Minnesota, health insurance rates through the marketplace in 2017 are expected to soar between 50 and 67%.

The same pattern can be seen in Arizona and many other states (Tuttle, 2016).

Importantly, this price increase does not apply to the vast majority of Americans, who get health insurance through work and who qualify for federal subsidies. Premium subsidies are available to exchange enrollees whose income is between 100 and 400% of the federal poverty level. In other words, eight out of ten Americans buying insurance on Healthcare.gov get their coverage for less than $100 per month because they are eligible for a tax credit. These tax credits increase if insurance premiums go up, so their out-of-pocket costs stay about the same. For Americans who don't obtain insurance through work, and who are not eligible for federal subsidies, the price hikes will hit them hard. According to the department of Human and Health Services estimates, approximately 10 million Americans in the ACA markets, and an additional seven million who buy health plans outside the marketplace, will be most affected by the rate hikes (Department of Human and Health Services, 2016).

Insurers attribute these price hikes to sicker and costlier enrollees they have gained under the ACA, failure of the risk corridor, a key part of the law, and the inability to charge older people and women more. Prior to the ACA, insurers could deny coverage to Americans with pre-existing conditions; ACA rules dictate that insurers can no longer do that. This has allowed sicker individuals, previously denied or unable to purchase insurance to enroll. Furthermore, the ACA forbids insurers from charging older subscribers more than three times what they charge younger ones for the same plan in the same state. While both ideas are very good and must be commended, they have unfortunately pushed up medical expenses for insurers. This rising cost of premiums has undercut the law's popularity with the customers it needs the most: relatively healthy people. Their participation is key to offsetting the costs of sicker people, and as they stay on the sidelines additional upward pressure is applied on premium prices.

The ACA includes an individual mandate clause that compels everyone to have health insurance or pay a penalty called the Shared Responsibility Payment (SRP); however, the penalty is less expensive than the premiums. In 2014, the SRP averaged only $150 per noncompliant person based on data from H&R Block (Williams, 2016). The Kaiser Family Foundation estimated that the average household penalty in 2016 was $969. This is less expensive than the lowest-cost bronze plan in each state, which was $2,484 for the year 2015. Until the SRP is equal to the cost of the annual bronze-level plan, many young adults will continue to stay on the sidelines.

Also, the risk corridor, which was supposed to help struggling insurance companies deal with increasing costs, has proved to be a failure. It was supposed to be a sort of risk-pooling fund among those insurance companies operating within the ACA marketplace exchanges. Insurers who were excessively profitable would be required to put some of those excess profits into a fund to compensate those that were losing excessive amounts of money. It unfortunately, didn't work out as thought, because most insurance companies weren't overly profitable. Many smaller insurers were forced to close. This has discouraged new entrants into the individual market and contributed to the rise in rates.

Another challenge the ACA faces is the declining number of insurer options for consumers to choose from. Several large insurers are leaving the exchanges. Aetna plans to pull out of all but four states almost entirely in the year 2017, due to heavy losses. UnitedHealth Group, just like Aetna, is reducing its offerings to just three states in 2017 from 34 in 2016 due to heavy losses. Humana is reducing its offerings from 19 states in 2016 to about 11 in 2017, while also cutting the number of counties in which it's offering coverage from 1,351 in 2016 to just 156 in 2017 (Haislmaier and Senger, 2017). Even the ACA's healthcare cooperatives are in trouble. Many of the approved co-ops have shut down or announced their intention to do so, by the end of the year 2016. According to the Kaiser Family Foundation, Alabama, Alaska, Oklahoma, South Carolina and Wyoming will have only one insurance company offering plans through the ACA's health insurance exchange in 2017. Nine other states (Arizona, Delaware, Hawaii, Mississippi, Nebraska, New Jersey, North Carolina, South Dakota, and West Virginia) will have only two insurance companies offering plans through the ACA's exchanges (Cox, 2016). For 2018, Aetna will completely withdraw from the ACA's exchanges, and other Insurers may follow suit (Goldstein, 2017). As more and more insurers exit the exchanges, competition is reduced, and the few insurers left will be compelled to take on more high-risk enrollees, prompting them to either raise rates further or exit themselves.

Also, the ACA places a huge burden on employers. It mandates that all plans cover adult children on their parents' policies until they're 26 years of age. In 2015, employers with 100 or more full-time employees were required to provide health insurance to full-time employees or pay a fine. As of 2016, those with 50 to 99 employees are expected to comply. Also, the ACA put a lot of levies on employers. Large employers must pay a Temporary Reinsurance Fee to help "stabilize" premiums in the individual insurance market. There is also a 40% excise tax that goes into effect in 2018 on expensive insurance plans with premiums greater than $10,200 for individuals and $27,500 for families. Over the next ten years, the ACA could cost large employers $150 to $185 billion (Pipes, 2014). Employers are likely to pass along these costs to their workers. Large employers may decide to pay the penalty for not providing health insurance and leave their workers to get coverage in the exchanges, as it makes more financial sense for their profitability. Companies could even decide to push their costliest employees onto the exchanges to save money (Pipes, 2014).

All these problems with the ACA have raised concerns and increased the call for healthcare reforms. In the 2016 election cycle, politicians on both sides of the political spectrum offered different solutions for healthcare. Speaker of the House Paul Ryan unveiled a plan similar to that of Congressman Tom Price of Georgia entitled "A Better Way". Many of the proposals in this plan have made it into the healthcare bill titled "The American Health Care Act" (AHCA) passed by the house of representatives and the senate healthcare bill titled "Better Care Reconciliation Act". In a nutshell, the AHCA includes:

- repealing the ACA,

- abolishing the ACA's individual and employer coverage mandates,

- expanding the use of private health savings accounts (HSAs),

- allowing people to purchase health insurance across state lines,

- providing tax credits to subsidize the purchase of private health insurance and reduce dependence on employer-sponsored plans,

- devolving Medicaid to the states, through a block grant or a "per capita allotment,"

- giving states the option to waive certain consumer protections, including essential health benefits, community rating and age rating.

- providing $115 billion toward the Patient and State Stability Fund for high-risk pools.

Some people on the political left have advocated for a public option to be added to the ACA. Others, like Senator Bernie Sanders, have argued for a government-run health insurance scheme or Medicare for All (also known as a single-payer system) because the ACA does not go far enough. He argues that healthcare is a right, and a single-payer or Medicare for All system will achieve universal coverage at lower cost.

An examination of the different proposals to improve upon or replace the ACA shows that none will achieve what the ACA failed to do, which is to provide both lower costs and access for all. The Congressional Budget Office (CBO) estimates that the AHCA as passed by the House of Representatives on May 4, 2017, would lower cumulative federal deficits over the 2017-2026 period by $119 billion. However, it would cause an estimated 14 million Americans to be uninsured by 2018, 19 million in 2020 and 23 million in 2026. Put simply, an estimated 51 million people under age 65 would not have health coverage in 2026, compared with 28 million under the ACA. This reverses all work done to get more Americans insured in the last eight years, a key achievement of the ACA.

Furthermore, the AHCA tax credits are expected to be the same for everyone, adjusted only for age and not by income with a phase out for individuals with incomes above $75,000. So, the growth in tax credits will not be tied to premium costs, making the credits grow more slowly than premium costs over time. While this would save the government some money, it leaves low-income enrollees to shoulder an increasing share of costs on their own. Under the AHCA, people who are older, lower-income, or live in high-premium areas will receive less financial assistance and have higher starting premiums (Kaiser Family Foundation, 2017).

Also, while the AHCA keeps the ACA protection for people with pre-existing conditions from being discriminated against or denied coverage by insurers, people who do not maintain continuous coverage for 63 days would be open to price discrimination for pre-existing conditions. This means if the tax credit is too small or premiums are too high, such that a person must drop their coverage, then they are open to price discrimination for any pre-existing conditions. This continuous coverage proposal is nothing short of the much-despised individual mandate in the ACA and the price hike for lapse in coverage could discourage healthy people from buying insurance.

Moreover, according to the Kaiser Family Foundation analysis, in 2015, 27.4 million non-elderly American adults nationally had a gap in health coverage for at least several months and 6.3 million of these people had serious pre-existing conditions like cancer and diabetes. In states that apply for the AHCA community rating waiver in the individual insurance market, such people could be charged prohibitively high premiums for up to a year (Levitt, et al. 2017). Also, the CBO Cost Estimate of March 2017 states that about one-sixth of Americans resides in states that would obtain waivers for both the essential health benefits and community rating and this will lower average premiums. However, less healthy people would face extremely high premiums, despite the additional funding from, patient and state stability fund for high-risk pools. And over time, it would become extremely difficult for less healthy people in those states to purchase insurance because of the high cost of premiums.

The AHCA proposes to allow the sale of health insurance along state lines. This proposal is based on the idea that by eliminating different state regulations in favor of a basic federal requirement that applies in all states, insurers will be able to offer national plans with lower administrative costs. Following the rules of a state of their choosing, insurers will be able to sell health coverage across state lines or to any customer regardless of where they live. Proponents argue that this would promote competition among the states, since there would be an incentive to attract insurers. The problem with this argument is that demographics, not state regulation, are primarily what drives healthcare costs. New York has an older, less-healthy population that uses more medical services compared to a state like Colorado, where most people are young and healthy. The result is that it is quite simply impossible to get the same plan at a similar price in both states. Another factor that drives the cost of care is the number of local doctors, as well as the cost of doing business.

Furthermore, selling insurance in a new region or state involves establishing a network. This means setting up contracts with doctors and hospitals so that customers will be able to get access to health care. Establishing those networks of healthcare providers can be hard for new market entrants. Also, attracting enough customers to create a large enough risk pool is another reason why it is unappealing to insurers to pursue this option. This is the reason insurance markets tend to be uncompetitive. Consequently, eliminating state regulations is not the solution because the problem lies with the financial and network barriers to entering a market (Sanger-Katz, 2015). In 2011, the state of Georgia passed a law allowing people to buy insurance from out-of-state carriers. Interestingly, not one out-of-state insurer has sought to participate (Roy, 2012). Another problem with this proposal is that insurers could cherry-pick the youngest, healthiest patients in states with high regulations and this would inevitably drive the cost of healthcare for older, less-healthy people in those states. In time, this would result in a vicious cycle, as sicker and older consumers are compelled to drop their insurance altogether or purchase less-generous out-of-state coverage themselves pushing the cost of health coverage for older and less healthy patients to rise even further. Any insurers left in those high-regulation states would inevitably pressure regulators to loosen coverage requirements to push prices down which will result in the availability of plans that don't cover much of anything (Rampell, 2017).

The use of high-risk pools is not a sustainable solution for Americans in poor health. It is unclear how many will be in this pool, and what the eligibility requirements will be for joining the pool. According to a recent Kaiser Family Foundation analysis, about 52 million adults under 65 or 27 percent of that population have pre-existing health conditions (Claxton, et al. 2016). In other words, about 1 in 4 adults under 65 live with at least one chronic illness that qualifies as a pre-existing condition. The big question is whether all these people will be included in the pool. Even if eligibility is initially limited, it is highly likely it would be expanded over time to cover more sick people and such a pool could consume hundreds of billions of dollars in a few decades. Also, the proposed dedication of $115 billion to fund this pool is unlikely to be enough, regardless of the eligibility criteria, because the cost of healthcare grows too fast. Therefore, it is very likely that this program will face cost cutting in the future and this could put the healthcare needs of people in the pool in jeopardy.

Another proposal in the AHCA is the expansion of healthcare savings accounts. A health savings account (HSA) is a special medical savings account to pay for qualified medical expenses. The AHCA increases the contribution limits for tax-exempt HSAs, from $3,400 for individuals and $6,750 for families to $6,550 and $13,100, respectively. Also, it allows individuals to use HSA money for over-the-counter drugs. HSA is touted as a great way to reduce healthcare costs because the individual is in control of making decisions about their healthcare needs with their own money. Proponent argues that it allows patients to shop around for the best possible care, based on the amount they have. However, information about the cost and quality of medical care can be difficult to find. Also, the unpredictability of illnesses and the cost of treatment makes it hard to accurately budget for healthcare expenses.

One could save up to $100,000 and suddenly find themselves in serious debt because they were met with a sudden illness that amounted to $200,000 or more. In addition, low income earners, people with little cash to spare, and those needing long-term care may find it challenging to set aside money to put into their HSAs. People who are older and sicker may not be able to save as much as younger, healthier people. Pressure to save the money rather than spend it might increase the chances of people not seeking medical care until their condition might have worsened. HSAs places too much financial burden on the individual to carry, and with the cost of healthcare always rising, its place as a serious solution to reduce healthcare cost is questionable.

Under the AHCA, Medicaid coverage expansion would remain in place until the end of 2019. It would fundamentally change the structure of Medicaid by converting it into a block grant, a lump sum rather than a per-each Medicaid patient payment. This will shift costs onto state budgets and force them to roll back Medicaid expansion and could result in millions of low-income people losing coverage or seeing their benefits cut. According to the Congressional Budget Office estimate, the AHCA would cut $880 billion in federal funds from Medicaid in the next 10 years (2017-2026). Lower enrolment would result in 14 million fewer people in Medicaid coverage in 2026, a 17 percent reduction relative to current law. (Congressional Budget Office Cost Estimate March 2017). While these cuts would save the government money, they would ultimately result in millions of people to lose vital health coverage. There are many other proposals in the AHCA but ultimately like the ACA it will not resolve the problem of cost and access.

The Senate's Better Care Reconciliation Act (BCRA) as posted on the website of the Senate Committee on the Budget on June 26, 2017, is similar in many respects to the AHCA. According to the CBO, over the 2017-2026 period, the BCRA would result in a net reduction of $321 billion in the deficit. Although these savings would be offset by the effects of other changes in the law, they would largely come from changes to the ACA's subsidies for nongroup health insurance and reductions in outlays for Medicaid spending which is expected to decline in 2026 by 26 percent in comparison with CBO projections under the ACA. The CBO and the staff of the Joint Committee on Taxation (JCT) estimate that, in 2018, 15 million more people would be uninsured under the BRCA than under the ACA and this would reach 19 million in 2020 and 22 million in 2026. Also, the BRCA would decrease the number of young and healthy people in the insurance pools because it eliminates the ACA's penalty for not having insurance. This would cause premiums to rise. There are many other proposals in the BRCA but just like the AHCA, it fails to resolve the problems of cost and access.

The next proposal is for the addition of a public option to the ACA which is advocated by many on the political left. Some Republicans argue that a health insurance plan run by the government is a bad idea because it will drive all private sector insurers out of business. Those on the left see the exit of insurance companies from the ACA exchanges as proof that a public option is necessary to bring genuine competition to the healthcare industry and save the ACA. If the public option does not have to break even or make a profit, then it must rely on endless government subsidies to keep it afloat, which of course is unsustainable. If it runs a deficit, this might lead to an increase in taxes to cover the cost, and with the cost of healthcare ever growing, that would put it on an unsustainable path. If the government uses its leverage as a very big purchaser to negotiate lower prices with providers, this will give it a massive advantage over private insurers. The public option would likely have lower administrative costs, and won't have to spend money on marketing, further increasing this advantage. This could push private insurers out of business leaving it as the sole insurer.

If it competes on the same terms with private insurers to maintain competition, then its sole purpose is negated. If it simply reimburses lower than private insurers like Medicare, or slightly more than Medicare but lower than private insurers, such a move gives it an unassailable advantage. Hospitals and medical personnel would vehemently resist this option. Physicians might decide against participation, further reducing access for people with public insurance.

Another proposal, and one that is gaining interest is overhauling the entire healthcare system in favor of a single-payer system. The presidential campaign of Senator Bernie Sanders made it a talking point, identifying Scandinavia, Canada, and other developed countries as models that the United States should emulate. Many on the political right see single-payer as government-run insurance and the next thing to socialism, pointing to the many problems with such systems like rationing and endless wait times for elective procedures to articulate their point. Single-payer systems are often confused with socialism, but this is wrong.

Simply put, there are two ways to deliver healthcare: directly or indirectly. The direct method is between healthcare providers and patients without any third party in between. Such a system includes cash-based medicine where patients pay directly for their healthcare needs; membership medicine where patients sign up as members to a clinic or hospital paying a monthly fee; government-owned healthcare systems like the National Health Service in the UK, where the government directly owns the hospitals and pays the healthcare personnel from taxes; and insurance companies like Kaiser Permanente that directly own the hospitals and clinics that its members use.

The indirect method involves a third-party payer. Examples of this kind of system include the single-payer in Canada and many parts of Europe, where the government acts as a third-party payer between patients and private hospitals. Multiple payer systems, like in the United States, where the government in the form of Medicare and several private insurance companies act as third parties between patients and private hospitals, are also indirect systems.

A single-payer system, as advocated by Senator Sanders, would provide access to all Americans and clearly be more efficient than the current US multiple payer system. However, it will not solve the big problem of healthcare costs. First, Medicare, in its current format which for the most part takes care of Americans 65 and older, is already on an unsustainable path and is one of the largest drivers of federal spending and debt. According to Medicare Trustees estimate, gross Medicare expenditures will increase from $613 billion in 2014 to more than $1.2 trillion by 2024 (Centers for Medicare and Medicaid Services, 2015). Gross Medicare spending is expected to increase from 2.6 percent of GDP in 2015 to 5.6 in 2040 and then to 6.0 percent by 2090. Under the illustrative alternative projection, it is projected to rise higher from 6.2 percent of GDP in 2040 to 9.1 percent in 2090. (Centers for Medicare and Medicaid Services, 2016). Moreover, the office of the actuaries of the Centers for Medicare and Medicaid Services estimates that Medicare's 75-year unfunded obligation is 28.5 trillion and using its illustrative alternative scenario that figure soars to $35.2 trillion (Codespote 2014).

Making it open to everyone means many sick people currently in the ACA exchanges and under employer-sponsored insurance would be free to join, and this would increase the financial burden on the government. While taxes from more people would shore up its account in the short run, it would inevitably become unsustainable in the long term with endless tax increases to shore up its account.

A detailed analysis of Senator Bernie Sanders' single-payer (or Medicare for All) plan by researchers at the Urban Institute showed that it would most likely cost the government double what the campaign proposed, and this does not come as a surprise. Their analysis found that under Sanders plan, national health expenditures would increase by almost $7 trillion between 2017 and 2026, and federal expenditures would grow by almost $35.0 trillion over the same period. Sanders's revenue proposals would raise $15.3 trillion from 2017 to 2026 which is insufficient to fully finance his health plan (Holahan et al., 2016).

Also, another analysis by Kenneth Thorpe of Emory University found that the Sanders plan is underfinanced by an average of nearly $1.1 trillion per year, and covering that extra spending would require a combined 20% tax on income (Thorpe, 2016).

The States of California and Vermont provide prime examples that a single-payer system would simply be unaffordable nationally. California's push to enact a statewide single-payer system in 2017 was shelved after an analysis by the Political Economy Research Institute at the University of Massachusetts Amherst estimated the yearly cost would be $331 billion. A legislative analysis pegged the cost at $400 billion — far exceeding the state's entire budget. In 2014, the state of Vermont toyed with the idea of a single-payer system but ultimately abandoned it after the government realized it was simply unafford-able. To fully fund the program required new taxes of 11.5% for employers and up to 9.5% for individuals (McDonough, 2015). This could have crippled the state economically. Even if the government had moved forward with the plan, the cost would likely have skyrocketed over time, exceeding projections. If implementing a single-payer system is financially difficult for California and Vermont, it would be even more daunting to try such a scheme nationally.

The world has changed and healthcare systems, including single-payer sys-tems which have satisfied the healthcare challenges of the past, are unable to meet our nation's emerging challenges cost-effectively. Today, advances in medicine mean more diseases and health problems can be treated than in the past. However, many of these treatments are increasingly expensive. Also, increased life expectancy means an increase in the number of old people in the population who are much more likely to require long-term care. A rapidly growing population, because of either higher birth rates, mass migration, or both, is adding to the increase in healthcare expenditures. Rising incomes, improved technology, and advances in medicine—as well as the explosion of information due to the Internet—have made patients more aware of healthcare possibilities. Knowledgeable patients want the best treatment, even if very expensive. Diabetes and heart diseases are on the rise, also adding to the burden of the healthcare system. These emerging challenges are caus-ing the cost of healthcare to soar, regardless of the healthcare delivery system.

Countries with single-payer or government run healthcare systems are struggling with the cost of healthcare, just like the US, and costs are expected to rise. Health spending over the past 20 years in all OECD (Organization for

Economic Cooperation and Development) countries—many of which use single-payer systems—continues to rise faster than economic growth. According to OECD projections, without cost containment efforts, public expenditures on health and long-term care in OECD countries is set to grow from around 6% of GDP to almost 9% of GDP in 2030, and as high as 14% by 2060 (De la Maisonneuve and Martins, 2013). According to Mckinsey, if current trends persist, most OECD countries will spend more than a fifth of GDP on health care by 2050 and by 2080 the U.S and Switzerland are projected to spend more than half of GDP on healthcare with most other OECD countries reaching this level of spending by 2100 (Drouin, Hediger and Henke, 2008). This problem of healthcare cost is already causing many countries around the world to cut back on their generous single-payer healthcare systems. Many services that were once free are now paid for, and costs are increasingly being passed along to patients.

In France, where the government provides healthcare for its entire population, the cost of care is leading to serious changes to the system. In 2011, France spent 11.6% of its GDP on healthcare, or US $4,086 per capita. Assurance Maladie, French taxpayers' funded state health insurer, which everyone pays into proportionally to their income, has been in the red for many years. With an average life expectancy of 81.3 years, and a steady increase in chronic diseases including diabetes, Assurance Maladie has consistently exceeded its budget by billions of Euros, forcing the government to impose reforms to cut benefits like spa treatments and free taxi rides to the hospital. Patient co-pays have been introduced in an attempt to throttle back prescription drug costs, and state hospitals are being forced to crack down on expenses. Inevitably, this trend will continue, and the cost to patients will increase (Torsoli, 2013).

In China, because of its one-child policy, its population is aging at one of the fastest rates ever recorded. Massive economic growth in the past three decades has increased wealth, life expectancy, and the prevalence of chronic diseases. According to Deloitte's 2015 China healthcare outlook report, China's health care spending is predicted to grow at an average rate of about 12 percent a year in 2014-2018, and reach $892 billion by 2018. According to Mckinsey, spending is projected to reach a trillion dollars by 2020 (Le Deu, Parekh, Zhang and Zhou 2012).

In Malaysia, economic growth in the past three decades has changed the demographic landscape and lifestyle patterns. Life expectancy has increased as well as the prevalence of chronic diseases. These changes require expensive long-term treatments that government spending cannot sustainably match (The Economist, 2014). In the budget for 2014, the government allocated RM22.1 billion (US $5.1 billion) to healthcare spending, representing almost 10% of total government spending. This is projected to increase almost four-fold to as high as USD $20 billion by 2020 (Frost and Sullivan, 2016). Also, according to Deloitte 2015 Southeast Asia healthcare outlook report, Malaysia's health care spending is projected to rise by an average of about 11percent a year, to $22.9 billion by 2018. This is a significant chunk of the national budget.

In Saudi Arabia, healthcare is universal and funded by the government. According to the Deloitte's 2015 Middle East Healthcare Outlook, the Saudi government spent an estimated $35.9 billion, or 4.8% of GDP, on healthcare in 2013. This is projected to rise to almost $50 billion between 2014 and 2018. In the UAE, a sister Gulf Cooperation Council (GCC) country, health care constituted 3.5% of GDP in 2013, but that share is expected to rise. Overall healthcare spending is projected to increase 6.9% a year, from an estimated $14 billion in 2013 to almost $19.6 billion in 2018 (Deloitte's 2015 Middle East Healthcare Outlook). According to McKinsey, healthcare delivery in GCC countries will cost about US $60 billion by 2025, a fivefold increase. The prevalence of cardiovascular diseases, which account for 12% of total healthcare expenditures in GCC countries, is expected to rise by 2025, placing an enormous burden on government resources (Mourshed, Hediger and Lambert). Across the region, governments are cutting back and enacting reforms due to a slump in oil prices. For the first time, many are allowing the private sector to invest in healthcare. However, all these cutbacks are unlikely to put the cost of healthcare in the region on a sustainable path in the long run.

Japan's healthcare system is one of the best in the world but it is under severe stress from its rapidly aging population. It is the third-largest spender on health care in the world after the U.S. and China. In 2013, it spent an estimated $480 billion, or 9.8% of its GDP on health care. Healthcare spending is expected to reach 10% of GDP by 2018 and continue to outstrip GDP growth, putting pressure on Japan's budget deficit and the national debt (Deloitte's 2015 Japan Healthcare Outlook).

In Canada, the cost of healthcare puts the sustainability of its single-payer system into question. According to the Canadian Institute for health information, health expenditure is forecast to represent about 11% of Canada's gross domestic product (GDP) in 2016. From 34.3 percent of total program spending in Quebec to 43.2 percent in Ontario in 2016, it is the single largest budget item for every province (Barua, Palacios and Ames, 2017). Furthermore, according to the Ontario government, health care's share of provincial program spending is projected to rise to as much as about 55 per cent by 2024-25 (Ontario Ministry of Finance, 2005). Using current Canada Health Transfer, actuarial analysis of the Canadian health care system concludes that a whopping 97% of total funds available to provinces and territories will be used on healthcare expenditures by 2037, compared to 44% in 2012 (Canadian

Institute of Actuaries 2013). Put simply, the Canadian single-payer system is not fiscally sustainable in the long term in the face of current challenges.

There is no easy solution to the problem of healthcare cost. A focus on prevention and education to reduce the incidence of lifestyle diseases can only go so far. Also, significant cost-cutting and rationing can be helpful in the short term, but they are not solutions for keeping costs down in the long term. More rationing would only lead to lower access and poorer quality of care. Raising taxes to keep up with costs is not possible because of the limits of what can be taken in taxes before it is met by resistance. The world has changed, and new solutions are needed to provide quality care and access for all, at a sustainable cost. The days where government provided healthcare for all, as a right to its citizens, has reached its natural end because no government can handle the cost of healthcare in the long term with the current challenges. Existing healthcare solutions like Obamacare, Medicare, Medicaid, single-payer, or universal healthcare, are solutions to yesterday's healthcare challenges. They have outlived their purpose and usefulness.

De-entropification Solution.

According to the Administration on Aging, there were 46.2 million persons 65 years or older in the US in 2014. This represents 14.5% of the population, or about one in every seven Americans. By 2040, they are projected to be 82.3 million older persons representing 21.7% of the population. Research shows that most babies born in the US and most developed Nations since the year 2000 are likely to live to be more than 100 years old (Christensen, Doblhammer, Rau and Vaupel, 2009). Living long is not simply a passing phenomenon, but one that is here to stay. This has serious implications for healthcare costs because the elderly tend to be sicker than younger people, thus requiring more care and services, resulting in a significant strain on the entire system. Any solution must take this fact into account.

Although the ACA could be fixed, it is an outdated solution for American healthcare challenges; such efforts would be at best palliative. To create a better system that will effectively deal with current and future challenges of the healthcare system, there are several key principles that should be applied to the current system.

1. Secondary Contributors (Third Parties and Middlemen) Should Always Be Avoided, And Only Employed When Necessary or Unavoidable.

For many decades, the government—through Medicare, Medicaid etc., and private insurance companies—has acted as a third party between hospitals and Americans. Although third-party payers help patients overcome the cost disadvantage they face with the high cost of care, their use leads to overutilization and higher overall healthcare costs. It results in a lack of transparency, accountability, waste, and abuse (Buff and Terrell, 2014). It is estimated that fraud and abuse account for between 3 to 15 percent of annual expenditures for healthcare. The estimated cost of fraud and abuse could be placed at around $100–170 billion annually (Rudman, Eberhardt, Pierce, and Hart-Hester, 2009).

A better approach would be to create healthcare associations, or cooperatives, to establish a direct connection between patients and medical services. These healthcare cooperatives would be non-profit and owned by members collectively to take care of their healthcare needs. They would be run by the people and for the people. Unlike Obamacare cooperatives that couldn't compete with well-established insurance companies, they would directly own the hospitals and clinics their members use and finance their operations from the premiums, co-pays and deductibles of their members. Also, cooperatives would be free to borrow money from the private market to expand and acquire new facilities. To get an operating license, cooperatives would be required to gain a membership of between two to five million people. Members could join across state lines, and cooperatives could open facilities around the country for their members. All cooperatives would be required to cover everything from inpatient to outpatient care; primary care to specialty care, including long-term and palliative care; vision, hearing and oral health care; preventive to emergency care; and mental health and substance abuse services.

Admission to a cooperative must be open to all citizens and legal residents, and no one should be prevented from joining a cooperative based on a pre-existing condition, race, ethnicity, gender, age, religion, national origin, etc.

Key advantages of these healthcare cooperatives

- Plans would be strictly individual or family. This means that membership and thus coverage would be unlinked from employment. Employers will help pay a portion of the premiums or membership fee of the cooperative of their employee's choosing, or the one they want all employees to join, and if the employee leaves their job they retain their membership as long they maintain their premiums.

- Competition between healthcare cooperatives would lead to an explosion of new ideas in the healthcare industry, generating smart solutions for the healthcare needs of members and creative ways to reduce cost. From telemedicine to mobile clinics, different cooperatives would have different plans to meet the needs and financial abilities of their members. Also, due to competition, cooperatives would have different annual caps that a member can spend on premiums, deductibles, or co-pays. Some could even eliminate deductibles or co-pays if they think they can provide services to their members without it. How long a child can stay on their parent's plan would differ between cooperatives, and members would choose what cooperative they join based on the attractiveness and affordability of their offerings.

- Competition between cooperatives would increase quality. A cooperative would only thrive and gain new members on the merits of how well it manages costs, and the quality of its services.

- Efficiency would be increased. A direct link between patients and medical services would significantly reduce fraud and abuse and eliminate most of the high entropic contributors engaged in such activities.

- Since the cooperatives are non-profit and owned by the people and for the people, they would work in the interest of their members. Services would not be arbitrarily denied as would be the case when it is privately owned and motivated by profit making.

- Cooperatives would increase the number of health care professionals in the healthcare system as they invest in health care professionals their members need. According to the American Medical Colleges, the United States faces a shortage of more than 90,000 physicians by 2025 to treat an aging population that will increasingly live with chronic disease. These include primary care physicians, nurses, and surgeons. These cooperatives could fill this gap very well by sponsoring medical students and signing contracts with them to work for them for specific periods of time to cover their educational costs. They could actively seek to bring foreign medical graduates to the United States and help them through the residency programs so that they could join their network of hospitals and clinics.

- Costs could be cut through the exploitation of overseas medical services. These healthcare cooperatives could take some of their services overseas to cut costs. In places like Mexico, Cuba, the Caribbean, Canada, Ecuador, Costa Rica, Japan, the United Kingdom, and many parts of Europe, healthcare services are much more affordable than in the United States. From the cost of prescription drugs to surgery, healthcare in the United States is just out of reach for ordinary Americans. Americans pay more for prescription drugs compared to many countries (Jick, Wilson, Wiggins and Chamberlin, 2012).

Too much demand within national borders is one of the reasons for spiralling costs, and this demand is only going to increase. The recent price hike of drugs like EpiPen, Ursodiol, and Daraprim is only possible because demand is constantly or excessively high. With healthcare cooperatives taking advantage of overseas services, such things wouldn't happen as demand would slow or balance out. This will make the American internal healthcare market restructure itself for the better.

Cooperatives could move expensive services like surgeries, and short-term care of their members overseas. Even accident and emergency situations could see a patient stabilized and flown overseas for a treatment deemed too expensive in the US. Cooperatives would have to negotiate with overseas hospitals to use their facilities for certain procedures. They could even acquire facilities overseas if conditions permit. Cooperatives would provide different plans, and based on ability to pay some plans would cover all services in the US, while others would be both in the US and overseas.

Importantly, this flexibility to move services overseas is one of the reasons healthcare cooperatives would be better suited to the meet the challenges of cost than any universal government healthcare system. This, together with the fact that these cooperatives own and operate their hospitals and clinics, means they will be more efficient and would therefore, be more effective at keeping costs down. Healthcare plans are likely to be extremely cheap and affordable by most Americans regardless of age or health status.

2. The Principle of General Homogeneity.

i. The healthcare needs of everyone are not the same, and a good healthcare system must take this into consideration by allowing for homogenous groups to have their own cooperatives. High entropic groups, like the elderly and veterans, must have their own dedicated healthcare cooperatives since their healthcare needs are different from those of the general population. Most veterans and military officers need healthcare services focused on long-term care, surgery, critical care, mental health services, orthopaedics, radiology and physical therapy, audiology and speech pathology, dermatology, dental care, neurology, podiatry, prosthetics, urology, and vision care, and a healthcare cooperative dedicated to and financed by them will do a better job at managing their affairs. These cooperatives would support themselves from the premiums of their members, and with two or more competing for members, smart and creative solutions would drive membership up or down. Members will be free to join a general health cooperative if they think they will get a better bang for their money.

Health care cooperatives focused solely on the elderly would be good, since the elderly have special healthcare needs. Such cooperatives would do a better job of managing their needs in a more cost-effective way, and with competition, quality will not be compromised. This approach is better than plans to move Medicare into a premium model, as cooperatives could keep costs down for seniors far better than the premium model, which could see premiums, deductibles, and co-pays soar over time.

Also, there should be healthcare cooperatives exclusively for children and for women. Women's healthcare needs differ from those of men, from adolescence to the reproductive years, and through menopause and beyond. Healthcare cooperatives dedicated to women's health would be beneficial to the system.

General healthcare cooperatives would continue to cater to the healthcare needs of all people regardless of gender and age. However, these special homogenous cooperatives are more likely to do a better job at cost control over time. Homogeneity promotes trust and solidarity, so in more homogenous healthcare associations people may be willing to do more for other members. These cooperatives could have annual newsletters or a magazine that highlights the healthcare needs of fellow members, and in more homogenous associations, members are more likely to help those in need of an organ transplant or other health issues than in general healthcare cooperatives.

ii. **Homogeneity: Homogenization of the system to stabilize it.**

The US healthcare system is unique compared to that of other developed nations because it does not guarantee health coverage for all citizens. This creates a situation where there are many citizens and legal residents who are low entropic contributors in the negative homogenous group; young and healthy people with no health coverage. According to the Kaiser Family Foundation, 28.5 million Americans remain without coverage as of 2015 despite the ACA's expansion of health coverage (Kaiser Family Foundation, 2016). This includes millions of both low and high entropic contributors. This lack of coverage creates a big problem for the system. The low entropic contributors are needed to balance or stabilize the system and the high entropic contributors without coverage suffer financial hardship and cause the system millions of dollars in uncompensated care. According to the Kaiser Foundation, medical care spending for the uninsured population totalled $121 billion in 2013, 21%, or $25.8 billion, was paid out-of-pocket by the uninsured and 70%, the majority of expenses were uncompensated, totalling $84.9 in 2013 (Coughlin, Holahan, Caswell and McGrath, 2014).

Therefore, to achieve a stable system, it would be necessary to homogenize the system by pulling the low entropic contributors into the positive homogenous group through the provision of subsidies for them to purchase health coverage and subsidizing the health coverage of low income high entropic contributors who cannot afford coverage. This will reduce disparities in the system, financial hardship and most importantly, help tackle the problem of uncompensated care.

The federal government should provide most of the funds towards these subsidies, in a 70/30 or 80/20 arrangement with states. However, to make it efficient, it should be left to individual states to determine the criteria for eligibility and how much to provide in subsidies. Also, to reduce healthcare burden on the poor (those below the federal poverty line), premiums and select medical and dental expenses should be made tax deductible if it exceeds 5% of adjusted annual income.

3. Negative Consequences Must Be Equal to Severity of Wrongdoing.

With the ever-increasing high entropic contributors (The old and sick) in the system, the system cannot achieve stability without an individual mandate to compel all especially low entropic contributors to get coverage. Therefore, all citizens and legal residents must be compelled to have health coverage, and this must be enforced vigorously.

To make this work, the penalty for not having coverage must match the harm that failure to purchase insurance poses to the system. A penalty that is equal to or twice the cost of the cheapest healthcare coverage must be put in place to make this work and enforced by states since they determine eligibility and criteria for subsidies. To strengthen adherence, anyone (except those unqualified for subsidies who are temporarily unemployed because of a job loss with no alternative source of income) that goes without health coverage for at least six months should face a forty percent surcharge on premiums when they want to purchase coverage and if they fall sick without coverage, this surcharge should increase to as much as 80 percent.

Also, an employer mandate is required to ensure that employers do not take advantage of government subsidies by discontinuing the provision of health coverage for their low-income workers who qualify for such subsidies. The employer mandate would also be enforced by the states. To ensure some consistency, the federal government could set a standard minimum requirement that all states must meet to qualify for federal dollars. For example, that all state health plans cover certain minimum benefits, all states provide subsidies for workers whose income is between 100 and 400% of the federal poverty line and employers with 100 employees or more provide health coverage for their employees. States are free to expand the minimum benefits that all individual and employer health plans must cover and to expand the employer mandate to employers with less than 100 employees or to individuals whose income is more than 400% of the federal poverty line.

In this scenario, some states could have a requirement that employers with 30 or more employees provide health coverage for all employees whether full or part time while another could mandate employers with 90 or more employees to provide health coverage for all their employees. States are better suited based on their finances and economic needs to make this judgement. A penalty is triggered if an employer fails to provide coverage for a qualifying employee and the employee receives a subsidy to purchase health coverage. Employers that fail to provide health coverage for qualified employees would be required to pay a penalty that is equal to the annual cost of the cheapest health coverage in the state and if a qualified employee receives government subsidies due to the failure of an employer to provide health coverage, the erring employer would be required to pay a penalty that is double the annual cost of the cheapest health coverage in the state. Since states are putting up some of the money towards these subsidies, they would vigorously enforce both the individual and employer mandates because it's in their interest to keep their spending on subsidies as low as possible.

Also, immigration policy should be reformed to make it compulsory for all visitors and immigrants to purchase and provide evidence of health coverage before the issuance of visas. Failure to provide evidence of health coverage for the duration of stay for non-immigrant visa applicants and at least the first three months for immigrant visa applicants, should result in rejection of application. This would help reduce the problem of uncompensated care.

4. Third Parties Should Be Employed to Ensure the Rule of Law and Proper Oversight.

The government should create a third-party agency to ensure that all cooperatives are complying with the law. This agency should be under the department of health and human services and should be empowered to register, deregister, suspend, monitor and bring criminal and ethical violation charges against any erring cooperative. The will ensure that cooperatives act within the law and patients are getting the best care possible.

Conclusions and The Future of Healthcare.

An overview of the healthcare system reveals a system in dire need of reform. The challenges facing it remain the same; high cost to both patients and the government and lack of universal access. The current third-party approach will not solve these two problems and any solutions like the ACA or AHCA will ultimately fail to overcome these challenges because they structurally depend on third-party approach. The best way forward is to significantly reduce the role of third parties or eliminate them altogether from the system.

However, for practical reasons, and to give people more choices, private insurance companies should be allowed to continue to operate in the system. The presence of insurance companies would allow hospitals and clinics that are not part of a cooperative to continue to operate in the system. People should be free to buy health insurance from them to supplement their membership in a cooperative, or simply use their private health insurance for all their healthcare needs and not join a cooperative.

Health care in the future will be more advanced, personalized, and expensive. Citizens will increasingly live longer, become well informed, and demand better care. In the face of these challenges, the government must not involve itself in the direct provision of healthcare because it is a service it simply does not have the financial wherewithal to keep providing. However, it must remain a key player in the healthcare industry in enforcing the laws, provision of subsidies to indigent citizens and legal residents, maintaining public health, promoting mental healthcare, and supporting research. To keep the cost of subsidies from rising too fast, state governments could direct people receiving subsidies to purchase health coverage from cooperatives with the least expensive plans and with good customer satisfaction. This would force cooperatives whose plans are too expensive to keep cost low to be able to compete for government-subsidized patients.

The future of health care is outside of national borders, and healthcare cooperatives are the best way to exploit it fully. This will allow for the true advent of globalized healthcare. Currently, medical tourism is on the upswing by individuals who are dissatisfied with the quality of their country's healthcare system. Countries like India, Cuba, Costa Rica, Israel, Malaysia, Mexico, Singapore, South Korea, China, Canada, Taiwan, Thailand, Turkey, and the United States are at the forefront of this nascent industry. However, with healthcare cooperatives this would become the standard practice in a coordinated way, driven by market forces. Nations—especially developing ones that can keep costs down and encourage investment in their healthcare infrastructure to meet or match those in developed countries—will make a fortune from healthcare and tourism. Globalized healthcare is the untapped goldmine of the century. For some nations, healthcare is likely to become the top foreign exchange earner.

For the United States, countries like Canada, Costa Rica, Cuba, Mexico, Ecuador, Japan, Europe, Caribbean countries, Central and South America would be good destinations for healthcare cooperatives to take a significant portion of the healthcare needs of their members to bring down costs. This would mean a future where people are inundated with health coverage advertisements that are comprehensive and affordable, but where a large part of treatment occurs outside the country. For example, a person based in New York, who belongs to a healthcare cooperative in New York, might be flown to the Caribbean, Cuba, Costa Rica, Ecuador or Mexico for their routine check-up, elective surgeries, short-term care and rehabilitation, and even accident and emergencies after being stabilized. They would be flown in for treatment, accommodated, and flown back to the States at no additional expense, or perhaps a small deductible or co-pay. All this would be done at a fraction of the cost in the US. To make this happen, however, there would need to be substantial private investment to get the infrastructures in these countries up to US standards.

Canada would also benefit by moving in the direction of healthcare cooperatives, because the current cost of healthcare in Canada cannot be overcome by rationing or cost-cutting. Canadian cooperatives could take some of the healthcare needs of their members to the United States, Mexico, the Caribbean, Costa Rica, Europe, and even to India to bring down costs. Also, healthcare could become a huge source of foreign exchange for Canada, if it can keep health costs down.

Health care cooperatives will allow countries in Europe to take advantage of the strengths of their different healthcare systems. Instead of the current government-controlled, top-down healthcare system, healthcare cooperatives in the UK, for example could move some of the healthcare needs of their members to Greece, Turkey, or even Kazakhstan to bring costs down.

Currently, most wealthy Africans go to Singapore, South Africa, Europe, and the United States for their healthcare needs, while many in the middle class go to India. The use of healthcare cooperatives will ease the individual financial pain of seeking overseas treatment. Health care cooperatives will look after members better, and would pursue the most cost-effective strategy for members.

In the Gulf Cooperation Countries (GCC), health care cooperatives would help bring down costs by moving their healthcare needs within countries in the GCC, or go as far as China, Japan, or the EU for their healthcare needs. In South Asia and Australasia, health care cooperatives would allow people to enjoy the strengths of the different healthcare systems in the different countries. Countries that can bring down costs and allow private investment in new hospitals and clinics would become the top attraction for health care cooperatives. Latin America and the Caribbean would also benefit from the ability of cooperatives to keep costs down at home, and the freedom to move to where cost and quality are most affordable overseas.

Chapter 3

The Criminal Justice System

The American criminal justice system is broken. According to data from the center of prison studies, the total prison population in the US in 2014 was almost 2.3 million. This gives it the unenviable title of housing about 25% of the world's prisoners while having less than five percent of the world's population. According to the Bureau of Justice Statistics, the imprisonment rate in the United States was 458 prisoners per 100,000 U.S. residents of all ages in 2015 and state and federal prisons had jurisdiction over more than 1.5 million prisoners at yearend 2015 (Carson and Anderson, 2015).

Also, the system is rife with significant racial disparities. According to a 2014 report by the sentencing project, blacks and Latinos together makeup about 30% of the US population, but account for almost 60% of the prison population. According to the ACLU, 1 in every 15 African American men, and 1 in every 36 Hispanic men are incarcerated, compared to 1 in every 106 white men (ACLU, 2011). Aside from these disparities, the recent unfortunate deaths of several unarmed black men and law enforcement officers show that serious underlying tensions exist between the police and the communities they are supposed to protect. With these appalling statistics and the current state of affairs, one can't help but wonder: how did we get here?

Close examination shows that there are several reasons for this situation, with the first being the system's punitive approach since its declared "war on drugs." Since the early 1980s when mandatory minimum sentences were introduced for low-level drug offenders, there has been an unprecedented increase in the federal prison population. Prior to mandatory sentencing, many offenders received probation or a fine for the same violations, but after the law's passage, drug convictions went up significantly. Between 1980 and 2013, the federal prison population increased, on average, by almost 6,000 inmates annually (James, 2016). According to Bureau of Justice Statistics, nearly half of federal prisoners incarcerated on September 30, 2015 had been sentenced for drug offenses. In 2014 alone, there were more than 1.5 million drug arrests (Drug Policy Alliance, 2016). Mandatory minimum sentencing does not distinguish between someone possessing drugs because they are a dealer, or because they are an addict.

The next reason for the crisis in the US criminal justice system is the fundamental lack of trust between law enforcement and many Americans. A Gallup poll found that blacks have a significantly lower level of confidence in the police as an institution than do whites; 59% of whites have a lot of confidence in the police, compared with just 37% of blacks. Also, the poll found that blacks give police officers lower honesty and ethics ratings and were more likely than whites to say new civil rights laws are needed to reduce discrimination (Newport, 2014). A 2015 Pew Research Center polling found similar lack of trust; almost "seven-in-ten whites (71%) expressed a great deal or fair amount of confidence in local police to treat blacks and whites equally, compared with only 36% of blacks" (Drake, 2015). This difference in racial perception reveals the existence of bad blood between blacks and the police.

Also, according to an analysis by the Washington Post, black Americans are 2.5 times as likely as white Americans to be shot and killed by police officers. The same research found that since January 2015, about 13% of all black people who have been fatally shot by police were unarmed, compared with 7% of all white people (Wesley, 2016).

Unsatisfactory police contact erodes legitimacy, as indicated in research in several countries, and people who regard the police as lacking in legitimacy express less willingness to cooperate or defer to the police. Inequality in police treatment, whether perceived or real, results in hostility and distrust towards the police. Research shows that fair and respectful treatment by the police generates trust and bolsters police legitimacy (Jackson, Bradford, Stanko, and Hohl 2012: Hough et al., 2010). This negative perception of the police as a biased force is a significant problem in the criminal justice system.

The next reason for the crisis in the US criminal justice system is the huge racial disparity attributable to systemic failures, some level of racial bias, and wealth inequalities. According to data from the National Registry of Exonerations, there have been 2000 exonerations since 1989 with almost half of them black. Also, the registry reports that about half of the people exonerated for non-drug related crimes and roughly two-thirds of those exonerated for drug possession or sale in 2016 were African Americans. According to data compiled by the Innocence Project on 297 individuals wrongfully convicted and exonerated through DNA evidence in the United States, 70% were people of color, with 63% being black (Grimsley, 2012).

Racial bias has also been documented in traffic stop and search. Research of more than 13,000 officer-initiated traffic stops in a Midwestern city found that minority drivers were stopped and searched for contraband at a higher rate than whites. Yet, there was no difference in the likelihood of officers finding contraband on minority motorists than white motorists (Leinfelt, 2006). Police use of force is also higher for blacks compared to whites. A study by the center of policing equity, found that although officers employ force in less than 2 percent of all police-civilian interactions, the use of police force is more than three times high for African-Americans than for whites. The study found that the disparity is consistent from mild physical force, baton strikes, pepper spray, Tasers, canine bites, to gunshots (Goff et al., 2016).

Moving forward, nearly three-quarters of a million people are locked up in local city and county jails and about 60 percent of them have not been convicted of anything. In other words, they're innocent in the eyes of the law, awaiting resolution in their cases. Many of these inmates are there because they cannot afford to pay the bail that has been set. The poor are disproportionately affected by the cost of making bail while awaiting trial, and inability to make bail makes it harder for defendants to prepare a defense. Many end up with a conviction and prison time when they might have had their cases dismissed, or gotten a better plea deal if they had been able to negotiate from the outside. This contributes to the racial disparities in incarceration. Moreover, it disrupts family life and employment (Pinto, 2015).

Flaws in jury selection also contribute to the miscarriage of justice that disproportionately affects minorities. Jury selection can influence deliberations and verdicts. Unfortunately, blacks are underrepresented in juries, and systemic striking of blacks is one of the reasons for this underrepresentation (Benokraitis, 1982). A study found that prosecutors used peremptory challenges three times as often to strike black potential jurors compared to others during the last decade and the likelihood of an acquittal rose with the number of blacks on the jury (Noye, 2015).

Inequalities in access to effective counsel between the rich and poor is another systemic flaw. Good counsel can determine whether defendants receive the most severe of punishments: life without parole, and the death penalty. The poor are often poorly represented, and with inadequate counsel, they are more likely to be unfairly punished by the criminal justice system. According to the ACLU, although defendants who cannot afford a lawyer are appointed one by the state, many especially capital defendants are frequently represented by over-worked, inexperienced, and in many cases incompetent lawyers.

The next reason for the crisis in the system is the destructive culture of some law enforcement officers and black youths in the inner cities. According to Redditt Hudson, a former cop, police officers see young black and brown men as targets and would respond with force to even minor offenses. In his book, former police officer Norm Stamper provided a first-hand account of the problems with police culture. He identifies a police force with a destructive culture that breeds excessive militarism, racism, corruption, brutality and sexual predation. Stamper describes a culture of not reporting colleagues, or collusion between officers even in the face of wrongdoing, and the endless layers of police bureaucracy that undercut accountability. He notes the curso-

ry evaluation, supervision, and oversight that many officers receive. A culture
where officers' performance or productivity is judged on the number of tick-
ets they write and arrests they make. This culture ultimately makes officers
view citizens as numbers or revenue sources, and transforms them into hunt-
ers and citizens into prey.

A Department of Justice study revealed that almost 65% of police officers
admit they don't always report criminal violations that involve abuse of authority by fellow officers, about 25% agreed or strongly agreed that whistle
blowing is not worth it and almost 70% reported that police officers who report incidents of misconduct are likely to be given a "cold shoulder" by fellow
officers (Weisburd et al., 2000).

A lack of consequences and accountability for police misconduct has only
encouraged this culture of acting outside the law. Police officers rarely face
prosecution for wrongdoing, and even when they do convictions are rare.
Nationwide, many complaints against the police are not even investigated. In
Chicago, a 2008 study by University of Chicago law professor Craig B. Futter-
man found that 10,000 abuse complaints were filed against the Chicago Police
Department between 2002 and 2004, but fewer than 20 resulted in significant
disciplinary action. In almost 90% of the cases, the complaint was dismissed
without even interviewing the accused officer. On a national level, a significant number of police misconduct cases referred for federal prosecution are
declined by prosecutors because it is very hard to get a conviction. Local
prosecutors don't often charge police officers with whom they must work
closely, creating a situation where police go free even in cases where they have
overstepped their authority. Officers who are found guilty of abuse of authority do not have to personally pay for their behavior. Typically, the settlement to
their victims is paid from city coffers. In larger cities, these settlements easily
cost the public tens of millions of dollars annually. In 2014, the 10 cities with
the largest police departments paid out almost $250 million in court judg-
ments and settlements in police-misconduct cases (Elinson and Frosch,
2015).

The culture of black youths in the inner cities also contributes to the crisis in
the criminal justice system. In all inner-city neighborhoods, there is a problem minority between the ages of 16 and 25 who revel in a culture that sees
breaking the law as cool. They equate blackness with rejecting mainstream
culture, education, personal responsibility, and gainful employment. Many
belong to gangs and revel in a street or thug way of life which idolizes hyper-
masculinity, respect, extreme individualism, materialism, violence, and guns.
This culture is reinforced by the severe socioeconomic conditions in these
inner cities, breakdown of family structure, racial discrimination, a chemically
toxic, neurologically injurious environment and chronic unemployment (Pat-

terson, 2015). This destructive culture contributes to the uneven incarceration of blacks compared to the rest of the country.

According to the US Department of Justice using data from 1980 to 2008, the offending rate for blacks was almost eight times higher than whites, and the victimization rate is six times higher. Almost 70% of drug-related homicides were committed by black offenders (Cooper and Smith, 2011). In 2013, according to FBI data, blacks accounted for 4,379 out of 8,383 or 52.2% of all arrests for murder and nonnegligent manslaughter, and whites accounted for just 3,799 or 45.3%. For robbery, blacks account for 56 percent while whites accounted for only 42%. So, the problem is not simply police brutality or systemic bias, there is a serious problem with the culture and socioeconomic conditions in the inner cities that must be tackled to eliminate or significantly reduce the huge racial disparities in the criminal justice system.

Another reason for the crisis in the criminal justice system is with the prison system, which has failed to live up to its mission. Prisons are supposed to rehabilitate offenders, not destroy or condemn them. According to the American Civil Liberties Union (ACLU), rape and sexual abuse of prisoners by staff and other prisoners are serious problems in detention facilities and prisons. Also, according to the ACLU, a senior prison official in Georgia watched while guards brutally beat handcuffed inmates, and in California, correctional officers encouraged combat between prisoners by placing rival gang members together in the prison yard. A human right watch report based on information collected from over 200 prisoners in thirty-seven states found serious problem of rape in US prisons. Furthermore, a 2015 New York Times report on Clinton correctional facility found many cases of inmate abuse that go unpunished (Winerip and Schwirtz, 2015). Many prison staff members abuse their authority with impunity, and harass prisoners for no reason. Instead of being rehabilitated, these practices leave many offenders scarred and worse off. This defeats the entire purpose of the criminal justice system.

Racial disparities also exist in discipline in many prisons, negatively affecting minorities. In a review by The New York Times of disciplinary cases against inmates in 2015, hundreds of pages of internal reports and several years of parole decisions revealed serious racial disparities in New York prisons. According to their analysis, in most prisons, blacks and Latinos were disciplined at higher rates than whites, and were sent to solitary confinement more frequently and for longer durations. In addition, the report found that even after accounting for age, which is correlated with a tendency to break prison rules, the racial disparities in discipline persisted. (Schwirtz, Winerip and Gebeloff, 2016).

An important negative outcome of this racial disparity in prison discipline is that it prevents access to jobs, educational and therapeutic programs, and most importantly reduces an inmate's chances of being paroled. The Times analysis of first-time hearings before the New York State Board of Parole found that one in four white prisoners were released, but fewer than one in six black prisoners were released. Racial disparities in discipline contributed to the disparities in parole.

The next reason for the crisis in the criminal justice system, and arguably the most serious problem, is the barrier to reentry that many ex-offenders face. For the over 100 million Americans with a criminal record, getting a job is almost impossible (Bureau of Justice Statistics, 2012). Ex-convicts with a felony are denied the right to have a professional license in nearly 80 professions, including barbers, cosmetologists, electrical contractors, plumbers, scrap metal processors, conditioned air contractors, auctioneers, utility contractors, registered trade sanitarians, and nurses, among others. These restrictions severely curtail the number of professions available to people coming out of prison (Rodriguez and Emsellem, 2011). With such restrictions, it's probably fair and accurate to say the system just wants those convicted to keep failing. Shut out from legitimate job opportunities, many ex-offenders resort to illegal means of survival and soon find themselves back in prison. According to a study by the Pew Center on the States, more than 40% of ex-cons commit crimes within three years of their release and end up behind bars, despite billions spent on prison rehabilitation. Approximately 43% of prisoners who were released in 2004 were sent back to prison by 2007, either for a new crime or for violating the conditions of their release.

Recidivism has devastating consequences, not only for the individual offender, but also for the family, the community, and society at large. It contributes to the increasing prison population, and disproportionately affects minorities. Apart from difficulty finding a job or getting a professional license, many ex-offenders also face housing discrimination and felony disenfranchisement. The widespread disenfranchisement of formerly incarcerated persons disproportionally impacts minorities, and is a barrier to successful reintegration into society.

De-entropification Solution.

Eight principles could be used to de-entropify the criminal justice system.

1. Principle of General Homogeneity.

A. Barriers to Reentry

Figure 3-1: An Ideal Criminal Justice System.

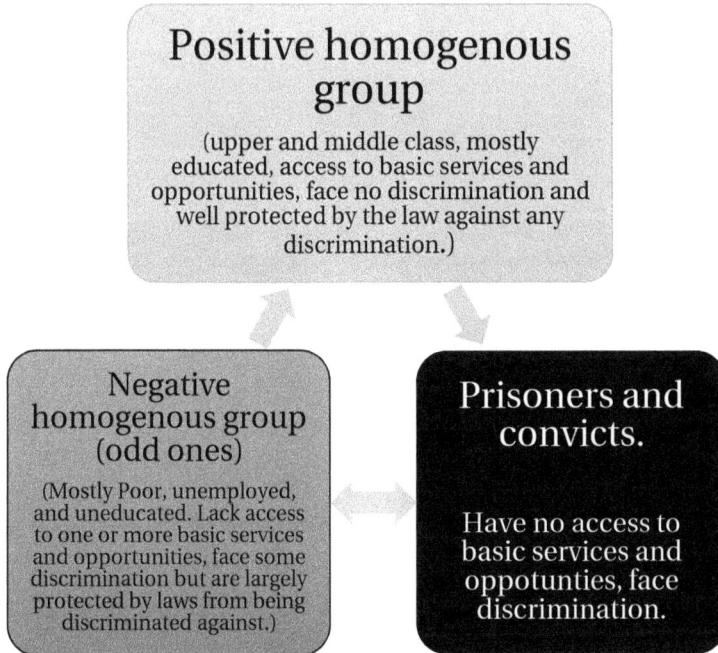

Positive homogenous group
(upper and middle class, mostly educated, access to basic services and opportunities, face no discrimination and well protected by the law against any discrimination.)

Negative homogenous group (odd ones)
(Mostly Poor, unemployed, and uneducated. Lack access to one or more basic services and opportunities, face some discrimination but are largely protected by laws from being discriminated against.)

Prisoners and convicts.

Have no access to basic services and oppotunties, face discrimination.

A good criminal justice system must be one that properly identifies people who need rehabilitation and on rehabilitation give them all the opportunity to rejoin the positive homogenous group. This includes lifting barriers to enter many professions, get a job, to vote etc. Unless the system works like this, its purpose is defeated no matter how much money is thrown at it.

The figure 3-2 demonstrates one of the most serious problems with the current US criminal justice system: barrier to reentry. The system condemns for life, giving almost no chance for the offender to join the positive homogenous group, as shown by the one-way arrows. With over 100 million or 1 in 3 Americans having a criminal record, the current laws and policies shut out a large chunk of the population from ever joining the positive homogenous group.

Figure 3-2: The Current US Criminal Justice System.

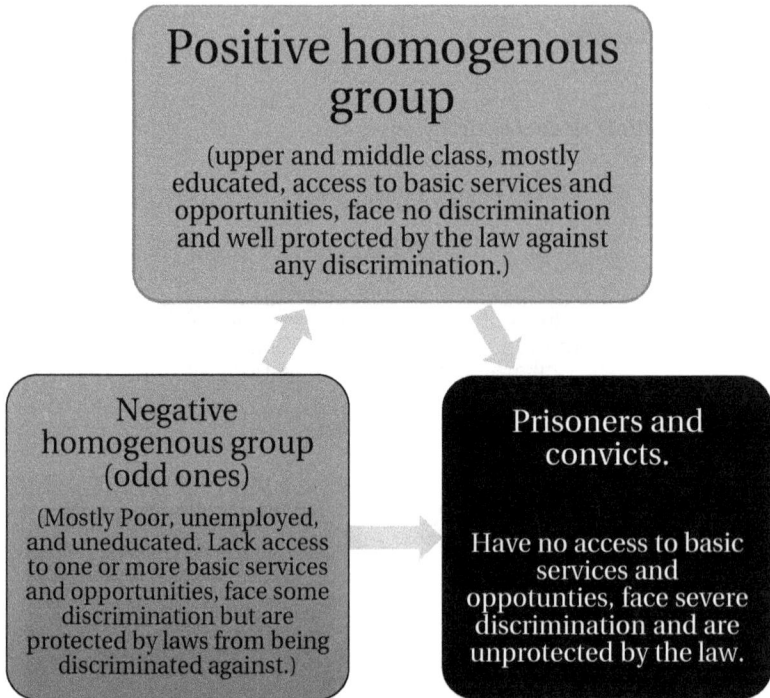

To rectify this problem, it would be important lift all barriers that prevent ex-offenders from joining the positive homogenous group. Ban-the-box policies, which prevent employers from seeking information about an applicant's criminal history until later in the hiring process, should be implemented across the country. Employers should be forbidden from discriminating against ex-convicts whose record is not connected to the particular job they are applying for. Also, ex-offenders who do not constitute a threat to the safety of others should be protected from being discriminated against by employers. This can help ex-offenders enter the labor market more easily. President Obama has already taken such steps on federal government employment applications in 2015, and a total of 25 states, over 150 cities and counties have adopted it in some form (Rodriguez and Avery, 2017). However, more should be done to see this become standard across the country.

Additionally, more effort should be made to lift existing restrictions on professional licenses. Many states have blanket restrictions on some of the professions most suitable for ex-offenders' skillsets. These restrictions should be substituted with clear and reasonable criteria to determine whether a person is suitable for a particular profession given his or her criminal history. This means every person should be evaluated on a case by case basis and eligibility to receive or be denied license should be based on the nature of their crime and how it affects their ability to do the job. Many states are already working towards removing these barriers, and this process should continue. Also, criminal records should be wiped clean after several years of demonstrable good behavior by an ex-offender. The current system, in which criminal history is eternal, makes no sense. Some states have begun permitting people convicted of drug offenses, minor crimes, or violations as juveniles to have their records expunged sooner, or more easily. However, more still needs to be done.

Education and vocational training is another important way to make it easy for offenders to integrate and join the positive homogenous group on return. Many people enter prison with educational deficits. According to a 2003 Bureau of Justice Statistics report, about 75% of State prison inmates, almost 59% of Federal inmates, and 69% of jail inmates did not complete high school (Harlow, 2003). Unsurprisingly, employment rates and earnings histories of inmates in prisons and jails are often low before incarceration (Holzer, Raphael & Stoll, 2003). Adults inmates have no right to a public education like Juveniles but could benefit from education and job training to help them on their return to the outside. A 2014 study published by RAND Corporation, "How Effective is Correctional Education, and Where Do We Go from Here?" found that adult inmates who participated in correctional education programs had "43% lower odds of recidivating than inmates who did not." This represents a reduction of 13 percentage points on the risk of recidivism. The study also found that, among inmates who participated in correctional education, the odds of obtaining employment after being released were 13% higher than for those who did not and those who participated in vocational training were 28 percent more likely to be employed after release than those who did not receive such training. The report concluded that correctional education is a cost-effective initiative (Davis et al., 2014). Similar research by the Minnesota Department of Corrections found that earning a post-secondary degree in prison significantly increased the odds of securing post-release employment by 59 percent and was associated with less recidivism (Duwe and Clark, 2014). So, there is clear evidence that education can help in the rehabilitation of an offender and reduce recidivism which, by the way, is the primary purpose of the criminal justice system.

Some states have been investing in education. In 2014, New York Governor Cuomo announced a new initiative to introduce college programs that will offer associates and bachelor's degrees at ten prisons throughout the state. The Obama administration has chosen 67 colleges and universities for a pilot program called Second Chance Pell that will offer Pell Grants to incarcerated students. The program will enroll 12,000 prisoners at more than 100 correctional institutions across the country. This effort by the Obama administration, although a step in the right direction, is quite small since there are millions of people currently in prisons. More must be done to make education and vocational studies compulsory in prisons and detention centers to give all inmates a chance to join the positive homogenous group upon their return to the outside.

B. Homogeneity: Homogenization of the police and the community they serve.

The Justice Department investigation of the Ferguson Police Department following the death of Michael Brown found evidence of discriminatory policing, racial bias and stereotyping. Justice department investigation of Baltimore police department found that the department used strategies that wrongfully subjected African Americans to disproportionate rates of stops, searches and arrests. Also, the Justice Department investigation of the Chicago police department found serious concerns about the prevalence of racially discriminatory conduct by some officers which was largely tolerated and a disproportionality of illegal and unconstitutional patterns of force on minority communities. All these cities have one thing in common; the police departments were not representative of the community they served.

Across America, there are serious disparities in the racial makeup of police departments and their communities especially in suburban towns where the population had grown increasingly diverse the past few decades. In Ferguson, Missouri, where Michael Brown was killed August 9, 2014, by Officer Darren Wilson sparking nationwide protests, minorities make up at least two-thirds of the population, but the police department is predominantly white. Like Ferguson, Maple Heights, Ohio, has a population that is nearly two-thirds black but a police force which remains predominantly white. In parts of Orange County, like Buena Park, Tustin, and Garden Grove, the police force is failing to keep up the growing Asian and Hispanic communities and the same trend can be seen in cities in the Los Angeles county like West Covina and Pomona. Also, Cicero in Chicago, Pembroke Pines and Lauderhill in Miami, Chelsea in Boston, Massachusetts, Dallas and South Houston in Texas, Daly City, Hayward, and Fremont in San Francisco, as well as Phoenix, Arizona to mention just a few, the same trend can be seen (Ashkenas and Park, 2015).

Homogeneity influences the level of trust between police and the communities they protect. Positive homogeneity of the police force means it is dominated by people with positive traits (integrity, honesty, and professionalism), and at the same time, it is culturally competent and highly reflective of the gender, racial and ethnic makeup of the community it serves. On the other hand, negative homogeneity occurs when the police force is not at all culturally competent or reflective of the community it serves and it is dominated by officers with negative traits (unprofessional behavior and a tendency to abuse their authority).

Any police force tends to move from positive to negative homogeneity. In other words, the police force tends to fail to keep up with the speed of ethnic or racial changes in the community in its hiring practices and tends to fail to get rid of bad officers and administrators quickly enough. For this reason, the tendency for distrust and lack of cooperation between the police and the community it protects is always very high. The recent riots over the deaths of unarmed black men, as well as the deaths of several police officers, shows a deep lack of trust—some of which can be traced to the negative homogeneity between the police and community they protect. To achieve positive homogeneity, it is important to make sure that the police force reflects the gender, racial and ethnic makeup of the community it serves and it develops mechanisms to quickly rid itself of officers with negative traits. Only when this is the case will trust be restored and sustained between the police force and the community they protect. Furthermore, the police department must make efforts in its hiring practices to keep up with demographic changes in the community lest it slide into negative homogeneity again.

A recent study by Public Administration Review concluded that the rate of fatal police-involved incidents levels off only when black officers reach a 25% ratio in the force. The study found that the more black officers a police department has after the 40% point, the less likely the incidence of fatal encounters with black people. It argues that police departments need to hire more black officers so that they would be overrepresented relative to the local black population (Nicholson-Crotty Sean et al., 2017). An overrepresentation of black officers relative to the local black population may create problems of trust and cooperation in neighborhoods or communities that are mostly white or other racial groups. Moreover, hiring more black officers would not solve the problem of negative culture in many police departments. Minorities police officers are not immune from unprofessional behavior if it is imbedded in the culture of the police department they find themselves. For instance, a 2004 study that examined the behavioral differences between Black and White police officers in handling interpersonal conflicts using observational and survey data from St. Petersburg, Florida, and Indianapolis, Indiana found that black officers are more coercive than their White counterparts in responding to conflicts (Sun and Payne 2004). Also, in 2009, the Detroit police department which is dominated by African Americans got only 18 percent approval rating from black residents of Wayne County of its work.

So, to ensure positive homogeneity between the police force and the community and within the force itself there should be; proper training that inculcates positive traits and professional conduct; recruitment that selects the best and most qualified; the police department must reflect the gender, racial and ethnic makeup of the community it serves; and mechanisms to quickly flush out officers with negative trait must be put in place.

C. Homogeneity: Homogenization of the Prison systems.

A review by The New York Times of thousands of disciplinary cases against inmates in 2015, three years of parole decision and thousands of pages of internal reports found significant racial disparities in the prison experience in New York. According to the report, blacks and Latinos were disciplined at higher rates than whites. At Clinton Correctional Facility, "black inmates were nearly four times as likely to be sent to isolation as whites, and they were held there for an average of 125 days, compared with 90 days for whites". Importantly, at Clinton, only one out of the 998 guards is black; however, blacks make up a significant portion of the prison population. In contrast, at Sing Sing Correctional Facility in Ossining, blacks and whites are treated more equitably. According to the Times review, of the 1,286 violations issued to inmates for breaking prison rules, there were no disciplinary disparities between whites and blacks. Importantly, blacks make up a significant portion of the inmate population, and black officers make up the majority of the uniformed staff at Sing Sing (Schwirtz, Winerip and Gebeloff, 2016).

A prison system is in a state of positive homogeneity when the prison staff and officers have positive traits, are culturally competent and they are reflective of the racial and ethnic makeup of the prison population. In positive homogeneity, abuse of offenders by prison staff is low or nonexistent, and disciplinary actions are fair and equal to the severity of wrongdoing. Also, racial disparities in prison discipline are absent. In negative homogeneity, the prison staff and officers are not at all culturally competent or reflective of the racial or ethnic composition of the prison population and it is dominated by bad apples, or officers with negative traits. In this state, inmates are routinely abused by prisons guards or staff, unjust punishment is meted out, and racial disparities exist in opportunities, access to services, and discipline.

If the prison system is to be the place for prisoner rehabilitation, positive homogeneity must always be maintained between the prisoner population and the prison's uniformed worker population. To achieve this, prison hiring practices of must evolve with the ethnic demographics of the prisoner population. This is by no means easy, but it is an effort that the prison system must expend to make it fairer and more effective. Also, the prison system must be able to quickly rid itself of officers who abuse their authority. Any correctional officer with negative traits allowed into the prison system damages the lives of prisoners and blocks their efforts at rehabilitation. So, firing bad officers quickly is crucial to keeping the prison in a state of positive homogeneity.

D. Homogeneity: Homogenization of the Parole Board.

An analysis by The New York Times of thousands of parole decisions from the past several years found that about one in six black or Hispanic men were released at his first hearing. In contrast, one in four white men were released at their first hearing. The times found this disparity to be particularly striking for small time offenders. According to the Times analysis, since 2006, white inmates serving two to four years for a single count of third-degree burglary were released after an average of 803 days, black inmates, in contrast, served an extra 80 days on average for the same crime. Also, when the Times analyzed almost 14,000 parole decisions for male inmates over a three-year period for only first-time appearances before the board, taking into account factors such as an inmate's crime, age, race, and previous stints in state prison, it found that the Board released more than 40% of white inmates for third-degree burglars who had no previous prison sentences. In contrast, it released only 30% of blacks and Latinos with the same crime and criminal history. Among male prisoners under 25 with no prior state prison sentences, the board released 30% of whites but only 14% of blacks and Latinos. Importantly, the board members or commissioners who made these parole decisions were mostly white, and mainly from upstate New York. According to Times, there is currently only one black man and no Latino men on the parole board. However, blacks and Latinos make up nearly three-quarters of the state prison population (Winerip, Schwirtz and Gebeloff, 2016).

The parole board should always be in a state of positive homogeneity. In a state of positive homogeneity, the parole board members or commissioners have positive traits (honesty, professionalism, fairness, objectivity, respect, etc.), are culturally competent and they are reflective of the racial or ethnic makeup of the offenders in the prison population. On the other hand, negative homogeneity occurs when the board members are not at all culturally competent or reflective of the offenders in the prison population and it is dominated by commissioners with negative traits (unprofessionalism, prejudice or racial bias, etc.). In negative homogeneity, bias corrupts the parole decision-making process and contributes to racial disparities in favorable and unfavorable parole decisions.

Furthermore, parole commissioners' tenure should have term limits, and selection of people into these boards should be based on merit rather than politics, with people with experience in rehabilitation given preference. Also, consideration should be given to developing a better mechanism for inmates to appeal the decisions of parole commissioners, and parole decisions should be reviewed from time to time by the corrections department for inconsistencies.

E. Homogeneity: Homogenization of Police Training Standards.

According to the Bureau of Justice Statistics, the United States has some 17,985 separate police departments that include town and city police, state police, sheriff's offices, university police, transport system police, and 73 federal agencies. Half of those departments have fewer than ten officers (Reaves, 2015). These departments, for the most part, have different recruitment policies, training programs, disciplinary policies, and police cultures. Also, there are over 600 different law enforcement academies offering different content. Some police academies operate like colleges with extensive training on de-escalation and how to handle mentally ill citizens. Some others adopt a military-style "boot camp" approach with focus on skills such as firearms use, and arrest procedures (Brooks, 2016).

This variation in standards, recruitment, and training is a big part of the problem especially in small agencies with fewer than ten officers. Small agencies often lack the resources for training and equipment that are readily accessible to larger departments. This causes serious disparities in the quality of police officers within a state and between states. The Justice Department investigation of Albuquerque Police Department determined that there were structural and systemic deficiencies including insufficient oversight and inadequate training. These findings align with findings from the Justice department's investigations of other police departments.

To fix this problem, it would be important to homogenize the system. National standards in recruitment and training for all police departments across the country must be instituted. One approach to creating uniform standards is the consolidation of police agencies. Another would be for the federal government to ensure that aspiring police officers go through a West Point kind of college where they are all well-trained on the same tactics and methods. Upon graduation, police officers would be given a license that would allow them to work anywhere after passing any necessary supplemental exams required by the state, municipality, city or university police agency. This would ensure uniformity in tactics and standards, eliminate mediocrity, and promote excellence and professionalism.

F. Homogeneity and A More Efficient Court System

The risk for crime is different for different groups, and a court system that punishes without regard to the underlying factors that drive people to crime will ultimately fail to dispense justice effectively. The use of homogenous courts, such as drug and mental health court that cater to the needs of specific risk groups, allows for efficiency and increased effectiveness at helping those at risk of committing crime. Drug courts have proven to be very good at reducing substance abuse and recidivism and are much more cost-efficient than only punishment (Brown, 2010: Krebs, Lindquist, Koetse and Lattimore, 2007: Fielding, et al. 2002). However, the current number of drug courts is insufficient to address the needs of drug users.

A study by the Rand Corporation on the fiscal impact of Allegheny County mental health courts found that mental health courts are effective at cost savings (Ridgely, et al. 2007). Also, studies have shown that mental health courts reduce the number of new arrests (Moore and Hiday, 2006). Other studies have found that mental health courts can reduce recidivism and violence for people with mental disorders in the criminal justice system (McNiel and Binder, 2007).

These courts should be expanded nationwide, and even tried for at-risk youths in the inner cities, involved in gangs who cross paths with the criminal justice system. Putting inner city youths involved in gangs through traditional courts does not help the justice system because their needs are special. Overall, there should be an expansion of homogenous courts to more at-risk groups to create a smarter and more effective criminal justice system.

2. All Contributors Must Act Within the Established Rules or Laws, and Everyone Must Be Equal before Them (Rule of Law).

When too many people act outside of or break the law, the system cannot hold. The destructive culture in the inner cities and in some police departments contribute to police abuse of power and some aspects of the racial disparities in the justice system. And unless these cultural and sociocultural issues are tackled so that these contributors conform or act within the rules, the system will never work optimally.

To address the police culture of acting outside the law with impunity, the use of body cameras should be made standard. Knowing with sufficient certainty that one's behavior is being observed or judged makes people—in this case, police officers and the person they were interacting with—more likely to adhere to socially acceptable behavior, and to follow the rules.

A year-long experiment conducted at the Rialto, California Police Department found dramatic changes in behavior and rates of complaint with the use of cameras. According to the findings, for three years prior to the experiment, the department posted roughly 65 use-of-force incidents per year. During the experimental period, the use-of-force rate dropped significantly, to 25 incidents total—a reduction of 58% to 64% compared to previous years. Citizen complaints dropped dramatically to just three from twenty-four or from 0.7

complaints per 1,000 contacts to 0.07 per 1,000 contacts, representing an 88% drop (The Rialto Police Department, 2013). Furthermore, according to a report developed by the police department for the San Diego City Council's Public Safety and Livable Neighborhoods Committee, the use of body cameras by San Diego police resulted in fewer complaints by residents and use of less force by officers. Complaints fell 40.5%, use of force by officers reduced by 46.5%, and use of pepper spray by 30.5% (Bonk, 2015: Repard, 2015: Perry, 2015).

Researchers at the University of South Florida randomly selected 46 officers to wear body cameras on a yearlong (March 2014 through February 2015) pilot program at the Orlando Police Department. Compared to 43 officers who did not wear the cameras, researchers found that use-of-force incidents dropped 53% among officers with the cameras and the number of complaints filed against the officers dropped over 60%. Also, the study found that officers wearing body cameras had a significant reduction in reported civilian injuries and injuries to themselves compared to officers without body cameras (Jennings, Lynch and Fridell, 2015). Positive findings on police use of body cameras have been found in Arizona (Ready and Young, 2015) and other places.

So, without any doubt, cameras affect police behavior positively. Their use improves transparency and accountability and helps curtail the tendency to act outside of what the law permits. Thus, the use of cameras should be a nationwide standard for all police departments. President Barack Obama recently announced a $75 million initiative to help departments cover the costs of expanding their programs. This is a good first step, but more resources and effort must be dedicated to ensure that on-duty police officers interact with members of the public only if they are wearing a working body camera. Also, these cameras should be made available to correctional and detention officers who must be mandated to wear them whenever they interact with prisoners or detainees. This would ensure that prisoners are not unfairly disciplined, and it would push back on the culture of impunity that has been documented in many prisons and detention centers.

Comprehensive and continued training is essential to keep the police informed and more professional. Compared to other developed countries around the world, police training in the United States is quite poor. In the US, the national average of academy training required is just over 600 hours. In Louisiana, the police academy lasts a mere nine weeks (360 hours), but in Washington, D.C police recruits have 28 weeks (1,120) of full-time academy instruction before supervised patrolling (Ramsey, 2015). In the state of Idaho, a police officer is required to complete 400 hours of training (a mere ten weeks of training), and in California, police are required to complete 833 hours, only 21 weeks of training. In Alabama, 12 weeks (480 hours) of training is the requirement for its officers. In contrast, in Germany, police train for at least 130 weeks. Police officers in Nordic countries are required to receive at least two full years of college-style classroom training before they become officers (King, 2016).

The fact that police training in America is less rigorous than that of many European nations raises serious questions. Training can make a difference in how police think and approach deadly situations. If police officers are not adequately trained on the use of non-violent tactics as their first option, then they are more likely to resort to their guns, pepper spray, batons, or Tasers, resulting in violent encounters that are avoidable. With better or more comprehensive training, the culture of policing would shift from an aggressive or assault mindset towards an approach that emphasizes de-escalation. This would result in a reduced incidence of tragic encounters. Moreover, police should have continuous education, as is the case with many professions. Research shows that there is little to no requirement of continued education for police officers and for states that mandate continued education it is no more than 40 hours per year (King, 2016). Officers should be required to earn continuing education credits to learn new ways of dealing with people, tackling emerging threats and behaviors, and dealing with cultural and demographic changes in their communities. Certificates from such programs should be linked with licensing or permission to work as an officer of the law.

Training should also be expanded, and continuous education credits should be made compulsory for detention and correctional officers. In Mississippi, prisons guards get only four weeks of training, compared with 16 weeks in Michigan and 12 months in New York (Hager, 2015). Inadequate training allows mediocrity and bad behavior to flourish. Addressing these concerns will correct some of the failings associated with correctional officers in the system.

Moving beyond the police department culture, the inner city culture to which many black youths in the inner cities subscribe that celebrates thug or gang life, reverence for guns, and a lack of respect for the law contributes to the racial disparities in the criminal justice system. The inner-city culture is first and foremost a product of the criminal justice system. The revolving door in the criminal justice system, combined with the barriers that prevent many young blacks who have a criminal record from being gainfully employed, contributes to the sense of disconnection and victimization that is pervasive in the inner cities.

Aside from criminal records that hamper gainful employment, the playing field is not level between blacks and whites. According to findings from the Economic Policy Institute, the unemployment rate of college-educated blacks is nearly two times that of their white counterparts. For blacks who have only a high school diploma, or who failed to finish high school, the rate of unemployment is worse (Wilson, 2015). With this difficulty getting jobs, many young black people in the inner cities naturally gravitate towards gangs and crime. Poverty, coupled with a sense of alienation and marginalization, fuels a sense of victimhood and a tendency to push back at the system they consider to be at the heart of their problems. Blacks have faced many problems in America, from slavery to Jim Crow laws, and this negative history adds to the sense of victimization that is ingrained in the inner-city culture. Unfair police treatment adds to the sense of alienation that drives the disconnectedness and violence in the inner cities.

These problems coupled with the rise of single parenting or family disintegration has resulted in a culture of deep cynicism towards society, the pessimism of possibilities, and the gravitation towards crime. According to a study from the Centers for Disease Control (CDC), 73% of African American births in 2010 were out of wedlock (Martin et al., 2012), and estimates for the percentage of African American children growing up in single-parent households is almost 70%. Family disintegration is one of the primary causes of poverty, despair, and a gravitation toward gangs and crime in the inner cities. Research shows that active parental monitoring of children was relatively strongly linked to delinquency (Hoeve et al., 2009).

The situation in Chicago clearly shows the effect of poverty, family disintegration and marginalization. According to data reported by the Chicago Tribune, almost 3,000 people were victims of shooting in 2015 in the city of Chicago and that increased to a staggering 4,365 for 2016. For a city, not at war, these numbers are simply insane. In Chicago, by the Labor Day weekend of 2016, the city had hit the tragic number of 500 homicides—and nearly all those killed were black men by other black men (Glanton, 2016). Much of the violence is driven by gangs. Boys are joining gangs at younger and younger ages, and dying like fleas. A similar situation exists in many inner cities across the country. Unless there is a reversal of this trend in the inner cities, little or no progress can be made in tackling the overrepresentation of African Americans in the criminal justice system which stands at about 40% of all inmates in federal prisons according to the Federal Bureau of prisons and 38% at state prisons according to the Bureau of Justice Statistics (Carson, 2015).

One solution to the situation is a better educational system in the inner cities. Many of the public schools are terrible, and more must be done to improve them. A supplementary after-school and weekend education program should be created to help young people in the inner cities. The supplementary school would give inner-city kids a chance to add to whatever the school is teaching them. Stipends could be provided to encourage attendance. Such enticement would make the program succeed and keep kids from the street. This program could be put together and financed by wealthy African Americans and well-wishers. Many government-sponsored after school programs have seen significant cuts, so betting the lives and wellbeing of inner city black youths on the whims of government spending is not a serious move. National and regional televised quizzes, and spelling and debate competitions for young black kids could be sponsored to help create heroes for many inner-city kids and inspire them to love education. For when people get an education especially to college level, they are less likely to join gangs or have an unplanned teenage pregnancy.

This is not a panacea to the problem, but it will go a long way to reverse the overrepresentation of blacks in the criminal justice system.

Furthermore, to ensure equality of all citizens before the law, changes should be made in jury selection and service. Noye (2015), found that prosecutors used peremptory challenges more frequently to strike black potential jurors compared to other races, and this had a negative impact on trial outcomes. In the last decade, blacks were routinely excluded from jury service by prosecutors for being too young or old, single or divorced, failing to make eye contact, having bad posture, served in the military, having a hyphenated last name, long hair or even for wearing a beard (Liptak, 2015). According to the Caddo Parish study, no defendants were acquitted when two or fewer of the dozen jurors were black. However, when there were at least three black jurors, the acquittal rate rose to 12 percent and with five or more, the rate rose to 19 percent (Noye, 2015). Other studies have shown that the composition of the jury pool has a large impact on average conviction rates for black versus white defendants. A 2012 study published in the Quarterly Journal of Economics showed that defendants of each race do relatively better when the jury pool contains more members of their own race. It concluded that interaction of defendant and jury race fundamentally alters the mapping of evidence to conviction rates (Anwar, Bayer, and Hjalmarsson, 2012).

So, to ensure fairness, the credibility of trial outcomes and equal application of the law, jurors selected for service must hold no hostility, negative feelings, or prejudice whatsoever against the defendant, and at least 40-50% of them must be of the same gender, race or ethnicity as the defendant. In civil cases, this must apply both to the defendant and the plaintiff. All energy must be expended to achieving this to improve fairness in judgments or verdicts for all citizens regardless of race or ethnicity, religion, gender, etc. and eliminate wrongful convictions. There should be very strict selection criteria, and a test to determine if potential jurors hold any malice towards the defendant. Also, minorities are frequently excluded from jury selection, because members of a jury are usually selected from registered voters. A more comprehensive pool, such as those with driver's licenses, would improve the chances of having a jury that can ensure the equal application of the law.

3. Negative Consequences or Punishment in any form Should Always Be Limited or Confined to The Wrongdoer and Not the Group.

Those who break the law must always face the consequences of their actions, and such consequences must always be limited or confined to the wrongdoer. When law enforcement, or any group for that matter, spreads negative consequences or punishment in any form to a contributor or contributors who share the same background, race, ethnicity or culture as the wrongdoer, then mistrust, anger and hostility increases. Unfortunately, people tend to profile, stereotype, and spread blame. This tendency must be resisted, especially among members of law enforcement, since their effects are always counter-productive.

A study of the Los Angeles Police Department showed that unfair targeting of minority communities results in greater mistrust and fear of police officers (Stone, Foglesong and Cole, 2009). Racial or ethnic profiling alienates communities from law enforcement, makes communities live in fear of law enforcement, and causes law enforcement to lose credibility and trust among the people they are sworn to serve. It undermines public safety and generates a reluctance to cooperate with police officers since they are perceived as biased. Moreover, it wastes resources on false positives as many members of the profiled group are decent, law-abiding people who have no business with crime.

In many states in the US, racial profiling remains a problem. Since September 11, 2001, ethnic profiling has become much more prevalent for the Muslim, Arab, and South Asian communities. The Demographics Unit—a branch of the New York Police Department that tracked New York's Muslim communities is a good example of racial profiling. This policy sowed fear and mistrust among members of the Muslim community as well as between the Muslim community and law enforcement. The New York Police Department's controversial stop-and-frisk program targeted blacks and Latinos about 85% of the time. Unsurprisingly, in nearly nine out of 10 searches, police find nothing according to the ACLU office in New York. Furthermore, according to the ACLU office in Illinois, Black Chicagoans were subjected to 72% of all stops, although they constitute just 32% of the city's population. The justice department investigation of Ferguson and other police departments have found similar patterns of the use of profiling.

Fortunately, since the death of several unarmed black men, the outcry against this policy has led legislators in many states to propose measures to tackle profiling. In California, Governor Jerry Brown has approved legislation that requires local law enforcement agencies to collect demographic data on all the people they stop. However, more needs to be done to push back on the use of profiling in all its forms. The End Racial Profiling Act should be passed without further delay. Positive homogeneity of the police would help to reduce the incidence of racial profiling and efforts should be made to achieve it in all police departments. Also, it must be made compulsory that police alert people to their right to refuse a search, that is arbitrary and unjustifiable or without the approval of a judge. Police officers must be required to present documented proof of consent to search, and if they don't, the search should be considered inadmissible in a court of law, and unconstitutional.

4. Negative Consequences Should Always Be Equal to Severity of Wrongdoing.

The bail system and the use of mandatory minimum sentencing both violate this principle, with quite terrible and far-reaching consequences. The use of bail keeps people from fleeing because it gives them something of real consequence to lose. Unfortunately, bail in America has a disproportionately negative impact on the poor. Most defendants who are unable to make bail fall within the poorest third of society and it is simply unrealistic to expect them to be able to quickly put together $5,000 to $10,000, or a portion thereof, for a bail bond (Rabuy and Kopf, 2016). For many poor defendants, bail has become an additional punishment for the crime alleged to have been committed.

A pilot program called the Freedom Fund, set up in 2007 by the Bronx Defenders, posted bail for poor clients charged with misdemeanors and resulted in more than half of their clients' cases being dismissed. This shows the significance of being able to post bail (Walshe, 2013).

The vast majority of criminal cases are resolved by guilty pleas (Hessick, & Saujani, 2002). Prosecutors use plea bargains to reduce backlog and save money, and this gives them an advantage especially against those who cannot make bail. In 2010, Human Rights Watch issued a report titled "The Price of Freedom" which found that instead of offense committed, poverty dictated a defendant's fate. The report found that only 13% of defendants among defendants arrested in 2008 on non-felony charges and given bail of $1,000 or less, could post bail at arraignment. Research shows that when a person is kept in jail before their hearing, it seriously damages their ability to fight the charges and they are often offered harsher plea deals than those who are fortunate enough to make bail and negotiate from the outside. According to the same human rights watch report, in New York City, about 99% of all misdemeanor convictions come from plea deals and negotiating terms from jail puts a person at a great disadvantage.

According to the Bronx Freedom Fund, Defendants who await trial in jail are four times more likely to be sentenced to time in prison. For defendants, able to come up with $500 or $1,000 to make bail, their chances for no prison time and dismissed charges increase exponentially. Those stuck behind bars are faced with a terrible choice: plead guilty and go home with a criminal record, or maintain their innocence and remain in jail. Many reluctantly take the plea deal even if they are innocent, just to get out. Many people who are unable to pay end up on Rikers Island, and sometimes for years. There are stories of people placed in solitary confinement on Rikers Island for a long time while awaiting trial.

Bail has quite simply become a ransom to extract or coerce guilty pleas from poor people. It has resulted in a two-tier justice system that on one hand unfairly punishes the poor, who can't afford to pay their way out, while those who are well-off find themselves off the hook or with better deals for the same crime. This plunges the poor deeper into poverty, and in many cases, precipitates their return to jail. Families suffer enormously from this unfair system, and it contributes to the racial disparities in incarceration of minorities in the criminal justice system, as well in the high level of poverty and unemployment. The bail system has failed to serve its original purpose. In its current form, it quite simply doesn't serve the public.

To ensure that negative consequences is equal to the severity of wrongdoing, it will be important to consider annual income in determining bail. For the poor charged with a misdemeanor, 10-15% of a paycheck (from the defendant, or a family member or friend if necessary) could be withheld as surety until the case is closed. For a poor offender who has no means of paying this 10-15% of income, bail should be free and based solely on risk of flight and return to criminal activity. This would allow the poor who are arrested for misdemeanor or low level non-violent crimes not to be swallowed up by the criminal justice system. It would level the playing field and connect the negative consequences only with the actual wrongdoing for which the person was brought to court in the first place. A more stringent version of this same approach should be applied to the poor who have no criminal history, or pose no risk to public safety, but who are charged with a felony. Withholding a percentage of pay from the defendant or a family member, implementing electronic supervision, and receiving guarantees from several people of good moral standing who could go to jail if the defendant were to flee, could be employed. For the well-off, property or a fixed cash amount could continue to be used for bail. The bottom line is that the bail system should work fairly for all, regardless of socioeconomic circumstances. The current focus on money or property as bail misses the entire point of what bail should stand for, and unfairly punishes the poor. It creates a system where the poor suffer more for the same crime, defeating everything the criminal justice system stands for.

Mandatory sentencing also violates the principle that negative consequences and severity of action should be equal. Although mandatory sentencing laws help set the standard or guidelines that judges or juries should follow for sentencing, as opposed to relying on the discretion of judges which is fraught with problems, it is like a bull in a china shop because it ends up destroying more than it fixes. With mandatory sentencing laws, a single mother, for example, with no criminal history could be sentenced to 10 years in prison for mailing a package that contained a few grams of crack cocaine on behalf of someone that she didn't know. It would not care if she was taken advantage of by the person who instructed her to mail the package due to her naiveté and desperation for money. This punishment simply does not match the woman's wrongdoing, nor does it in any way help the justice system or the safety of the community she resides in. Such a woman needs help with a job to alleviate her financial situation.

The law must consider everything about an offender and try to help them. For those who can be rehabilitated, it must expend all energy to do so, while those who are clearly unredeemable it must lock away in the interest of public safety. Current mandatory laws should be reserved for career criminals, and those bent on committing crimes even after efforts at rehabilitation, or people to whom the system has given all opportunities at redemption. Low-level offenders who pose no harm to the community shouldn't be made to suffer excessively.

Thankfully, a program called Pretrial Intervention (also known as diversion) is now available in many states. This is distinct from mental health and drugs courts. Diversion is intended to spare low-risk offenders from the devastating consequences of a criminal record and mostly applies to nonviolent cases— offenses like shoplifting, drug possession, and theft. It is truly a step in the right direction.

However, many diversion programs are poorly run and benefit the rich rather than the poor. An examination by The New York Times of statutes and fee schedules on 225 adult diversion programs run by prosecutors in 37 states, and interviews with more than 150 prosecutors, found that in many states, only people with money could afford diversion and many jurisdictions have turned it into a source of revenue. Prosecutors decide who can join the program, and at what price. Even when in the program, failure to pay can cause a person to be kicked out, and the prices are not cheap. Although prices vary widely from town to town, according to the Times, it can reach $5,000 for a single offense. Not many working Americans can afford this. So, in a nutshell, two people who commit the same crime that qualifies for diversion face different negative consequences. The one who is poor and unable to pay the exorbitant fee is put through the justice system, and the one who is well-off walks away without a record. Diversion has quite simply become like the unfair bail system (Dewan and Lehren., 2016).

To ensure that negative consequences is equal to the severity of wrongdoing, just like bail, diversion programs should take into account the income of the offender. If the person is poor, fees for entry should be eliminated and a fixed percentage (10-15%) of the salary or monthly wages of the offender, their family, or friends should be taken for the period of the program. For a poor offender who qualifies for the program but has no means of paying this 10-15% of income, all fees should be eliminated. This would equalize access for all offenders, regardless of ability to pay.

In some states, diversion programs fail to protect defendants who are granted diversion from avoiding prosecution and a criminal record. According to The New York Times, cases that are dismissed after finishing the program can still show up in a background check. Also, many district attorneys require defendants to enter a guilty plea and impose strict requirements, like hundreds of hours of community service, five years of probation, or even a month in jail. Such strict requirements are tantamount to excessive punishment and undermine the entire idea behind the program. Diversion programs are about correcting the underlying problem for low-level offenders and giving them a second chance. If it imposes draconian requirements and a guilty plea while the defendant pays a lot of money to be in the program, then the negative consequences become greater than the severity of the wrongdoing.

Changes should be made to the program with a focus on counseling, rehabilitation and job training. People in diversion programs should not be made to take a guilty plea or serve a day in jail. While they must be supervised, they should be allowed to go about their lives. They should be allowed to keep going to school, if they still attend school, and to work if they are working adults while reporting for their classes. Restrictions on alcohol or drugs, staying outside late, or other forms of restrictions that pertain to their offense may be placed on them during this period. However, these restrictions should be reasonable and not excessive.

Prison and harsh jail terms are not the solution to crime. As a matter of fact, unjust prison terms end up ruining lives. Many offenders need help with some underlying problem, and unless the justice system decides to address these problems, it will continue to be a system of waste and ineffectiveness, a system that preys on the poor and results in the perpetuation of poverty and despair while claiming to serve everyone.

5. Rules Should Be Clear, Simple, and Consistent.

One tragic hallmark of 2016 was the violent and often tragic interaction between several unarmed people and the police. The shooting of Charles Kinsey on July 18, 2016, in North Miami, while he had his hands up, and the shooting of Philandro Castile on July 6, 2016 in Falcon Heights, Minnesota, while trying to retrieve his license and registration according to his girlfriend, raises concerns about how people should behave when confronted by a cop. This lack of simplicity, clarity and consistency in what is the appropriate behavior to be displayed by both the cop and the person in question only increases the mistrust as well the risk of violent encounters between law enforcement and people in the communities they serve.

Simplicity, clarity, and consistency about what is expected when stopped by a cop while driving, when a cop comes to one's house, when a cop stops one on the street, even when a suspect is in hiding, would help a great deal to allay the fears and worries of many who see the unnecessary shooting of people even when they seemed to have followed the rules. A media and outreach campaign to show what is considered appropriate and inappropriate behavior in all circumstances when interacting with a cop would go a long way in making the rules clearer. How police should act, and how the person in question should respond, must be made a national standard or protocol that everyone follows. Justifiable force can only therefore be used when a person knowingly violates this standard.

Furthermore, clarity and consistency on what to do for people with mentally challenged relatives who need help with the police needs to be established. The death of Alfred Olango, an immigrant from Uganda, by police in El Cajon, California, shows the need for such clarity. Before his sister called the police, should she have sedated him, locked him up in his room, or restrained him? With some clarity, his death could have been avoided. People with mental and emotional illnesses make up a significant portion of those police officers deal with every day, so the need for simplicity, clarity, and consistency to reduce the incidence of unnecessary tragic loss of life cannot be overemphasized.

Also, the rules for which an inmate is granted parole should be simple, clear, and consistent. An analysis by The New York Times of thousands of parole decisions from the past several years found that parole hearings in New York are hurried and often disorganized. Board members' first impressions of an inmate, whether he is well-spoken or inarticulate, neat or disheveled, black or white, can have an outsized impact on his future. Such excessive use of discretion allows for unfairness and inconsistency in parole decisions. Also, according to the Times report, it was often hard to pinpoint the deciding factor for parole commissioners. Some board commissioners were interested in the inmate's criminal record or problems with drug abuse. Some others were more interested in family ties. In some cases, their minds are made up before the offender comes into the room (Winerip, Schwirtz and Gebeloff, 2016).

In place of human discretion, a simple scoring algorithm should be used to determine whether a prisoner should be released or not. An algorithm that takes age, criminal history, prison behavior, mental competence, drug abuse, and family ties into account can be used for each prisoner, and a passing score would require the parole commissioners to release the prisoner. Such an algorithm would constantly be fine-tuned as new data accumulate about how parolees behave when released. Only such consistency, clarity, and simplicity will bring fairness to parole hearings and decisions. Inmates especially minorities are disproportionately affected when parole commissioners are allowed to use their discretion in making parole decisions.

Furthermore, prosecutors shouldn't be given too much power to decide who qualifies for diversion programs and how much they should pay. Such excessive power results in unfairness. Qualification or eligibility criteria for diversion programs and amount to be paid should be simple, well defined and consistent. A scoring algorithm would serve better than a prosecutor to determine eligibility. Such an algorithm will take many things into consideration like type of crime, criminal history, socioeconomic circumstance etc. and provide a passing score. A person is then allowed into the program or excluded from it because of their score and not the whims of the prosecutor. Also, amount to be paid for the program should be affordable, consistent and transparent. Clarity and consistency of amount to be paid will avoid the variations and unfairness that inevitably accompanies a persecutor deciding how much to pay for every defender.

Finally, the rules for which bail is set should be simple, clear and consistent. Across the country, the bail system is complex, unclear and arbitrary. In some places, bail is based on the charges alone while in others, court officials weigh a host of factors like criminal record, substance-abuse history and employment status. Under such a system, some of the decisions will inevitably be influenced by the biases of magistrates, commissioners and judges. Such hidden biases tend to be more against the poor and minorities and results in a two-tier justice system. To achieve clarity and consistency in the bail system, an algorithm should be used in place of human judges. The state of New Jersey recently implemented an algorithm called the Public Safety Assessment, which mathematically determines a defendant's risk of flight or to commit another crime. The use of this algorithm is not perfect but it will put simplicity, clarity and consistency in bail decisions and ensure that everyone regardless of their race or socioeconomic status gets an equal chance to make bail. More states should adopt such algorithm and fine-tune it over time to make it more perfect.

6. Primary Contributors Must Always Communicate or Interact Directly and Frequently.

The police and members of the community are considered primary contributors in the criminal justice system. When primary contributors communicate directly and regularly, trust and cooperation between the police and members of the community is strengthened and overall the system works better.

So, to promote and sustain trust, the police must engage all relevant groups in the communities they serve. Being aloof or divorced from the affairs of the community they serve makes them to be perceived negatively. Many police departments already have outreach programs; however, with the increased sense of distrust because of the recent shooting of several police officers and members of the public, efforts must be doubled on such programs. More resources should be put into police community outreach programs across the country to increase police engagement. Youth engagement would help decrease tension and hostility toward the police. Regular engagement and contacts with the community, so that grievances are addressed, would help foster trust and increase the reporting of suspicious behavior to the police.

7. Third Parties or Secondary Contributors Can Be Applied or Introduced to Uphold the Rule of Law

Too many people have died at the hands of police, with no punishment or consequence, and often no finding of wrongdoing by investigating committees. From the deaths of Amadou Diallo, Gidone Busch, Richard Watson, and Eric Garner, many law enforcement officers have gotten away without criminal charges or criminal conviction. It's rare that an officer gets charged with a homicide offense resulting from their on-duty conduct, even though people are killed on a regular basis. According to a study by the Cato Institute, in which researchers tracked allegations of misconduct involving nearly 11,000 police officers in the US from April 2009 through December 2010, only 33% of the 3,238 of those cases with criminal charges resulted in a conviction (Packman, 2011). Rates of criminal charges are low, and rates of conviction are even lower. This only increases public distrust of the entire system and emboldens the bad eggs among the police to continue in their behavior.

Police work is hard, and they must be given credit for what they do, but the law must apply equally to everyone, regardless of place or authority. While there is no easy way to fix this problem, one thing that can be done is to introduce third-party, independent prosecutors to look at allegations of wrongdoing and objectively pursue cases where sufficient evidence of wrongdoing is found. Third-party independent prosecutors are needed to overcome the very close working relationship between prosecutors and the police, which to an extent contributes to the low level of criminal charges brought against many officers. Although the Justice Department investigates allegations of wrongdoing in police departments, they often step in when the problems are widespread. A state-wide, independent body should be created that reviews police officers' wrongdoings and brings charges when they think there is a case to answer. This is likely to result in more prosecution and indictment of officers who act outside the law, and could help curtail the culture of acting outside the law that has been associated with some police departments. While this is not a perfect solution, and conviction is not guaranteed, it would help ensure that everyone is equal before the law regardless of their position or authority. Importantly, it would help increase overall confidence in the justice system.

Third parties can also be used to review disciplinary actions taken against prisoners. Prisoners are very vulnerable to abuse because of their status, and they are particularly at a great disadvantage in prisons where they live in isolation with prison staff. To increase transparency and accountability, state departments of corrections could institute monthly reviews and overturn or reprimand prison officers found to be abusing their authority. Leaving the prison system to run itself without much oversight results in a culture of impunity, and this is bad for the entire criminal justice system.

8. Third Parties Should Be Employed to Achieve Fairness and Equality in the System.

More than five decades ago, in the case of Gideon v. Wainwright, the United States Supreme Court declared that the Sixth Amendment guarantees to every criminal defendant in a felony trial the right to a lawyer. The ruling ensured that a defendant who is too poor to hire a lawyer is provided counsel to assure a fair trial.

Today, across America, the right to counsel is violated. In many courts, many poor people plead guilty without lawyers. In some counties, the poor are charged as much as $200 as application fee for free legal representation (Kim, 2105). This goes against everything that public defender system is supposed to do. Lack of proper funding and explosion of criminal cases means most court-appointed lawyers are often underpaid and grossly overworked. This compels them to triage and results in less than adequate representation (Cohen, 2013).

According to a Brennan Center for Justice, many courts appointed lawyers often spends less than six minutes per case at hearings where their clients plead guilty and are sentenced. There are cases of people learning about plea offers from lawyers they barely knew and will never see again (Giovanni Thomas, 2012). For many poor defendants, their court-appointed lawyer is perceived as working together with the prosecutor because prosecutors often determine outcomes in cases with little or no input from defense counsel.

Many states use a combination of public defenders and court appointed lawyers. Some states like Colorado have a good statewide state-wide public defender system, but they are far from perfect. Others like New York, and Texas have left selection and administration of their system to their counties resulting in different quality of representation across county lines. (Cohen Andrew, 2013). At the federal level, many indigent defendants rely on salaried public defenders and appointed lawyers paid by the hour. A study found that defendants represented by court-appointed lawyers received sentences averaging about eight months longer than those represented by federal public defenders and took longer to resolve cases through plea bargains. The results were considered to be consistent with the hourly wage structure of court appointed lawyers which create incentives for them to take longer to resolve cases (Iyengar, 2007).

To fix this problem, third party private independent lawyers should be employed state wide and at the federal level to defend indigent citizens, and these lawyers should be salaried. The State of Maine currently provides representation through assigning private counsel, but it could use some improvement. An electronic social network system that allows defendants to choose the lawyer they want to represent them from a pool, see their records and availability should be put in place. In this network, defendants should be able to provide feedback, rate the quality of representation they got from an attorney and these ratings should be connected to attorney contract extension. Furthermore, defendants should be given the privilege to select or fire as much as three lawyers during their trial. This will improve the quality of representation and spur lawyers to go the extra mile for their clients.

Also, it will ensure that the criminal justice system works equally for all regardless of socioeconomic status.

9. Third Parties Should Always Be Avoided Except When There Is an Insurmountable Disadvantage to a Primary Contributor or Doing It In-House.

The prison system is a key element of the criminal justice system. It is meant not merely to house criminals, but to reform them. In recent years, there has been an explosion in third-party, for-profit private prisons and the excuse for their use is to cut costs. The problem with this approach is the profit motive. With private prisons, the interest of the prison becomes to keep as many people locked up for as long as possible while spending little or no money on quality care. It results in powerful interest groups lobbying against prison and criminal justice reforms, and even the criminal collusion between prison investors or owners and the justice system. The case of Judge Mark Ciavarella and Michael Conahan of Pennsylvania, who were involved in the sentencing of youngsters to prisons they had a hand in building is a clear example of this problem. Kids as young as 10 years old were sentenced for crimes such as possession of drug paraphernalia, and posting web page spoofs about an assistant principal (Urbina and Hamill, 2009).

Figure 3-3: The goal of the criminal justice and prison system.

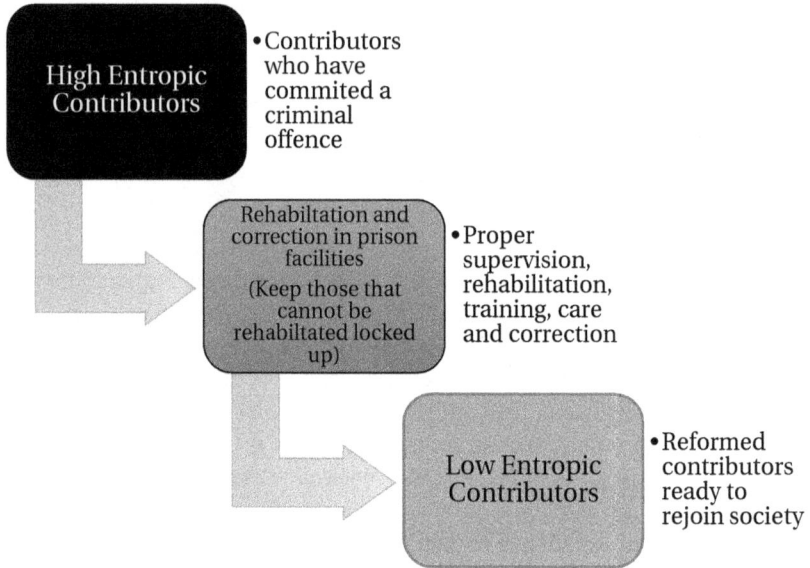

Furthermore, since for-profit entities are in business to make a profit, they are likely to do anything, including food rationing, denying needed health care, hiring poorly trained staff, reducing investment in educational and job training programs, and other important rehabilitative services in other to keep costs down. These services are essential to reducing recidivism and improving public safety. Evidence from research in Minnesota found that private prisons are not more effective in reducing recidivism (Duwe and Clark, 2013). According to the ACLU and the Southern Poverty Law Center, who investigated problems with two Mississippi prisons operated by the GEO, one of the biggest for-profit prison operators in the world, there are horrifying patterns of abuse against juveniles and the mentally ill. According to their investigation of the GEO-run East Mississippi Correctional Facility, the GEO has been "starving the mentally ill prisoners, denying them basic mental health care, punishing them with solitary confinement, and exposing them to such systemic abuse and neglect that suicides and suicide attempts are rampant." (Eber and Winter, 2012).

The Obama Justice Department recently announced that it was phasing out its relationships with private prisons; this is a step in the right direction. According to the Justice Department, private prisons did not save substantially on costs. Hopefully, this same policy will be adopted by states and cities across the country as third-party for-profit prisons are not the solution to cutting costs or improving the quality of services. Third parties can be useful, but must only be employed when there is an insurmountable problem that cannot be overcome—and in this case, the costs and problem of overcrowding in prisons are not insurmountable to the government. They can be fixed with criminal justice reforms that correct mandatory sentencing laws.

10. Power or Authority Must Never Exceed or Go Beyond Contribution.

This means power and contribution must always be equal. Contribution in this case entails competence or qualification. Power or authority must always be given to those who are most competent and qualified. When this is violated, the repercussions are far-reaching. The job of the police is perhaps one of the most important in any community, making it even more important that only the most competent are granted police powers.

Recruitment is critical, and for this reason, a lot of attention should be paid to the quality of people allowed to join the force. Community colleges are responsible for educating the bulk of recruits in police departments around the country, but this qualification is too low with the complex levels of tasks that an officer manages. Raising the bar to college and graduate degrees would be a step in the right direction, with a focus on people with degrees in the social sciences. Also, many police departments give preference to people with aggressive tendencies in recruitment, but aggression is not a necessary trait to do police work. Such people may be more likely to abuse their power. People who have solid social skills, who are more cerebral, more sensitive, empathetic, rational and willing to learn should be given preference over those with aggressive tendencies (Lantigua-Williams, 2016).

In the United Kingdom, police recruitment is a rigorous selection process of fitness tests, psychological appraisals, and marksmanship exams, followed by a tough screening process. Officers must serve for years before they can apply to carry a gun, and the selection of those deemed worthy is intensely competitive (Witte, 2015). This is not the case in the United States, where gun laws are lax. So, to get a more professional and effective police force, the selection process must be rigorous and the bar for entrance raised from its current level.

The same attention should be paid to the recruitment of officers in detention and correctional facilities. Currently, at the city, county, and state levels, correctional officer education requirements vary. State, county, and city correctional jurisdictions usually require that correctional officers hold a minimum of a high school diploma or its equivalent. This should be raised to a minimum of bachelor's degree. Correctional officers deal with very complex problems, and a bachelor's degree would better prepare them better for the rigors of the job.

Also, judges in any capacity should be people in good standing with the law, who have earned a law degree and passed the bar. In some states, all judges presiding over misdemeanor cases are required to be lawyers but in others, non-lawyer judges can hand down jail sentences for misdemeanors. In some states that allow non-lawyer judges, a defendant who receives a jail sentence from a non-lawyer judge has the right to seek a new trial before a lawyer-judge while in others like Montana, Arizona, Colorado, Nevada, New York, Texas, South Carolina, and Wyoming, the defender has no right to a new trial before a lawyer-judge (Ford 2017). Criminal procedures are complex and if the judge has poor grasps of the law then they cannot perform their job in a fair and effective manner. To ensure that power and contribution are equal, changes should be made so that all judges whether in rural or sparsely popu-lated areas are lawyers. This would go a long way towards creating a better criminal justice system.

Conclusion.

An overview of the criminal justice system in its current form reveals a system in crisis, and in need of serious reforms. The use of mandatory sentencing is one of the biggest problems with the system and reforms are necessary to calibrate them towards punishing serious offenders. More resources should be put into diversion programs to ensure that low-level drug offenders are not excessively punished. Homogenous courts like drug, mental health, and gang courts should be expanded for special at-risk groups so they can receive the care and rehabilitation they need.

Better and more robust legal representation should be made available at the state and federal level to indigent defendants. Furthermore, the culture of violence and poverty in the inner cities must be addressed to give people there a chance to choose a different path. The government should double its efforts toward the chemical detoxification of ghetto neighborhoods, consider-ing the well-documented relationship between toxic exposure and youth criminality (Patterson, 2015). More resources should be put in community-based programs that focus on improving life skills and keep boys away from the streets. President Obama's "My Brother's Keeper" program is a great initi-ative, but more still needs to be done. Failure to do something about the inner cities would result in a criminal justice system that continues to be bedeviled by significant racial disparities.

Furthermore, bail reform is needed to make sure the poor are not unfairly punished. If the law cannot protect the weak and vulnerable, then it becomes a tool of witch hunt and oppression. Barriers to reentry, like barring offenders from professional licensing, should be amended to fight recidivism and give offenders a chance to make something of their lives. More resources should be put into prisoner education, and criminal records should be sealed after a set number of years of demonstrable good behavior. When the criminal justice system keeps people permanently from joining the positive homogenous group, it works against its own interest and mission.

Also, efforts must be doubled to keep the police force, parole board, and prison system in positive homogeneity. Use of body cameras should be made standard to help curtail abuse of power and cover-up by police officers.

These reforms would turn the criminal justice system around and make it a much fairer and effective system.

Chapter 4

Social Security

Social Security, also known as Old-Age, Survivors, and Disability Insurance (OASDI), is a very important benefit program that millions of Americans rely on. It has two parts, both funded by payroll taxes: The Old-Age and Survivors Insurance (OASI), which pays retirement benefits, and Social Security Disability Insurance (SSDI), which pays disability benefits to workers unable to engage in "substantial gainful activity," as it is termed. Both programs are very popular among taxpayers. According to the 2015 Trustees' report, at the end of 2014 about 59 million Americans were receiving retirement and disability benefits from the system, and 166 million people paid payroll taxes into the system. Also, according to the Social Security 2016 Trustees' Report, social security has collected about $19.0 trillion, paid out $16.1 trillion, and as of 2016, the trust funds for both programs have reserves of more than $2.8 trillion in Treasuries.

For many decades, the OASDI produced big surpluses, collecting more in payroll taxes than it paid in benefits, and these surpluses were put in a trust fund. According to the 2015 report from the Social Security Trustees, in 2014 the program took in $769 billion and paid out $714 billion. The surplus $55 billion went into its trust fund. In 2015, according to the 2016 trustee report, $23 billion surplus went into its trust fund.

However, it is not all rosy for the programs. The OASDI combined income from payroll taxes and the interest earned on its reserves is expected to exceed total costs through 2019. Excluding interest income, its cost has exceeded its non-interest income since 2010, and this non-interest deficit is projected to average about $69 billion between 2016 and 2019. Past 2019, interest income and trust fund asset reserves will need to be redeemed to satisfy benefit obligations until 2034 when the reserves would be exhausted. After this, it will only be able to pay about three-quarters of scheduled benefits through the end of 2090 from ongoing tax revenues. The Congressional Budget Office estimates that the OASI will reach insolvency as early as 2030, four years earlier than the Trustees' reported insolvency date.

Although it is not yet in a state of crisis, reforms must be implemented to put the program on a sustainable path. On the 2016 presidential campaign trail, reforming Social Security (OASI and the SSDI) was one of the hottest topics, and politicians on both sides of the aisle offered different solutions, focusing primarily on the OASI. Proposals included privatizing it, raising the full retirement age, initiating longevity indexing, recalculating the cost-of-living adjustment, increasing or eliminating the payroll tax cap, means-testing for benefits, reducing benefits for higher earners, increasing the payroll tax rate, increasing the number of years used to calculate initial benefits, and covering all newly hired state and local government workers, among others.

Close examination of these proposals shows that none of them would solve the deep structural problems with the OASI. Proponents of the proposal to raise the full retirement age argue that this will help close the OASI's funding gap and put it on a sustainable path. Changing demographics is one of the biggest challenges the OASI faces. People now live much longer than they did in the 1940s. This means that beneficiaries will be getting hundreds of thousands of dollars more in lifetime benefits than they would have when the system was first created.

Also, there is a declining worker-to-beneficiary ratio, which is projected to fall from 3.3 in 2005 to 2.1 in 2040 (Reznik, Shoffner and Weaver, 2006). According to Social Security office of policy, by 2080, 23 percent of the total population will be aged 65 or older. According to CBO's 2016 long-term budget outlook report, the number of people who are age 65 or older will increase by 37 percent by 2026, and 75 percent by 2046. In contrast, it projects increases of only 3 percent and 14 percent over those same periods in the working age population; between the ages of 20 and 64.

This puts the program in a difficult fiscal situation as it is dependent on new enrollees to outnumber the beneficiaries to remain sustainable. Even with this change in life expectancy, full or normal retirement age will increase by only two years in 2027, to 67. Proponents of raising the retirement age, the early eligibility age or both want these changes taken into consideration. According to the American Academy of Actuaries, raising the full retirement age to 70 would wipe out up to half of the long-range actuarial deficit and raising it to 73 would almost eliminate the deficit. However, raising the full retirement age would result in a benefit cut. It will cause benefits for people retiring early at 62 to be only about 57 percent of the full retirement benefit (depending on the early-retirement reduction factors used), which is grossly insufficient and even more insufficient for non-working spouses, who receive about half of the worker's benefit.

Also, low-income workers do not live as long as wealthy Americans, and they often work in physically demanding jobs that compromise their health which forces many of them into early retirement. Raising the retirement age would unjustly punish them. Also, it will encourage more impaired workers younger than full retirement age to file for disability benefits, raising the SSDI program's costs. Importantly, raising the retirement age, the early retirement age or both is not a permanent solution because it would have to be constantly raised since life expectancy is anticipated to increase for future enrollees. With this strategy, full retirement age might someday have to be set at 85 to maintain solvency, which of course would be ludicrous.

Another proposal is to adjust benefits by using a different method of calculation. OASI benefits keep up with inflation through a cost-of-living adjustment or COLA. Since 1975, the Labor Department uses the Consumer Price Index for Urban Wage Earners and Clerical Workers, or CPI-W, to calculate inflation's effects on OASDI beneficiaries' costs. It measures changes in the prices of consumer goods and services. Proponents seek to replace it with Chained Consumer Price Index which is an index that reflects the substitution that consumers make in response to changes in prices. It is derived from the broader Consumer Price Index for All Urban Consumers (CPI-U), which covers 87 percent of the population. Supporters of this proposal argue that using Chained CPI means the rate at which benefits rise would be slower, and this would fill a significant portion of the funding gap.

The problem with using the Chained CPI is that a small reduction to the annual COLA will result in significant reductions in benefits over time. This would have a negative impact on the economic well-being of many seniors and their family members who rely on Social Security benefits for their income. Also, many seniors tend to have higher out-of-pocket medical spending and poverty rate than younger Americans and may not be able to absorb any cuts in benefits. Moreover, this proposal doesn't reform the structural problems with the OASI.

Another proposal is to increase or eliminate the payroll cap. Currently, OASDI payroll tax applies to annual earnings up to $127,200 in 2017, and any wages earned above this amount go untaxed. This amount usually increases each year at the same rate as average wages in the economy. Proponents argue that raising the cap to cover a higher percentage of total earnings would help close the OASI funding gap. Some politicians and experts have talked about raising the cap from its current 82% in 2016 to cover 90% of earnings, which in 2017 would mean a cap of about $245,000. According to the staff of the Joint Committee on Taxation, this would increase revenues by an estimated $648 billion over the 2017–2026 period. Some have proposed eliminating the cap altogether so that all earnings would be subject to OASDI payroll tax. The problem with raising the cap is that it would impose high marginal tax rates on middle income and upper-income earners, who already pay more in income taxes. Also, it would reduce individual incomes, hurt tax revenues, and overall economic growth without fully fixing the problem (Greszler, 2014).

As for eliminating the cap, the problem with this proposal is that only about 6% of workers earn more than the current cap of $118,500 (Reno and John, n.d.), and if this is implemented, those people and their employers would have to pay more payroll taxes. This would hit high-earning workers, and businesses hard, and could discourage investment and hiring. Importantly, it is unlikely to solve the OASI's financial shortfalls.

Another proposal is to reduce benefits for higher earners or higher lifetime earners. The argument for reduced benefits to higher earners is that many of them have little or no need for OASI benefits. The original intent of OASI was to protect against poverty in old age, so slashing benefits to higher earners maintains its promise while closing its funding shortfalls. The problem with this proposal is that it would cut benefits for many middle-class workers, including those making as little as $35,000 a year according to Virginia Reno of the National Academy of Social Insurance. Benefits are already modest, and many retirees are battling high healthcare costs. Importantly, reducing benefits for high-income earners who have paid into the program with the hope of getting their money back on retirement would be a serious breach of trust. It would be tantamount to robbing Peter to pay Paul.

Another proposal is to increase the payroll tax rate. Currently, for OASI, employees pay 5.3%, and this is matched by employers to make a total of 10.6%. The self-employed pay the full 10.6% themselves. Experts calculate that increasing the payroll tax rate by a few percent from 2018 to 2023 could fill a significant portion of the funding gap, and will help shore up its finances. Increasing taxes to shore up the OASI would affect all workers, regardless of income, and would leave many with even fewer resources to spend for themselves or save. For employers, payroll tax increases would result in higher labor costs, which would discourage hiring and investment. Importantly, this move will not put the program on a sustainable path because taxes would need to be raised many more times in the future until it becomes unbearable, or impossible. Put simply; it is a palliative solution to a deep-seated problem.

Another proposal is to cover all newly hired state and local government workers. OASI does not cover about one-quarter of state and local government employees. These workers are enrolled in retirement plans provided by state or local governments that are not part of the OASI program. Estimates by the staff of the Joint Committee on Taxation, show that including all state and local government employees hired after December 31, 2016, will increase revenues by a total of $78 billion over the 2017–2026 period. However, the problem with this proposal is that, although it would lead to an increase in revenue in the short term, it would leave the program saddled with paying more people benefits in the long term.

Another proposal is to increase the number of years used to calculate OASI benefits. OASI benefits are calculated from a worker's highest 35 years of annual indexed earnings that were subject to Social Security payroll taxes. If a person worked more than 35 years, the highest 35 years are used in computing their benefits and if they have fewer than 35 years of earnings, the missing years are simply assigned as zero earnings. One option to help close the OASI funding gap is to increase the number of years used to calculate benefits from 35 to 38, or even 40. This, it is argued, would reduce the benefits paid out and fill a significant portion of the solvency gap. The problem with this proposal is that it will force people to work longer with little or no change in benefits. This change would be harder for low-income workers. Also, it would reduce benefits for retirees and their dependents who need it the most.

Another proposal is to begin means-testing OASI's benefits. OASI's benefits have always been provided to anyone who has paid into the system and who meets the work and age requirements without any regard if they have other sources of income such as investment, pension, or savings. Mean testing would mean cutting benefits for higher-income recipients and retirees with other sources of income. The problem with means testing is that it is grossly unfair and could discourage some people from pursuing other sources of retirement saving, which should be encouraged. Furthermore, it would cost more to administer as the government has to spend time and resources to regularly check the income and assets of people to adjust their benefits.

Another proposal is to privatize the OASI. Proponents argue that the year-over-year growth rate for private investments is much higher than the return gained by retired workers in the current OASI program, and this makes personal retirement accounts a better option. Private accounts, they argue will give workers personal freedom, and control over their retirement funds, lower the entitlement burden and increase investments. To allay people's worries, these private retirement accounts would be restricted from being invested into high-risk ventures. This means people would not be allowed to invest their OASI savings in individual stocks or other highly volatile investments.

Although private accounts can be useful, switching to them, whether partially or fully, would make the OASI—which is supposed to be a guaranteed benefit—vulnerable to the vagaries of the stock market. During the 2008 financial crisis, the three main stock market indexes all dropped precipitously, resulting in massive losses. Such risks make it a very unattractive choice regardless of its many benefits. Furthermore, due to the "boom and bust" nature of the market, those who retire during an economic boom would be better off than those who retire during a downturn.

The OASI isn't supposed to be a gambling program or a wealth-building program; it's a guaranteed social insurance program for the elderly so that they can retire in dignity (Sloan, 2010). Changing it into an investment program would significantly favor higher-income people because they have savings they can depend on while they wait out the markets. Also, many people lack the basic financial literacy to make wise investment decisions on their own, and this makes them vulnerable to unscrupulous people who could mismanage their money. So, while private accounts are not necessarily a bad idea, the risk involved makes them unsuitable for a guaranteed income program like the OASI.

Just like the OASI, the Social Security Disability Insurance (SSDI), is facing serious fiscal challenges. According to the 2015 Annual Statistical Report on the SSDI Program, the number of disabled beneficiaries has risen from just under two million in 1970 to over ten million in 2015, driven mainly by an increase in the number of disabled workers. This breaks down to almost nine million disabled workers; over one million disabled adult children; and over 250,000 disabled widow(ers).

This increase in SSDI beneficiaries has resulted in significant financial strain on the program, and it has been running a deficit for many years. According to the 2014 OASDI trustee report, in 2013, the SSDI took in $111.2 billion in revenues and paid out almost $145 billion in benefits, resulting in a deficit of $32.2 billion. Furthermore, according to the 2016 Social Security Trustee Annual report, the SSDI Trust Fund reserves will increase until 2019, because its reserves were shored up by reallocating a portion of the payroll tax rate from the OASI but it will be fully exhausted in the third quarter of 2023. After this, incoming tax revenues will only be enough to cover 89% of promised benefits.

One reason for the SSDI financial situation is that too many people enter the program and very few leave it. Most SSDI benefit recipients remain on SSDI until death or retirement. In 1985, the Disability Insurance exit rate was 12.1 percent, but in 2004, it went down to a low of 7.2 percent, an exit rate of one in fourteen claimants (Autor and Duggan, 2006).

One reason for this increase in beneficiaries is that the workforce is getting older. As the Baby Boomers have gotten older, their disability rates have risen, and this has contributed to the increase in the number of people receiving SSDI benefits. Some analysts have pointed at retirement age as a culprit in the increase in SSDI payments. Previously, older SSDI beneficiaries became eligible for the OASI at age 65, but this has changed to 66 which means an additional year of waiting.

Another reason for the rise in SSDI recipients is due to the rapid increase in female labor force participation. Decades ago, few women worked enough quarters in jobs covered by OASDI but as their participation in the labor force has increased over the years, many of them have become eligible for benefits. Also, the expansion of the scope of the program from workers between the ages of 50 and 65 to include workers under age 50 and the temporarily disabled contributed to the increase in beneficiaries.

Another reason for the increase in the number of SSDI recipients, is the relaxation of the medical eligibility criteria to include medical conditions that are difficult to assess objectively. Several decades ago, strokes, heart attacks, and cancer were the leading causes of disability. However congressional reforms in 1984 resulted in the rapid rise in recipients suffering from back pain and mental illness. These medical impairments are harder to verify due to their lack of objective measures, and this makes them open to manipulation and fraudulent claims. Also, because these disorders have low mortality, more people remain in the program than leave and hence the size of the recipient population has increased (Autor and Duggan, 2006).

Another reason offered for the explosion in SSDI receipts is the rising financial incentives to apply for a disability award or its appeal to low-skilled workers who are facing a hard time in the stagnant economy. Wages for low-skilled workers with few skills have stagnated over the past four decades, and this has made SSDI look very attractive. The average monthly SSDI benefit which is about $1,200 is almost equal to what a full-time minimum wage worker earns before taxes. In addition, after two years they qualify for Medicare. While this is not enough income to live lavishly, for someone whose alternative is a minimum wage job that will pay them around $15,000 a year, with no certainty of health insurance, disability seems like a better option. Other reasons cited for the growth in the SSDI program include poor continuing disability reviews, adjudication process flaws and deficiencies, fraud and abuse, and less than optimal interaction or coordination with other government programs.

There have been calls to reform the SSDI just like the OASI. Reform proposals include; raising the payroll cap, raising the payroll tax rate, tightening eligibility, reducing monthly benefits to recipients to make it unattractive, raising the retirement age, continuing to transfer money from the OASI trust fund to the SSDI fund, and replacing it with private long-term unemployment insurance (PLUI) or with private disability insurance. Some proposals are impractical, while others will do little to put it on a sustainable path.

Although it is important that eligibility is tightened, past efforts have failed. The political backlash in pursuing this strategy makes it impractical. SSDI benefits are quite modest; the average monthly benefit is about $1,200. To cut it just to make it unattractive or force people to leave the program for work would harm many severely disabled people who depend on SSDI checks for their sustenance. The proposal to raise or eliminate the payroll tax rate is not going to put the SSDI on a sustainable path. Workers currently pay a tax of 0.9% of their wages up to $118,500 in 2016, and their employers pay an equal amount. Proponents argue that 0.9% is too small and it should be increased.

Raising the tax will not solve the SSDI's problems, as it would have to be raised many times in the future. The same problem applies to the proposal to raise the payroll tax cap.

The proposal to keep moving funds from the OASI to the SSDI accounts has been implemented many times before and has not put the SSDI on a sustainable path. The Obama administration has proposed to shift 0.9% of the OASDI payroll tax from OASI to SSDI over the years 2016 to 2020. This would only shore up the SSDI's accounts in the short term, and it's tantamount to a bandage on a deep, infected wound that needs multiple surgeries. The proposal to require firms to offer private disability insurance (PDI), and to provide SSDI only after private disability insurance runs its course is a good one. Such a policy would shift some of SSDI's costs onto private employers, and thus onto covered workers. PDI is likely to provide better income support as well as a tougher examination of disability applications. It would more effectively address fraud, which has been reported to be present in the SSDI program while increasing benefits for those who are truly disabled. The biggest drawback with PDI is that it could result in a situation where many people who truly need help are denied.

Another interesting proposal is to use private long-term unemployment insurance (PLUI) (Winship, 2015). The argument for this proposal is that the PLUI would ensure that workers insure themselves against the risk that they may become unemployed for longer periods in their lifetime. The problem with the PLUI proposal is that many low-skill workers who earn very little are unlikely to be able to afford this insurance. To make it work, an individual mandate may, therefore, be needed, and this would eventually mean that the government might have to provide subsidies to low-income workers (Pollack, 2015). This would be fraught with many problems and could end up costing more.

The SSDI and OASI programs are vital to millions of Americans, but for them to continue to serve these people, bold reforms are needed. In their current form, they are structurally defective, and that is why small solutions like raising or eliminating payroll taxes will not put them on the path of sustainability in the long term.

De-entropification Solution for OASI.

The OASI can be restructured and put on a sustainable path by applying two principles to it.

1. Benefit Must Never Exceed or Go Beyond Contribution

Benefit and contribution must always be equal. Looking at the structure of the OASI, it is quite evident that this principle doesn't hold true. An analysis by the Urban Institute found that the average earning couple who retired in 1990 would have paid $316,000 into the system, but would receive a total of $436,000—$120,000 more than they paid in. In contrast, those turning 65 in 2010 would have paid $600,000 in taxes but could expect to collect $21,000 less, for a total of $579,000. Furthermore, couples now in their early 40s will pay in more than $808,000 by their retirement but will receive only $703,000, representing a loss of $105,000 in benefits. A couple earning average wage of $44,600 each in 2012 dollars who turn 65 in 2030 would have paid in $840,000 in lifetime social security taxes but can expect to collect $725,000 in lifetime benefits (Steuerle and Quakenbush, 2012, 2013, 2015). Even allowing for inflation and investment gains, many OASI recipients receive much more in benefits than they paid into the system. Such a benefit structure puts it on an unsustainable path.

The OASI program uses the best or highest 35 years of earnings to calculate benefits. Therefore, if a person works more than 35 years, those earning are not calculated in their benefits. Put simply, those extra years of work are lost. Another structural problem is that the OASI pays recipients until their deaths, regardless of how much they paid into it. This means that someone who lives to 105 would receive more than someone who died at 75 with no dependents, regardless of their contribution.

Also, a surviving spouse who remarries at 60 or older can get thousands of dollars on their deceased partners 'earnings records, but those who remarry even a day before are ineligible for such benefits. A husband or wife who never contributed a cent into the OASI can get thousands of dollars in benefits over their lifetimes, based on their spouses' earnings records. A couple with only one spouse working and earning $80,000 annually gets thousands of dollars more in benefits than a two-worker couple each making $40,000, even though the two-worker couple pays the same amount of taxes and are more likely to have higher work expenses. Divorced spouses who were married for 10 or more years are eligible to receive thousands of dollars in OASI benefits based on their ex-spouse' earnings record while those divorced a day less are ineligible. Through several marriages, a worker can collect multiple spousal and survivor benefits, without paying anything into the system. Single people who never married for up to 10 years to any one person pay for spousal and survivor benefits, but do not qualify to get them. Collecting at a certain point can make a person get less than if they collect later. Those who understand the complex rules, and time their benefit collection just right, can collect tens of thousands in additional benefits. In contrast, those who don't understand the many rules cannot take advantage of these additional benefits (Steuerle, 2015: Kotlikoff, 2014).

The rules are very complex and the benefits sharing mechanism is haphazard. The receipt of benefits has little to do with what an individual paid into the program. The logic behind using the highest earning 35 years, and not 25 or 40, for example, is incomprehensible. The entire structure is very confusing. Although it is not a Ponzi scheme, it was not very far from it in concept. The system was designed to be perpetually dependent on new enrollees, and this is one of the key problems with it.

To reform the OASI, what an individual put into the OASI should never exceed what they get in benefits. Only when it adheres to this principle will it function optimally and be on a sustainable path. To achieve this, it will be important to personalize the program and focus on saving for the last 35 years of life. Although it remains a program run by the government, all enrollees would have their own accounts accessible online and tailored to their needs. They would contribute a percentage of their income in payroll taxes to this account until age 65. There is no need for a cap in payroll taxes to this account; individuals simply pay into their accounts until they reach the target amount they signed up for. The target amount they need to reach at 65 is decided at the time of enrollment.

Three levels of plans will make this work: gold, silver and bronze. This would give people choices. The gold pays the most benefits on retirement, and the bronze the least benefits. For example, the gold could pay an estimated $5,000 a month, the silver $3,000 and the bronze $1,500 for 35 years, after retirement at 65. That is $2,100,000; $1,260,000; and $630,000 respectively, unadjusted for inflation. Workers then select the plan they want and pay into their accounts to meet this retirement benefit. People can switch between plans if their employers agree to it, or if they are self-employed. The amount in payroll taxes would vary between all three plans. However, for simplicity, it should be the same for everyone. For example, the bronze plan could be the current OASI 10.6% in payroll taxes, the silver could be 12% and the gold 15%. Employers pay 75% and workers contribute 25% for the bronze plan; they pay 50% and workers 50% for the silver plan, and they pay 25% while workers contribute 75% for the gold plan. This arrangement makes it fair to employers and puts some burden on those who want to earn more in retirement. An employer could also choose to offer only the bronze or silver plan to their employees.

Enrollees will not be allowed to dip into this money until they reach the retirement age of 65. An enrollee who fails to meet their target at 65 could work a few more years to meet their target, or simply collect whatever they have saved. This, of course, would be lower than their target monthly payment. An employee could decide to increase their portion of the payroll taxes to meet their target faster, and although their employer would not be obligated to match it, they could do so. Such flexibility is necessary to avoid shortfalls on reaching 65, especially for low-income people or those who may have been without a job for some time.

On retirement, an enrollee receives this money monthly, and not a cent more, for exactly 35 years. Lump sum payments should be taxed heavily to deter people from collecting their retirement money and gambling it on ventures that could fail, causing them to fall into poverty. When an individual die, their spouse, and dependents will be eligible to receive whatever is left of their money, and not a cent more. It could be paid out in a taxed lump sum or monthly. Enrollees could also pass this money in their will to a specific dependent. With this arrangement, retirement age does not need to keep shifting. If people live longer, the program will need to extend the payment to last 38 or 40 years of life and ask enrollees to pay more in payroll taxes. Also, and importantly, the government cannot siphon money from this program to use on other programs, as its structure makes it impossible—unlike the current program.

This system solves many of the problems with the OASI. It is a sustainable system that doesn't require new enrollees to shore it up. It is simple, clear, and efficient.

2. Principles of General Homogeneity: Homogenization to Help Low-Income Workers.

According to a 2016 Pew research center study, there is been a steady decline in the number of middle-income Americans since the 1970s. This means many low-income workers may not be able to save enough for even the OASI bronze plan on retirement. This is likely to increase elderly dependence on welfare and poverty, as well as their healthcare needs. Most importantly, it doesn't speak well of the character of a nation to allow the elderly to live in poverty. To reduce the differences between retirees, a homogenization fund should be created to help fill the funding gaps of low-income workers for the bronze plan. This fund should be funded by taxing both employers and high-income earners (Workers making $250,000 and above), 1% in payroll taxes. To be eligible, a low-income worker should have paid into their OASI account for at least 15 years for the bronze plan. Funds from deceased workers with no dependents should be moved into the homogenization fund to increase its solvency. To avoid the constant raising of payroll taxes to shore up the fund and ensure its sustainability, it would be important to allow people to make tax deductible charitable donations to the fund. Also, would be immigrants on investors visa (EB-5 visa program), should be mandated to make a monetary donation of $10,000 to $20,000 to the fund as part of their eligibility criteria. This will help keep the fund in good shape.

De-entropification Solution for SSDI.

Four principles are needed to fix the problems with the SSDI.

1. Benefits Must Never Exceed or Go Beyond Contribution.

The SSDI benefit system violates this principle. Teenagers with a parent on SSDI benefits are usually eligible to receive benefits as far as they are unmarried. Also, children (18 or over) with a parent on SSDI benefits can receive dependents' benefits if they are disabled, the disability occurred before the child turned 22 years old, or the child is a full-time student at a secondary school and under 19 years old. These benefits continue until graduation or two months after the child's 19th birthday, whichever comes first. Grandchildren or step-grandchildren could also receive dependents' benefits in some cases if a grandparent is collecting SSDI benefits. An elderly parent dependent on an insured worker for more than half of his or her support can collect SSDI benefits. A spouse, and even an ex-spouse can collect SSDI benefits (Netter, n.d.). The list for eligibility goes on, and all these payments are funded by the mere 0.9% taken in payroll taxes from the qualifying worker. None of these qualifying dependents have contributed a penny to the fund, nor has the worker paid any additional money in payroll taxes to insure them. This puts it on an unsustainable path.

To match benefits and contribution, workers should be given the option to enroll their dependents in their plan. If they want their spouse, children, parents, etc., to enjoy SSDI benefits should they become disabled, they must pay more. To enroll dependents, the worker will pay an additional 0.5% in payroll taxes for every dependent added to the plan. This payment is optional. A worker who doesn't enroll dependents would therefore not get any benefits extended. Employers would continue to pay the standard 0.9% for the worker but could help to cover the cost of the worker's dependent(s) if they choose to. This extra money from the worker would help shore up the SSDI finances. It would equalize benefits and contribution, and help put the program on a more sustainable path.

Another way to match benefits with contribution is to increase the payroll taxes of employers whose employees or ex- employees are on SSDI benefits. Currently, all employers pay the same SSDI payroll tax rates regardless of how many of their employees are on SSDI benefits. This creates a situation where employers have lower-than-optimal incentives to prevent their workers from becoming disabled. By shifting the burden to employers as their workers receive SSDI benefits, benefits and contribution would be matched, and employers would be incentivized to prevent disabilities. Employers would then want to retain disabled workers, thus keeping them in the workforce.

Implementing this plan would mean that when an employee leaves a company and joins SSDI, the employer keeps paying the full 1.8% in payroll taxes (currently 0.9% each for both employer and employee) they were paying before the employee joined SSDI. In addition, when the employee becomes eligible for Medicare benefits, the employer starts to pay the full 2.9% in payroll taxes (currently 1.45% each for both employer and employee) that Medicare was supposed to receive before the employee left the company due to disability. This would be discontinued when the employee leaves the program. Another solution is to have employers pay a percentage of the annual benefits an employee collects from SSDI. A small business could pay 15%, and large businesses 25% to 40% of the annual benefits collected by their employees on disability. This would go a long way to shore up SSDI finances and would make employers look for ways to accommodate such workers.

Whatever approach is taken, the point is to put some of the burden on employers with too many of employees on SSDI. Only when contribution and benefits are matched can sustainability be achieved.

2. Rules Should Be Simple, Clear and Consistent.

The rules of eligibility for SSDI benefits are not simple and clear. This makes them vulnerable to abuse and misuse. A simple and well-defined definition of disability based on diseases that are incontrovertibly and objectively verifiable should be the standard for SSDI. Diseases without objective markers, like depression or anxiety, and musculoskeletal conditions such as back pain, should be removed from the program. While such a move would be politically impossible, it is the only way to make the program fair to taxpayers and rid it of dubious claims. Even if the program should continue to allow these diseases and conditions, consideration should be given in eligibility decisions to whether the conditions can be eased or ameliorated by treatment so the worker can return to work. Many musculoskeletal conditions can be treated with physical therapy or surgery, and mental conditions can often be managed by regular psychiatric or psychological therapy and medication. People with conditions that can be managed by treatment must be given all possible support to keep them in the workforce and should not be placed on SSDI benefits.

3. Negative Consequences Must Be Equal to Severity of Wrong Doing.

Currently, attorneys, physicians, healthcare providers assisting SSDI and other claimant representatives are not held accountable enough for the evidence and opinions they present at hearings. To make this system work well, the negative consequences for aiding and abetting a fraudulent claim should be raised. Physicians, healthcare specialist, and claimant representatives should be held liable for any payments to beneficiaries they assisted who are found to have obtained SSDI payments fraudulently. Representatives who aided the claimant, along with the claimant, would be required to pay back every cent that was paid out, and face severe criminal penalties. Furthermore, the negative consequences for withholding medical evidence during a hearing should be raised. Applicants and their representatives should be made aware that withholding any medical evidence would subject them to criminal and civil penalties. Before the hearings, all parties must certify and sign that they will not withhold any medical evidence, regardless how insignificant or irrelevant they might consider it to be, with the negative implications unequivocally spelled out to them.

4. Third parties should be introduced to increase fairness in the system.

While claimants can bring their treating physician's evidence and testimony, his or her views must not be given too much weight. A better approach is to have completely independent experts brought in to examine the claimants, and the views of such independent experts must be given the strongest weight. Three independent private physicians or medical experts randomly selected should be employed to assess the condition of the claimant from which a consensus position is then used to make a judgment on the claimant's case. This would result in a fairer system.

Conclusions.

Social Security (OASI and SSDI) was designed with a poor structure that is perennially dependent on new enrollees to shore up its accounts. The benefit structure which allows people to receive more than they contributed is at the heart of the problems both programs are facing.

The best way forward for the OASI is to reform it and ensure that in its structure benefits and contribution are equal. For the SSDI, tightening eligibility will make the program fairer to taxpayers. Allowing people with illnesses and conditions without objective markers into the program makes it vulnerable to abuse, and increases its number of beneficiaries far more than the program can sustain with 0.9% or 1.8% in payroll taxes. Furthermore, making employees pay for coverage for dependents would help SSDI shore up its finances. The current system, in which a worker and his or her dependents can enjoy SSDI benefits by paying a flat 0.9% of payroll taxes, is unfair to the program. Employers with too many people on SSDI should also have the burden or risk spread to them. This would not only shore up SSDI finances, but it would place some burden on employers who fail to take care of their employees.

Employers having some skin in the game could force them to investigate employees who are gaming the system and help SSDI fight fraud. This would reduce some of the work of the SSDI and save it money.

Also, SSDI should not be an early retirement program for people who are unable to find a job or a long-term unemployment program for those who have fallen on hard times. According to the 2015 Annual Statistical Report on the SSDI Program, in Alabama, Arkansas, Kentucky, Maine, Mississippi, and West Virginia, 7 percent or more of the population ages 18-64 receive SSDI benefits. Such a burden placed on the program threatens its existence. Expanding back-to-work programs would be a step in the right direction. Making SSDI hearings adversarial should also be considered to make the process fairer. Significant negative consequences should be put in place against claimant representatives, physicians, and health providers who collude in fraudulent activities. Independent examiners or physicians should be put in place, and their views should be given overriding authority over the views of the claimant's physician or healthcare personnel.

These and many other ideas would turn the SSDI and OASI around and put them on a path of sustainability.

Chapter 5

The Nation-State and Immigration

Immigration, the international movement of people to a country of which they are not native, or do not have residency or citizenship to settle or reside, is as old as man. People have always migrated to new territories in search of greener pastures, or to escape from persecution in their native communities. Many countries were founded, built, or developed by immigrants. The benefits of immigration are too numerous to mention.

Most immigrants enrich the culture of the host community with their own set of values, cultures, skills, and ways of life. Immigration has always been a source of labor, both low-skilled and high-skilled, which is vital for business and the economy of the host country. Immigrants often help fill skill gaps that the host country may be missing. This helps employers and the job market to remain competitive. For an aging population, immigration helps to replenish the workforce; this is particularly vital to help fill the pension gap and national healthcare systems which are sustained by taxes from younger workers. More immigrants mean more consumers, profits for companies, sales tax, real estate tax, more insurance, more loans, etc., and all these results in economic growth.

Immigrants bring innovation and energy to their host country. According to the Kauffman Foundation, from 2006 to 2012, nearly 25 percent of engineering and technology companies founded in the United States had at least one key founder who was foreign-born. In Silicon Valley, this number was 43.9 percent. These companies employed almost 600,000 workers and generated over $60 billion in sales in 2012 (Wadhwa, Saxenian and Siciliano, 2012). Immigrants have helped bring glory and fame to their adopted nation in international sporting events. The list of the benefits of immigration goes on.

With the numerous benefits from immigrants and immigration, it comes as a surprise that anti-immigrant sentiments are on the rise in the US and around the world. In the United Kingdom, immigration has become a very touchy subject and contributed to their vote to leave the European Union. In Germany, Angela Merkel is taking heat from members of her party for her open-door policy to Syrian refugees. Across Europe—in France, Italy, and Hungary—anti-immigrant sentiments are high, but are particularly prevalent among people on the right of the ideological spectrum, according to a recent Pew Research Center survey of seven countries in the European Union (Wike,

2014). Far right groups like PEGIDA, and far-right political parties like the Party for Freedom in the Netherlands, Austria's Freedom Party, the UK Independence Party, the National Front in France, and the Alternative for Germany, are making electoral gains that would have been unthinkable a few decades ago. Anders Behring Breivik's homicidal rampage in Norway, and the murder of Jo Cox, the British Labor Party Member of Parliament for Batley and Spen, are further evidence of this rising anti-immigrant sentiments.

In the United States, the 2016 presidential election campaign saw tough talk about immigrants, particularly against Mexicans and Muslims. Donald Trump's call during the campaign to temporarily ban Muslims from coming into the country, Ted Cruz's call for the police to "patrol and secure" Muslim neighborhoods, and former House Speaker Newt Gingrich's call for the US to test every person with a Muslim background to ascertain if they believe in Sharia law and deport those who support it are all signs of the strong anti-immigrant sentiment in the US. The electoral victory of Donald Trump as President of the United States is unarguably the strongest evidence of the high level of anti-immigrant sentiment in the country.

Many have attributed this rising anti-immigrant sentiment to recent terrorist attacks in Paris, Brussels, Nice, San Bernardino, Boston, and Orlando. Other reasons put forward include anti-establishment or elite anger by ordinary citizens left behind by globalization, economic worries, criminal activities by immigrants, and their fiscal burden on public services.

Most of these explanations have no basis in the facts. First, there is no significant relationship between immigrants and crime. Although high-profile incidents—like the killing of Kate Steinle in San Francisco by Juan Francisco Lopez-Sanchez, an undocumented immigrant and recidivist felon who has been deported several times to Mexico— makes it look like immigrants are more likely to commit violent crimes, the facts show otherwise. A research study found that in 1904 prison commitment rates for serious crimes were similar between immigrants and natives of all ages except for immigrant in age group ages 18 and 19. However, by 1930, immigrants were less likely than natives to be committed to state and federal prisons at all ages 20 and older. However, this advantage was absent for violent offenses (Moehling and Piehl, 2009). A study published in the Journal of Social psychiatry and psychiatric epidemiology found that immigrants whether from Asia, Europe, Africa, and Latin America are significantly less antisocial than natives (Vaughn et al., 2014).

A report from the American Immigration Council notes that immigrants, both legal and illegal and regardless of their country of origin or level of education, are less likely to commit serious crimes or be behind bars than native-born Americans. The report notes that although the illegal immigrant population in the US more than tripled between 1990 and 2013, rising to more than 11.2 million, data from law enforcement indicate that the violent crime rate declined 48% while property crime rate fell 41% (Ewing, Martínez, and Rumbaut, 2015).

Also, a 2008 report by the Public Policy Institute of California found that immigrants are underrepresented in the prison system, with the incarceration rate for foreign-born adults at 297 per 100,000 in the population, compared to 813 per 100,000 for US-born adults. The foreign-born, who make up roughly 35% of California's adult population, constitute just 17% of the state prison population. Immigrants were overrepresented in federal prisons, but this was due in part to immigration violations which are prosecuted under federal jurisdiction.

In the United Kingdom (UK), studies have shown no correlation between immigration and crime. A 2013 study using new evidence from England and Wales in the 2000s when there was considerable immigration to the UK due to the accession of Eastern European countries to the EU in 2004, found no evidence of an average causal impact of immigration on crime. Looking at London by itself, it found no causal impact of immigration on crime and no differences in the likelihood of being arrested between natives and immigrants (Jaitman and Machin, 2013).

Another study examined the crime rate of two waves of immigration into the UK. Firstly, in the late 1990s/early 2000s when there was a wave of asylum seekers, and the second was the large inflow of workers from eastern Europe following their EU accession in 2004. The first wave resulted in a slight rise in property crime, but the second wave had no such impact (Bell, Machin, and Fasani, 2013). Another study found no evidence that immigration has caused a crime problem across countries and no difference in criminal activity between immigrants with good labor market opportunities and similar natives. However, it found that immigrants facing poor labor market opportunities are more likely to commit property crimes (Bell, 2014).

So, stories of immigrants bringing crime are more hyperbolic than true. Being an immigrant, whether undocumented or legal, comes with a degree of fear that one must be careful not to get into trouble so as not to be deported back home. This fear of deportation has been found to be a strong crime deterrent among immigrants. The driving desire of most newly arrived immigrants is to make money and achieve a better life, not to commit crimes. However, there is evidence that immigrants that face poor labor opportunities just like disadvantaged native groups could take to crime. So, while immigration and crime have no relationship generally, an immigrant's ability to integrate into the labor market could play a role in the story of immigration and crime.

Another reason given for the rising anti-immigrant sentiment is wage depression and job loss. The veracity of this assertion is debatable. A 1990 paper by economist David Card examined the effect of Mariel Boatlift of 1980, who were disproportionately low-skill workers on the Miami labor market and found virtually no effect on the wage rates of less-skilled non-Cuban workers. Although the Cuban influx increased the labor force of the Miami metropolitan area by 7%, he found no evidence of any increase in unemployment among less-skilled blacks or other non-Cuban workers (Card, 1990). However, George Borjas examination of the effect of the same Mariel Boatlift found that there was a drop in the average wage of the least skilled Miamians between 1977-1979 and 1981-1986 and this was substantial, between 10 and 30 percent (Borjas, 2017).

A study conducted in the United Kingdom (U.K) by the Migration Advisory Committee found that between 1995 and 2010, for every additional 100 immigrants, an estimated 23 British workers would not be employed. The committee found a negative association between non-European immigration and native employment in the U.K. Notably, this only held true when the economy was performing below full capacity or was not in a boom period, and the non-EU immigrants have been in the U.K for less than five years. However, the report found no statistically significant impact of migration on employment when considering all immigrants, whether from the European Union or not and without regard to how long they had been in the country.

So, the research on the impact of immigration on wages and job loss, is not settled. There are many research and reports with conflicting conclusions.

Other reasons cited for the rising anti-immigrant sentiments include globalization, economic worries, fiscal burden on public services, and anger against establishment politicians who support mass migration. However, the primary force fueling anti-immigrant sentiment is threat to national identity and worries about security. Research finds that immigration attitudes are largely shaped by concerns about its cultural impacts and to a smaller extent its economic impacts on the nation (Hainmueller and Hopkins, 2014). A study, titled "Immigration, Wages, and Compositional Amenities," looked at several European countries and found that people place value on having neighbors and co-workers who share their language, ethnicity, culture, and religion. Although concerns about wages and taxes affected feelings toward immigrants, worries about "social, cultural, and linguistic cohesion" mattered far more (Card, Dustmann and Preston, 2012).

So, natives concern about encroaching social and cultural changes due to mass immigration and their declining place in the emerging order, is the primary driver of anti-immigrant sentiments. For natives, these changes fuel a sense that something that uniquely belongs to them is being lost.

Close examination of the immigration policies of different nations in the developed world, including the United States, confirms that the driving force behind the current anti-immigrant sentiment is the perceived threat to national identity due to cultural, demographic, and social changes.

In Britain, instability in countries in Africa, Eastern Europe and the Middle East and the addition of several Eastern European countries to the European Union (EU) in 2004 resulted in the mass immigration of many people from those countries. According to the Office of National Statistics, in the late 1990s, net migration increased from the tens of thousands to the hundreds of thousands. From 2004 to 2014 net migration increased the UK population by nearly a quarter of a million people per year on average.

Furthermore, the state decided that multiculturalism was the best way for all to live in peace and harmony. This meant that the new immigrants were free to maintain their identities, culture, and customs. This resulted in a country where shared ideals, values, and identity that are uniquely British were missing and supplanted by a profound change in, or even total confusion about, what it meant to be British. This multiculturalism policy combined with the welfare state has contributed to the formation of parallel communities, the segregation of people along national origin and religious lines, low levels of employment, and an overrepresentation of immigrants in the criminal justice system (Koopmans, 2010). According to the Casey Review, people of Bangladeshi, Indian, and Pakistani ethnicity live in greater concentrations at ward level than other ethnic minority groups, and these concentrations are growing in many areas. In 2001, there were 12 wards in 7 local authorities where more than 40% of the population were of Pakistani ethnicity but this increased to 24 wards in 2011. Also, in 2001, they were 16 wards within 6 local authorities where more than 40% of the population were of Indian ethnicity but that has increased to 20 wards in 8 local authority areas. As of 2011, there are wards in Blackburn, Birmingham, Burnley, and Bradford with great concentration of Muslims population of between 70% and 85% (Casey, 2016).

Aside from its segregation and identity crisis, the murder of Lee Rigby and Islamic terrorist attacks have added to native British worries of security, and thus to the anti-immigrant sentiments.

The Brexit vote was a resounding rejection of the immigration policies of the political elites by native British citizens, and unequivocally demonstrates the importance of national identity and security to natives. According to Britain's National Institute of Economic and Social Research, immigration had contributed to an increase in the country's Gross Domestic Product and reduced the cost of government services like health care and pensions (Lisenkova and Sanchez-Martinez, 2016), but for many who voted to leave, these benefits were unimportant. The gains of immigration often feel elusive for many natives, whereas the costs tend to be perceived as greater than they are. It shows that national identity trumps economics; in other words, people are willing to choose to stop immigration, without care that it will worsen their economic situation, just to protect their national identity.

In France, mass migration policies of the past five decades has led to an increase in its immigrant population. According to France's National Institute of Statistics and Economic Studies, in 2015, 7.3 million people born in France had at least one immigrant parent or 11% of the population. Forty-five percent of them were of European origin, 31% of were descendants of the immigration waves from the Maghreb (Algeria and Morocco), 11% have at least one parent born in sub-Saharan Africa, and 9% have at least one parent born in Asia (Brutel, 2017).

Unlike the United Kingdom, to integrate its immigrant population France rejected multiculturalism for assimilation, and pushed for all to live by its core values of secularism (or laïcité, as it is known in France), which is hostile to public displays of faith. In 2010, the French Senate banned the public wearing of face coverings, including the Muslim face-veil, the niqab. In 2016, several French cities banned the burkini. These actions clash with many French Muslim citizens' freedom to express their religious beliefs and put them on a collision course with the state.

On top of laïcité policies, many French citizens of immigrant background especially Muslim citizens face discrimination and feel marginalized and excluded from mainstream society. A 2010 study found that a Muslim is 2.5 times less likely to receive a job interview callback than a Christian (Adida, Laitin and Valfort, 2010). Also, a 2008 study found evidence of significant employment discrimination against candidates with a foreign origin (Duguet, Leandri, L'Horty and Petit, 2008). Moreover, residential segregation of immigrant populations from North Africa, sub-Saharan African, Turkey and Asia is high. According to the institute of national demographics, in 2008, 42% of immigrants from Sub- Saharan Africa, North Africa and Turkey represented 28% of the population of disadvantaged neighborhoods (Pan Ké Shon, 2011).

All this has increased many French Muslims' sense of being unwanted, and may have contributed to their gravitation towards extremism. The Kouachi brothers, who were responsible for the Charlie Hebdo killings, were born and raised in Paris. Mohamed Lahouaiej Bouhlel, who was responsible for killing more than 80 people in the Nice attack, was a French citizen. So was Amedy Coulibaly, the gunman who killed four hostages at a Jewish Hyper Cacher supermarket. These terrorist attacks, along with significant cultural differences between mainstream France and its growing Muslim population, have heightened anti-immigrant sentiments. Citing threats to national identity, the platform of far-right and nationalistic voices has seen a resurgence. In France, just like in Britain, worries over national identity and security are driving anti-immigrant sentiments.

In the United States, the 1965 Amendments abolished the national-origins quota system and numerical limits were raised from 154,000 to 290,000 (McCabe and Meissner, 2010). According to Pew Research Center, since the passage of the law nearly 59 million immigrants have arrived in the United States and the nation's foreign-born population has risen sharply from 9.6 million to a record 45 million in 2015.

Aside from the legal mass migration of people to the US, the porous southern border has allowed the unchecked immigration of illegal immigrants into the country. According to Pew Research, there are over 11 million illegal immigrants living in the country in 2015 (Krogstad, Passel and Cohn, 2017). Adding to the problem of illegal immigration is the significant number of people who overstay their visas. According to the Department of Homeland Security (DHS), which produced its first partial estimate of those who overstay their permits in the US, out of the 45 million nonimmigrant arrivals who were supposed to depart in Fiscal 2015, about 527,127 remained in the country, a rate of 1.17%. Due to continuing departures, by January 4, 2016, an estimated 416,500 were still in the country, a rate of 0.9%. The DHS report said that some have likely left since then, or obtained or renewed a legal visa. For 2016, the DHS determined that there were 50 million arrivals and calculated a total overstay rate of 1.47 percent, or 739,478 individuals. Due to continuing departures, by January 10, 2017, this number decreased to 544,676, bringing the overstay rate to 1.07 percent.

This mass migration, both legal and illegal, has transformed the country demographically. Terrorist attacks by immigrants in Boston, New York, San Bernardino, and Orlando have added to worries about security and have increased anti-immigrant sentiments. Globalization and economic worries, as well as the failure of politicians to fix immigration, has added to the frustration of many Americans. Nationalistic "alt-right" groups are seeing a resurgence, just like in Europe, and tensions are rising between groups. Just as in Britain and France, worries about US national identity, and security are driving these anti-immigrant sentiments.

Insulated from this anti-immigrant wave that is bedeviling most of Europe and America is Japan. In Japan, a no-immigration principle, or strict ethnic homogeneity, has been prioritized over mass migration for many decades. However, Japan is experiencing a demographic crunch; about 27% of the Japanese population is over the age of 65 and there are 1.4 million fewer people today than there were in 2007. The UN estimates that Japan would need to receive 17 million immigrants, an average of 381,000 immigrants a year between 2005 and 2050, for it to maintain its population level at 127 million. So far, to address its labor needs the government has made only modest policy reforms focusing on expanding temporary foreign worker programs to allow more semi- and low-skilled workers to enter the country on temporary work visas. Japan has also begun to increase its intake of highly skilled immigrants since 2012; however, by the end of 2015, only about 1,500 skilled workers had entered Japan through this system.

Japan is simply not ready to accept immigration as a solution to its population problems. Opinion polls show the Japanese public to be increasingly worried about the effects of the declining population but are not in support of mass migration to secure labor. Many public opinion polls consistently show that at least half the Japanese population is opposed to mass migration or increasing presence of foreigners in their country. Many see immigrants more as a potential problem than as a solution. The bottom line is that the no-immigration policy continues to receive broad support from the Japanese public (Peng, 2016).

Although Japan faces demographic challenges that it must overcome, her immigration policies can best be described as thoughtful and successful, because the country has avoided ethnic tensions and natives' feelings of losing their country's national identity, responses that are fueling anti-immigrant sentiments in Europe and America.

De-entropification Solution.

The flaws with the immigration system of the United States and around the world can be understood and fixed with several key principles.

1. The Principle of General Homogeneity.

A nation-state, like all large social systems, has a positive and negative homogenous group. The positive homogenous group is dominated by citizens and residents with positive traits such as highly skilled and educated, employed, wealthy or middle class, speak the common language, law abiding and who enjoy equality of rights and access to services and opportunities. On the other hand, the negative homogenous group is dominated by citizens and residents with negative traits such as illiteracy, low skill, joblessness or unemployed, poverty, unable to speak the common language, criminal record or behavior and who are discriminated against and have little or no access to opportunities and basic services. The dominance of the positive homogenous group signifies a state of positive homogeneity, and when the negative homogenous group is dominant, it is in a state of negative homogeneity.

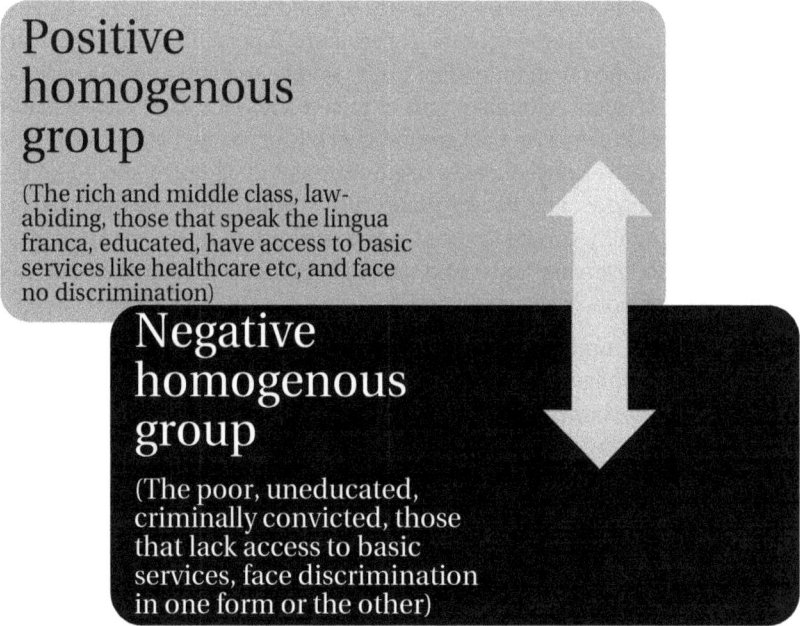

Figure 5-1 Positive and Negative Homogenous Groups of a Nation-State.

With this understanding, immigration policy can be divided into ideal and non-ideal.

1. Ideal immigration policy is
    a. highly controlled,
    b. strictly admits people who can join the positive homogenous group and
    c. admits people in very small numbers into the negative homogenous group on humanitarian grounds only.
    d. extensive and robust vetting and checks
2. Non-ideal immigration policy involves
    a. uncontrolled or mass migration, and
    b. admitting many people who will shore up the negative homogenous group.
    c. poor or inadequate background checks and vetting

An ideal immigration policy is cost-effective and highly beneficial to the host nation. It is highly controlled, takes in people who share a common identity with the host country or those whose values and beliefs agree with the core values of the host country and are of good character, highly skilled or with funds to invest in the country. Ascertaining a person's values, and world view must be done on an individual basis. Simply excluding people based on their names, religion, national origin or region without a direct conversation or interview plus extensive background check is unfair and violates the principles that negative consequences or punishment in all forms should be limited to the wrongdoer and not the group. Also, it could cause the nation to lose out on good quality candidates that can contribute to its prosperity and development. So, everyone must and should be given a fair shot regardless of their name, religion, or place of origin.

Also, an ideal immigration policy is one that accepts very few people into the negative homogenous group. This means taking in people who may or may not share a common identity with the host nation, are not highly skilled and do not have funds to invest. This must be done strictly on humanitarian grounds to fulfill international obligations and they should be adequately vetted to ensure that they pose no threat. An ideal immigration is highly controlled, and should be as low as 500:1 or as conservative as 1000:1. Going by 1000:1, this means for every one-thousand qualified people admitted into the positive homogenous group, one person should be admitted into the negative homogeneous group annually. Therefore, if 50,000 people were admitted into the positive homogenous group annually, no more than 50 should be admitted into the negative homogenous group.

For the few admitted into the negative homogenous group, concrete steps must be taken or put in place so that they can be integrated into the positive homogenous group over time. Education programs to acquaint them with the new culture and value system must be put in place. Everyone must be made to learn the language whether they are mothers who reside at home or fathers who maintain a job. Free schools that teach the standard curriculum, free language classes and everything they need to succeed, etc. should be available to them. The idea is to ensure that the positive homogeneity of the system is maintained.

A non-ideal immigration policy is uncontrolled, without adequate vetting or background checks and mostly takes in people who are unqualified to join the positive homogenous group. Such a policy is likely to result in a strain on social welfare programs, an increase in crime and unemployment due to poor labor market opportunities for many of the immigrants and discrimination by employers. Also, it could result in ethnic nationalism because the natives feel threatened, the formation of parallel communities, segregation along the lines of religion, culture and national origin and culture clashes as the host nation's identity, and value system cannot effectively hold the system together. The only way to hold such a system together would be by a major homogenization effort. Homogenization reduces the differences between contributors by enshrining certain core values that all must abide by and by promoting inclusion, equality, integration and constant contact between groups with the aim of achieving positive homogeneity over time.

In Britain, the immigration policy has been non-ideal, and this is why anti-immigrant sentiments are on the rise. Its policy of mass migration brought in people of all ethnic backgrounds, cultures, value systems, and skillsets, without regard to whether it was shoring up the positive or negative homogenous group. This immigration policy has resulted in large and growing ethnic minority populations. Looking at overall net immigration, total fertility, and mortality trends as assumed in the ONS 2008-based Principal Projection, the ethnic minority populations are projected to increase from 13% of the UK population in 2006 to 27 % by 2031 and 43% by 2056 (Coleman, 2010). This is a huge demographic change in a relatively short time.

More worryingly, and perhaps the most important reason for Britain's failed immigration policies, is her practice of multiculturalism. Put simply, multiculturalism, as practiced by Britain, is tantamount to having people in a soccer team wear completely different jerseys, practice separately, and then be expected to play together as a cohesive force against their opponent. With every group allowed to maintain its identity, the state has no umbrella of shared identity to hold it together and it has resulted in a fragmented society. To promote unity and strengthen social cohesion, the best way forward is to homogenize the system.

To homogenize the country, faith schools and home schooling should be eliminated in favor of secular schools that are well integrated. Britain has become more a multicultural and diverse society than it was a few decades ago such that these faith schools are not helpful towards homogenization. They should however, remain free to operate after school hours and on the weekends. Furthermore, consideration should be given towards state recognition of important Muslim and Hindu religious festivals due to the growing number of British Muslims and Hindu citizens. Affirmative action should be put in place to enhance integration into the higher educational system and labor market. Consideration should be given to the elimination of dual citizenship so that all citizen's identity and loyalty are to the state and to promote a stronger sense of being British. In addition, a mandatory military draft or an alternative one-year national service where people are transferred to different parts of the country to serve upon graduation from post-secondary education should be put in place. This will help promote a shared British experience, expose young people to the different ethnic groups in the country as well as strengthen trust and cooperation.

Most importantly, amendments should be made to the immigration policies from its non-ideal state to an ideal state.

In France, the immigration policies have also been non-ideal. Like Britain, its immigration policies have brought the same results; alienated minorities, resentful natives, and a country deeply divided along nativists and liberal political lines. Although assimilation is a form of homogenization, it is a policy that can best succeed with an ideal immigration policy and not the non-ideal immigration policy that France practices. Many of the immigrants brought into the country shored up the negative homogenous group and that is why the French assimilation policy failed. Instead of strengthening a single French identity it has resulted in exclusion and alienation. Many French immigrants especially those from North and Sub-Saharan Africa are having difficulties joining the positive homogenous group. According to an article published in the Economist, titled "Ethnic minorities in France, An edgy inquiry," youth unemployment is twice as high for French-born citizens whose parents are from sub-Saharan African countries and those of the Maghreb compared to French citizens with no immigrant background. About 30% leave high school without any diploma or qualification and they are more likely to live in poor neighborhoods (The Economist, 2015).

Mass migration has transformed France into a multicultural, multifaith and multiracial country and this has serious implications that must be recognized and integrated into its identity. The best way forward is to homogenize the system and create a France that all French citizens can identify with regardless of religion, national origin, ethnicity or race.

To homogenize the system, affirmative action and strong antidiscrimination laws should be put in place to help many minorities in the negative homogenous group to become integrated into the positive homogenous group. Mass immigration policies have created a new France in which immigrants are going to play a major role in future but current Laïcité policies are a denial of this fact. To promote inclusion, laïcité should be relaxed but not eliminated to allow minorities especially Muslims to express their religious heritage. This will go a long way to reduce feelings of alienation and humiliation. Integrated schools, housing, better representation in the criminal justice system and the political sphere will all help to create a France that truly represents all its citizens.

Immigration policies in the United States have also been non-ideal. From visa lotteries to bringing refugees en masse from different parts of the world, many of the immigrants have shored up the negative homogenous group. Also, this rapid, mass migration of people of different cultures from all over the world has transformed the racial demographics of the country. According to Pew Research Center, in 1965, 84% of Americans were non-Hispanic whites,

4% were Hispanic, and less than 1% were Asian. In 2015, just 50 years later, 62% of Americans were white, 18% of Americans were Hispanic, and 6% were Asians. This demographic change is projected to become more pronounced in the future. According to Pew Research Center projections, in 2065 the United States will have no racial or ethnic majority group, although non-Hispanic whites will remain the largest racial or ethnic group in the overall population. Currently representing 62% of the population, non-Hispanic whites will make up 46% in 2065, with Hispanics representing 24%, Asians 14%, and blacks 13%. Also, according to Pew Projections, "among the projected 441 million Americans in 2065, 78 million will be immigrants and 81 million will be people born in the US to immigrant parents" (Cohn, 2015).

This rapid demographic change is contributing to the racial divisions in the country, as seen in the resurgence of hate crimes and far-right nationalistic groups according to the Southern Poverty Law Center. In the political sphere, a battle between nativists and liberals is beginning to shape politics and identity politics is on the rise. The racial and partisan divide in perception of incidents like George Zimmerman's killing of Trayvon Martin and the police killing of Michael Brown in Ferguson are a testament to the division in the country. The riots and protests that greeted the election of Donald Trump is further testament to the deep divide in the country.

Terrorist attacks by immigrants in New York, Boston, San Bernardino and Orlando have added to worries about security, and increased anti-immigrant sentiments, adding to the divisions.

The need, therefore, to make significant changes and overturn decades of non-ideal immigration policies cannot be overemphasized. Firstly, changes should be made to the immigration policy from non-ideal to ideal. In other words, immigration should be controlled and focused on bringing in people who can join the positive homogenous group. Research shows that Americans of all classes and political spectrum view educated immigrants in high-status jobs favorably, whereas they view those who lack plans to work, do not speak English, or entered without authorization unfavorably (Hainmueller and Hopkins, 2015). So, this is a policy that would be embraced and supported by all Americans.

The diversity visa lottery program should be abolished and the EB-5 immigrant investor program should be reformed and expanded to bring in people who are willing and truly interested in investing in the country. For skilled immigrants, the H1B quotas should be expanded but remain tied to securing select high-end jobs that companies are unable to find suitable Americans to do. The US can take inspiration from Australia's immigration system, which is highly regulated and create a system like Australia's SkillSelect, an online system that ranks applicants based on information provided, such as nominated occupation, English proficiency, study and education, skills assessment, and business and investment experience. Qualification for immigration is then based on their score on the points system and immigration is capped annually.

2. Homogenization: To Reduce the Divisions in the Country and Pull the Illegal Immigrants with the Best Chance of Joining the Positive Homogenous Group from The Negative Homogenous Group.

To overcome the divisions in the country, some homogenization would be necessary. This can be achieved by the introduction of a mandatory one-year military service or an alternative national civilian service on graduation from college for all citizens to promote a shared American experience, trans-racial consciousness, instill a sense of patriotism and promote unity amongst the different groups in the country. In tertiary institutions across the country, programs to increase political contact, dialogue and debate between students of different political affiliations should be created. Elimination of dual citizenship should be considered to ensure that the loyalty of all citizens lie solely with the United States and promote an American identity. This is particularly important because of the rise in the number of immigrants and their children, many of which still maintain ties to their country of origin. Moreover, the fairness doctrine should be reintroduced and applicable to both mainstream and alternative media to reduce ideological polarization and ensure that all Americans get a balanced view of the issues. Also, more should be done by the executive branch to promote unity by recognizing the heritage and cultures of recent immigrants who have become part of the new America to give them a sense of belonging. President Obama's invitation of Muslims Americans to the White house in recognition of the Muslim celebration of Eid al-Fitr is a step in the right direction. All these efforts and more would go a long way to healing the divide in the country.

As for the undocumented or illegal immigrants currently in the country, some level of homogenization is necessary to pull those with the best potential to join the positive homogenous group. Many undocumented immigrants are educated and hardworking people, who often pay taxes into systems they do not enjoy. Being classified as illegal or undocumented means they are permanently in the negative homogenous group, with almost no chance to join the positive homogenous group. Tempering justice with mercy, it would be sensible to give an opportunity for those who have proof that they entered the United States before the age of 16 and who have continuously resided in the country for at least 10 years to join the positive homogenous group. This can be accomplished by giving them a two-year conditional residency that can be made permanent on expiration and after five years of permanent residency, they should be eligible to apply for citizenship. To be eligible, a person must have graduated from an institution of higher learning or served in the United States military for at least two years and if discharged, have received an honorable discharge. This would release many young people who are in the US illegally from the shadows, giving them a chance at a better life and would overall be good for the economy. In a one-time gesture, adults who arrived illegally across the border or who overstayed their visas should also be given the opportunity to join the positive homogenous group if they possess a bachelor or advanced degree, and have stayed in the US continuously for at least 15 years with no criminal record. They would have to pay back taxes that would be calculated based on how long they have stayed and how much they have earned. Those eligible would be granted a two-year conditional residency that could be changed to permanent residence on expiration and after five years of permanent residency, they should be eligible to apply for citizenship.

3. Benefit Must Never Exceed or Go Beyond Contribution.

A. Automatic citizenship: The benefit of U.S. citizenship by birth must be equal to contribution. This means U.S. citizenship by birth must only be available to the children of "U.S. citizens"—people whose allegiance is to defend the interests and security of the United States and who contribute to her growth and development. The current system violates this principle, and that's why it is vulnerable to abuse. Automatic citizenship for anyone born in the US, guaranteed by the 14th Amendment, has been one of the criteria for citizenship for a long time. This law has exhausted its usefulness and should be repealed and replaced. According to Pew research center estimates about 275,000 babies were born to illegal immigrant parents in 2014, or about 7% of the 4 million births in the U.S and illegal immigrants accounted for about one-in-three births (32%) to foreign-born mothers in the U.S. in that year (Passel and Cohn, 2016). All these children are automatically granted U.S. citizenship.

The simple fact that any child born in the United States is automatically bestowed with citizenship makes it open to abuse. There are documented cases of organized arrangements where people are brought in as short-term visitors just to gain citizenship for their children who, for the most part, will not live in the country for most of their young lives and as such are not accustomed to U.S. customs and values (Kim and Shyong 2015). They can, however, easily return when they choose—not as immigrants who need help with integration, but as full citizens. Notably, these foreign parents have allegiance to a foreign power sometimes even a hostile one. This is a serious problem, with national security implications.

Also, the fact that one can simply cross U.S. southern or northern border, deliver a child and be rewarded with a US passport opens it to abuse and contributes to the problem of illegal immigration. In addition, the fact that one can overstay their visa, give birth, and the child would be rewarded with US citizenship makes it attractive for people to overstay their visas.

Furthermore, automatic citizenship makes it difficult to deport illegal alien parents because of their child's legal right to live in the country. These children are instantly eligible for the full range of government welfare and medical benefits, adding to the cost of welfare.

Many Americans want this law to remain in place. Some people consider it inhumane to disallow a child born in the U.S., who has done no wrong, from being rewarded with citizenship. These emotions are misplaced. Most countries around the world do not offer automatic citizenship to everyone born within their borders, and even those that did have changed such laws, because of the tremendous abuse it attracts and its national security implications. Over the past few decades, countries including Australia, Ireland, India, New Zealand, the United Kingdom, Malta, and the Dominican Republic have repealed such policies. This policy should be discontinued, as it does more harm than good. By making available the benefit of citizenship by birth only to U.S. citizens, the abuse will be eliminated. Children born to tourists, students, temporary workers, and illegal immigrants should not be privileged to become automatic citizens.

One way to match benefit and contribution is to make wealthy non-citizens who wish to have their child conferred with U.S. citizenship to pay for it. At the cost of, say, $500,000, the child of an unqualified immigrant born in the U.S. would be granted the benefit of citizenship. This would be a conditional citizenship that would become permanent when the child is 21 or older and have stayed in the U.S. for at least five years. This would stop the abuse and whatever illegal immigration it attracts. It would also attract those who can easily join the positive homogenous group, which of course are people who have no need to use the welfare services of the nation. Most importantly, it would generate substantial income. Although this proposal might sound outrageous to some, there already exist programs to gain permanent residence or even citizenship in the U.S. and other countries for those who invest a certain amount of money in the economy. The truth is that unless this law is repealed, as every other developed nation has done, it will continue to be abused, costing taxpayers in welfare benefits, slowing the deportation process and hence the effectiveness of the entire immigration system.

Another way to match benefit and contribution is to give the children born by less wealthy noncitizens in U.S soil a conditional residency which can be made permanent after 10 years. This residency is voided if the child leaves the country for more than six months without return. Such a child becomes eligible to take the oath of citizenship when they are 21 or older if they have no criminal record and have paid taxes for at least three years. This will reduce the abuse that the system currently experiences, ensure that children born by noncitizens are well integrated into U.S. society and have contributed to the system before being granted the benefit of citizenship.

B. Secured borders. The benefit of being allowed into the country must only be available to those who meet the criteria to enter. A nation that cannot effectively police its borders, so that only immigrants or visitors who meet the entrance criteria get the benefit, is one that is deliberately investing in a bad future. Although the tide of illegal immigration has slowed because of the slowing economy and the Trump's administration hard line on illegal immigration, this issue is not one that should be treated with kid gloves. More money and resources must be invested in the border to make sure it is secure, and ensure that everyone allowed in meets the criteria to do so. Whatever needs to be done must be done to secure the border. If the proposed wall will help, then it should be built. Until such a time that the US border is secured, and only those qualified to come in can do so, all efforts to manage immigration will come to nothing.

4. Negative Consequences Must Always Be Equal to The Severity of Wrongdoing.

Even with a secured border, immigration violation cannot be tackled without a solid deterrent in place. The current deterrents are not equal to the severity of their violation. Violation of immigration law is a national security issue and must be met with a strong deterrent. To this end, very tough financial penalties must be imposed on employers who hire illegal or undocumented immigrants. For a first offense, an employer should face a fine of $10,000 per illegal employee and $20,000 per illegal employee for a second offense. Three or more offenses should cost an employer $50,000 per illegal employee. An employer who violates the law more than three times should be penalized with monetary fines and prison time of between 2-5 years. Only such a strong deterrent would stop employers from taking advantage of cheap, illegal, immigrant labor. When an illegal immigrant cannot work, then leaving the country becomes the only option. The knowledge that an illegal immigrant cannot find work would make it unattractive to violate the law.

Furthermore, illegal or undocumented immigrants should not be allowed to rent houses. Such laws already exist in many European nations. Landlords, or people who harbor illegal immigrants, should be fined heavily, and any subsequent violation should be met with at least six months in prison. Also, illegal or undocumented immigrants should not be allowed to get a driver's license or an identification card, instate tuition, and access to any government benefits.

Moreover, those who have overstayed their visas and who want to marry a US citizen to gain permanent residency must be compelled to go back to their country for at least two years before they can apply for a green card. Many countries already employ this strategy to make it less attractive for people who overstay their visa simply to marry a citizen to gain legal papers. Also, for those brought in on humanitarian grounds, negative consequences such as exclusion from welfare benefits, becoming a citizen and even deportation should be put in place for failing to be fully integrated (gainfully employed, crime-free record, good command of the lingua franca etc.) after at least fifteen to twenty years to reduce the negative homogenous group. Finally, legislation should be enacted in Congress against felons who reenter the country illegally after they have been deported. A mandatory minimum sentence of 15 years in prison will serve as a strong deterrent for deported convicted felons from reentering the country and help prevent crimes like that of Kathryn Steinle from happening.

5. All Contributors Must Act Within the Established Rules or Laws, And Everyone Must Be Equal Before Them (Rule of Law).

This entails strong enforcement of current immigration laws. People who crossed the border illegally into the United States, and those who overstayed their visas, have violated the law. The law unequivocally states that anyone who breaks immigration laws is subject to deportation, so all illegal immigrants—particularly those with criminal histories—should be deported. Sanctuary cities that protect illegal immigrants should be defunded or made to face some penalty. More resources and money should be committed to immigration, and especially to immigration courts that are facing huge backlogs. The 56 courts nationwide have become paralyzed by delays and bureaucracy (Preston, 2016), and more resources are needed for them to meet their goals. Also, there needs to be stronger enforcement of the E-Verify system. Employers nationally should be mandated to use it to screen new hires and current employees for their employment eligibility.

Furthermore, catch-and-release policies must be immediately abolished, and police should be required to hold and hand over illegal immigrants to immigration officials. Only strong enforcement of the law would make the system work optimally, therefore all efforts must be expended to enforce the law.

Conclusions.

The U.S. immigration system faces many challenges from lack of proper enforcement of the law, ineffective deterrence to having an unsecured border. All these challenges must be tackled concomitantly for the system to fulfill its mission.

Many nations in the western world including the United States have engaged in a non-ideal immigration policy, and this has sparked antiimmigrant sentiments, rise of ethnic, racial and religious nationalism, the polarization of the political sphere, and fragmentation of society. Immigration is vital for any nation-state, but it must be implemented in a controlled fashion to fill the nation's skill gaps, or to complement what the nation already has. The goal of immigration must be to bring in people who will join the positive homogenous group. Bringing in people who will join the negative homogenous group must be done strictly on humanitarian grounds, and must be highly controlled. When vast numbers of people unqualified to join the positive homogenous group are allowed in, efforts must be made to homogenize the system. This is a difficult process that could take decades to bear fruit.

Finally, there are mixed results about the immigration of low-skilled workers. Some research shows that they benefit the entire economy, while other research shows that they may lead to the displacement of low-skilled citizens and legal residents from the job market. Even if they do not depress wages or displace low-skilled natives, the most important thing in any immigration policy is to think in the long term. Most low-skilled jobs boom during periods of high economic growth and slow down during low economic growth, or as the economy transitions. When this happens, many of these workers never return to their home countries, and they shore up the negative homogenous group. The case of Turkish immigrants in Germany is a good example of this problem (Bartsch, Brandt and Steinvorth, 2010). For this reason, low-skilled immigration should not be prioritized. If it must be done, temporary work visas should be issued, and a clear path must be defined to leave the country when the job finishes.

Chapter 6

Higher Education and Student Loans

Education is vital to the prosperity of a nation and its citizens. Higher levels of educational attainment have been shown to enhance social mobility and improve overall national development. Higher education helps to create the business and political leaders of tomorrow. Also, students who have a college degree make more money in the long run compared to those who do not have a college degree. According to the US Census Bureau, in 2009, workers with a regular high school diploma earned about $27,000, and those with a bachelor's degree earned about $48,000 (Ryan and Siebens, 2012). A Georgetown University study found that by 2020, 65 percent of all jobs in the economy will require postsecondary education and training beyond high school (Carnevale, Smith and Strohl, 2013). College graduates thus have an advantage in employment opportunities compared to those with high school diplomas.

The importance of higher education in national development and employment is why governments around the world have for many decades made college access a priority for all citizens. Loans to students, free tuition, state selection of the most qualified students, etc., are just a few examples of different policies that governments have used to try to make education accessible to citizens. In the United States, loans to students have been the model for several decades. Student loans backed by the US federal government were first offered in the 1950s under the National Defense Education Act to encourage Americans to pursue science, technology, engineering, and mathematics (STEM) degrees after the launch of Sputnik by the Soviet Union. By 1965, student loans were expanded under the Higher Education Act, in hopes of achieving greater social mobility and equality of opportunity. The federal government gave loans directly through the Department of Education and guaranteed loans by the private market. Guaranteed loans were abolished and replaced with direct loans through the Student Aid and Fiscal Responsibility Act of 2010.

This policy of giving loans to help students is under scrutiny because, over the last ten years, students have struggled to repay their loans. According to student loan hero, a website that focuses on student debt issues, more than 44 million Americans hold student loans, and as of 2017, student debt stood at well over $1.4 trillion. According to a report from the Federal Reserve Bank of New York, 17% of borrowers are in default or delinquency, and only 37% of borrowers are current on their loan and actively paying down. Also, about 50 percent of the 2009 cohort are having payment difficulties on their loans with repayment difficulties more prevalent in borrowers from lower-income areas (Haughwout, Donghoon, Scally and Klaauw, 2015).

The consequences of these enormous debts are huge. Students face harassment from debt collectors, and those faced with financial difficulties or health problems find it nearly impossible to discharge their loans. Some people keep paying these debts even in their 50s and 60s, when they should be planning for retirement. Even after a student's death, many lenders still seek repayment from the student's estate or co-signer, and refusing to repay the debt can lead to terrible consequences, including; a damaged credit report, additional collection costs, tax refund and Social Security withholding, wage garnishment, inability to renew a state professional license, and even legal action for the total amount owed. This burden on student loans has major consequences for the economy. Research indicates that student debt may be preventing people from making important life decisions like getting married and having kids. Also, it prevents people from saving for retirement, starting a small business, and making big purchases that drive economic growth, like houses and cars.

To bring relief to students, President Obama, working with Congress, made some changes to the law. The recent repayment program, known as Revised Pay as You Earn, or REPAYE, represents an effort on this part. It caps borrowers' monthly bills to 10% of the borrower and their spouse's (if applicable) discretionary income, and the remaining balance will be forgiven after 20 or 25 years. This income-based plan is quite helpful because it reduces the likelihood of default, which can severely damage a person's credit rating or ability to buy a car or a house. These plans, however, are not for everyone. Only direct federal loans that are not in default are eligible.

Also, some colleges, including Harvard, Princeton, Columbia, Yale, University of Pennsylvania, Cornell, Brown and Dartmouth, have taken it upon themselves to have a "no loans" policy for low-income students who are eligible for the Federal Pell Grant, to reduce their debt burden. However, most colleges with these "no loans" financial aid policies aren't truly eliminating all loans; many still require a student contribution that could include working part-time and even some borrowing. Other colleges have adopted a low cap on the amount students can borrow. All these efforts have done little to tackle the problem.

On close examination of the student loan crisis, it becomes clear that government policies which made loans readily available to anyone who wants to go to college are at the heart of the problem. To understand this, it is important to bear in mind that one of the fundamental purposes of government is to advance smart policies for the welfare of all citizens and create opportunities for all. However, if not handled carefully, such policies can have unfortunate economic and financial consequences. Not too long ago, in the name of affordable housing for all, government policies encouraged the granting of mortgages to people with poor credit history and scores and Fannie Mae, and Freddie Mac which are government-backed enterprises funneled securities with high-risk mortgages into many important financial institutions. When housing prices unexpectedly dropped in 2007, these mortgage-backed securities became valueless, and the financial crisis ensued. In the same vein, government's good intention to expand access to higher education for all by making loans available is inadvertently harming the entire system.

The ready availability of loans has caused college enrollment to soar. This is in part linked to the fact that many high school graduates see college as the next step in their lives, without much thought about whether it is right for them or not. In other words, the decision to go to college is taken very lightly as loans are readily available. This has resulted in a situation where students who may not be qualified or ready for college education enter the system. Many who enroll in colleges do not necessarily want to be there, and many have no clear notion of what they're doing there. Some take a break after a semester or two and never return. Some switch to a different major after realizing that the one they enrolled for isn't right for them. This delays their graduation and adds to their debt burden. Other students drop out after realizing college is not for them because of coursework demands, cost, family problems, etc. Unfortunately, they drop out with debt and no degree.

According to Complete College America 2014 report, more than 31 million students have gone off to college but never earned a degree over the last 20 years. The 2011 "Pathways to Prosperity" study by the Harvard Graduate School of Education showed that almost 70 percent of high school graduates go to college within two years of graduating. However, just 56% complete four-year degrees within six years, and less than 30% of those who seek a two-year associates degree finish within three years (Schwartz and Keppel, 2011). According to the National Center for Education Statistics, in 2008, this 6-year graduation rate was 58 percent at public institutions, 65 percent at private nonprofit institutions, and a mere 27 percent at private for-profit institutions. Also, according to a 2016 report from the Third way, a Washington-based think tank, when students don't earn a degree within six years, they are unlikely to complete their studies (Hiler, 2016).

The ready availability of loans and easy access to borrowing for students has also spurred the emergence of many bad-acting for-profit colleges. A 2-year investigation by the Senate Committee on Health, Education, Labor, and Pensions found that although for-profit colleges enroll between 10 to 13% of college students, they receive 25% of all federal financial aid dollars, totaling $32 billion in education department grants and loans in the academic year 2009-2010. The investigation found that 54 percent of the students who enrolled at for-profit colleges for the 2008-9 year left without a degree and 63 percent enrolled in 2-year associate degree programs departed without a degree.

The investigation also found for-profit colleges to be very expensive. Bachelor's degree programs averaged 20 percent more than the cost of similar programs at public universities, associate degree programs averaged four times the cost of degree programs at similar community colleges and certificate programs averaged nearly five times the cost of such programs at similar community colleges. Furthermore, the investigation found that most for-profit colleges spend a lot of the tuition on marketing and recruiting efforts, leaving very little spent toward hiring high-quality faculty members, establishing a solid curriculum, and developing extracurricular programs that enrich students' overall academic experience. In 2010, 80 percent of the faculty employed at the for-profit colleges examined in the investigation were part time. In 2009, for-profit higher education institutions spent $4.2 billion or 22.7% percent of all revenue on marketing, advertising, admissions and recruitment and only 17.2% on instruction.

With their exceptionally high acceptance rate, these for-profit colleges target the most vulnerable people of society—those who may not have the necessary academic foundation to gain admission into the university system—with fantastic promises of a good life upon graduation. The vast majority of the students end up leaving without a certificate and student loan debt that may follow them throughout their lives.

The federal government has taken several measures to clamp down on the worst of them. ITT Educational Services, one of the nation's largest operators of for-profit colleges, was recently barred from using federal financial aid to enroll new students. Corinthian Colleges, once a leading network of for-profit schools, has also shut down its campuses across the country. However, despite this stepped-up scrutiny, the Education Department continues to pay out millions of dollars to many other for-profit schools that have been accused of substandard practices or illegal activity. Hundreds of schools, which include small beauty schools with huge loan default rates and online law schools that have terrible graduation records and have failed regulatory standards, are still receiving billions of dollars of government funds (Cohen, 2015).

The ready availability and accessibility of loans have also contributed to the ever-increasing cost of college education. The class of 2015 graduated with an average debt of $35,051, while those for 2016 graduated with an average debt of $37,172. One of the reasons put forth for the ever-increasing cost of college is the loss of government funding to state and public colleges. However, the simple fact that students can easily borrow money contributes greatly to the constant tuition hikes. It is undeniable that as federal subsidies increase, so does the purchasing power of students, and this allows colleges to ratchet up tuition rates with reckless abandon. A study by two researchers at the New York Federal Reserve Bank in 2015 found that the ready availability of easy federal money into higher education resulted in an increase in tuition and fees. The researchers found that for every dollar of new subsidized loans, tuition went up by 60 cents (Lucca, Nadauld and Shen, 2015). Simply put, a significant portion of the $1.4 trillion in student debt can be directly attributed to tuition inflation which is a byproduct of government student loan policies.

This ever-increasing tuition rate has not translated to higher quality education. Many colleges, including traditional non-profit colleges who have benefited extraordinarily from federal loans, have done little to improve the courses they offer, even as student numbers and tuition rates have risen. They are, however, spending a lot on administration and support services, driven by the need to compete in university rankings that tend to place excellence on almost everything about a university except the outcomes of its graduates (Arum and Roksa, 2011). Colleges have been investing in non-instructional student services like deluxe dormitory rooms, elaborate student centers, and expensive gyms sometimes at the expense of instructional spending. In 2011, despite revenue increases, public and private research universities cut back on education-related spending (Desrochers and Hurlburt, 2014).

In many colleges, students are increasingly taught by fewer full-time tenured faculty members. According to the American Association of University Professors, non-tenure-track positions of all types now account for over 70 percent of all instructional staff appointments in American higher education. More than 50 percent of all faculty appointments are part-time even though they teach the equivalent of a full-time course load. They are usually paid by the course, without benefits, health insurance and retirement plans. Just like court-appointed lawyers, these underpaid and overworked educators provide less-than-ideal instruction, and this hurts students' educational experience (Pros, 2015).

Most tenured professors spend most of their time on research and publishing articles, in part because they must obtain research grants to support themselves. Many of these published articles are never read by anyone outside the very narrow field of scholars, and many never receive a single citation.

In many colleges, students are increasingly treated as clients or customers who should be made happy or satisfied. Rigor and quality are not prioritized to avoid a decline in student enrollment, as well as to avert trouble from students who will complain about any low grade to school officials. Many colleges rely primarily on student course evaluations to assess teaching, which, unfortunately, makes professors to ask little from students and give out good grades (Arum and Roksa, 2011). Given this push toward grade inflation, it is unsurprising that a remarkable 43% of all grades at four-year universities are As, an increase of 28 percentage points since 1960. Grade point averages have risen from about 2.52 in the 1950s to 3.11 in 2006 (The Economist, 2012). Today, an average student can, with little effort, graduate with a GPA of 3.5 and above. GPAs of 4.0 have become so mundane that in a typical graduating class one can find more than a handful of students with such an accomplishment.

Further evidence of the declining quality of college education is reflected in an article published in The New York Times by Richard Arum and Josipa Roksa who, over four years, followed the progress of thousands of students in more than two dozen four-year colleges and universities. They found that "large numbers of students were going through college with little exposure to rigorous coursework, only a modest investment of effort, and little or no meaningful improvement in skills like writing and reasoning." According to their findings, in a typical semester, "32% of students did not take a single course with more than 40 pages of required reading per week, and 50% did not take any course requiring more than 20 pages of writing over the semester". Their research also found that many students showed no significant progress on the same "tests of critical thinking, complex reasoning, and writing that were administered when they began college, and then again at the ends of their sophomore and senior years".

Unsurprisingly then, on graduation many students are woefully unprepared for the job market and have a hard time getting employed. There are vast numbers of college-educated graduates working subpar jobs, like taxi driving, bartending, and working as waiters and waitresses. One of the reasons for this situation is the lack of skills that employers are looking for. A recent survey by The Chronicle of Higher Education and American Public Media's Marketplace found that employers had trouble finding qualified recent graduates to hire. Almost a third of the employer's surveyed gave colleges just fair to poor marks for producing successful employees. Bachelor's degree holders were considered lacking basic workplace proficiencies, like adaptability, communication skills, and the ability to solve complex problems (Chronicle of Higher Education, 2013). This contributes to the problem of unemployment, underemployment, and of course the student debt crisis, because underemployed (or unemployed) students do not have the means to repay their loans.

Aside from the negative effects of readily available loans, another reason for the student debt crisis is the fact that the return on investment of a college education is falling. Since the 1970s, the net job growth has been in occupations that require some post-secondary education. This is leading more students to sign up for college than ever before. However, because of the slow-growing economy, globalization, and a large number of graduates competing for fewer jobs, the return on college investment has fallen. Many graduates come out of college with large debt, only to be underemployed in an economy that cannot take advantage of their knowledge and skills.

The student loan crisis has put the higher education sector under scrutiny and was one of the topical issues in the 2016 presidential election campaign cycle. Some Democrats proposed debt forgiveness and a moratorium, or some relief to students burdened by debt after a period of time. Senator Bernie Sanders, and to some extent Secretary Hillary Clinton, proposed free tuition for public colleges and many young people warmed up to this proposal.

Senator Sanders argued that the use of taxes to fund public colleges is the responsibility of the government because education should be a right as it is in many other countries. He pointed to countries in Europe that have free tuition as the standard that the US should emulate. Donald Trump's education plan during the 2016 presidential campaign called for student loan repayments to be capped at 12.5% of the borrower's income, with any remaining debt forgiven after 15 years (Diamond, 2016). Many other Republicans argue that the best solution to the student loan crisis is to reduce access to federal loans and expand the private loan market.

Examining the different proposals put forth shows that none of them will solve the problem without creating more problems. Senator Bernie Sanders' idea of free tuition is quite a popular one. Polling conducted by the Campaign for Free College Tuition (CFCT) found that about two-thirds of Americans supported making colleges tuition free (Newman, 2016). This unfortunately is not the solution.

In Germany, by 2014, all states had abolished tuition fees following student protests and political pressure. According to the OECD 2016 annual Education at a Glance report, "the number of students in tertiary education increased by 28 per cent between 2008 and 2013. Germany increased total expenditure in tertiary institutions by 16 per cent between 2008 and 2013 (reaching $16,895 per student in 2013), but this has failed to keep up with the increase in the number of students, resulting in expenditure per student at tertiary level that is 10 per cent lower than in 2008". The report said, Germany's "annual expenditure directly related to instruction per student at the tertiary level is $9,085, which is below the OECD average of $10,222". In a nutshell, free tuition has caused participation to rise, outstripping public funding. The sustainability of such a venture in the face of increasing enrollment and cost is hard to envision.

Even with the disappearance of tuition, many students are still graduating with debt because they resort to jobs or loans to cover rent and food. This is particularly hard for students from low-income families, which the entire scheme was designed to help. Also, enrollment is still higher for students from families with college-educated parents compared to families with parents without a college education. Free college tuition does not change the demographics of students who go to college (Marcus, 2016).

Under the Bernie Sanders plan of free public college, the federal government would cover 67% of the cost without imposing new taxes on the middle class, while the states would be responsible for the remaining 33%. This means states would be forced to move existing resources from healthcare, K-12 education, and other important commitments into higher education, which is unlikely to happen. Importantly, Senator Sanders' proposal only applied to public schools, which means it does not cover 100 percent of college students in the US.

Also, Sanders' plan might not cover room and board, which interestingly, at many colleges, is one of the reasons students are incurring massive debts. According to the Sanders plan, students would receive federal, state, or college grants to cover the cost of other expenses if the cost is determined to be more than their family can pay. How this would be determined is unclear. Any plan that doesn't address this problem properly would not effectively tackle the student loan crisis.

Secretary Hillary Clinton's plan which is similar to that of Senator Sanders, called for an immediate three-month halt on student loan payments to all federal loan borrowers, and for the restoration of year-round Pell Grant funding. Her proposal called for the elimination of college tuition at in-state public universities for every student from a family making $85,000 a year or less, and this would be extended to families making up to $125,000 by 2021. Her proposal would cost $350 billion over a decade with the federal government providing tuition grants to states that agree to put up some matching money. Mrs. Clinton's proposal faces the same problem of state participation, which makes it hard to envision its success.

Furthermore, Clinton's proposal would increase enrollment at in-state institutions from 9% to 22%, according to the Georgetown University's Center for Education and the Workforce (Carnevale et al., 2016). This would lead to either a situation of overcrowding, which would inevitably reduce the quality of education or to higher selectivity by the schools, which is likely to shut out poor and minority students. Another concern of the Clinton plan is that it incentivizes people to go to their in-state public colleges. This limits choice for students who may want to study out of state. The Clinton plan is quite expensive, and like that of Sanders, Clinton's plan doesn't address the declining quality of education.

Donald Trump's plan calls for student loan repayments to be capped at 12.5% of the borrower's income, and after 15 years any remaining debt be forgiven. This is similar to the policy in the UK where borrowers earning more than an annual earnings threshold of £21,000 in 2016-17 repay 9 per cent of their income and any outstanding balance is written off after 30 years. It is a loss-making model and is therefore fiscally unsustainable. According to Rt Hon Margaret Hodge MP, Chair of the Committee of Public Accounts, there is around £46 billion pounds of outstanding student loans on the Government's account and the government assumes that 35% to 40% (£16 billion to £18 billion) of the total will never be repaid. This figure is projected to rise to £200 billion pounds by 2042, which will bring the amount expected to be unrepaid to between £70 billion to £80 billion pounds. UK taxpayers will end up paying the bill. Furthermore, this approach does not tackle the problem of declining quality of education because it places no burden on colleges to improve instruction.

Another proposal from Republicans is to shrink access to federal loan programs and to expand the private loan market. The problem with this proposal is that private student loans are too burdensome on students. Private lenders rely on predatory practices that include inflating billing statements, deceiving borrowers to maximize late fees, and harassing borrowers by calling them at odd hours. Their loans typically carry higher interest rates, many times more than federal loans (Johnson, Ostern, and White, 2012). Most importantly, the use of private lenders doesn't address the declining quality of education.

Another Republican proposal, and one that is quite interesting, is called income share agreements. This simply means students would obtain funding for their college educations from a private company, and students then pay back the loan from a percentage of their future income for a fixed number of years. This proposal is not fundamentally different from the federal guaranteed loans scheme; it's like changing the picture but leaving the frame. So, it will do nothing to address the declining quality of college education and the ballooning cost of college. On the contrary, it might inadvertently lead to lenders avoiding lending to students who may want to pursue a career in lower-paying but important fields like teaching, history, and social work.

Clearly, the entire higher education system is broken, and the proposals put forth don't address its core problems. With student debt rising, the need to find a smart solution that adequately addresses the problem of declining quality and cost both to the government and students cannot be overemphasized.

De-entropification Solution.

The higher education sector can be de-entropified by using three principles;

1. Benefits of Any Contributor in The System Should Never Exceed Their Contribution.

This simply means that benefits and contribution must always be equal. In the current system, benefit and contribution are far apart. The current system was greatly skewed to the advantage of colleges. No one doubts that colleges serve a public good, but they are first and foremost business entities whose primary goal is to expand, and perpetuate themselves. As the current system is set up, colleges have nothing to worry about. Loans were readily available for students to borrow and they can increase prices when they want to, hire adjunct professors to teach, graduate students, and bring in the next batch. The system does not hold them accountable for the quality of their product: in this case, the students. No business operates under these conditions. An analysis by the third way, a Washington-based think, concluded that colleges were being subsidized with tens of billions of dollars in federal aid which is taxpayer's money without any regard to results or accountability in return (Hiler, Hatalsky and John, 2016). Put simply, in the current system, the benefits of colleges exceeded their contribution.

Many students, on the other hand, graduated from colleges only to be saddled with huge debt and a certificate whose worth didn't match the amount they'd spent. So, on the part of the students, the benefit was significantly less than their contribution.

To match benefits to contribution, there are three possible approaches.

I. Approach one

Connect colleges and students such that colleges cover the entire cost of students' education directly, or guarantee it with their lending partner. With this approach, the college covers tuition, books and supplies, transport, and room and board while the student repays a fixed percentage of earned income to the college after they graduate, for the rest of their working life. Any person who is met with an accident or life circumstance that inhibits them from functioning optimally will be discharged from the loan burden. With payment made for the rest of working life, a few students unable to work due to clearly defined disability won't result in a loss of investment for the college.

With this arrangement, students and colleges communicate directly, and third parties like the government or private lenders are eliminated. This will make the system more efficient. Also, benefits and contribution would be matched. Students get a solid education for the money spent and look towards a good future. Colleges invest in their students, and their success or failure is tied to the quality of their product, like any other business. Colleges lend money to their students at a very low fixed interest rate, and they only make money from their investment over the working life of their students. With projected inflation, the interest rate would need to be fixed at between 4 to 6.5%. Students who are financially successful will make the college even more money.

The percentage to be deducted from the student's pay will be set at graduation, although an initial estimate must be discussed before admission. This percentage will not increase or decrease for the working life of the student; if the agreement is that the student will pay 12% of monthly pay at graduation, it remains 12% for life. The dollar amount fluctuates with the rise or fall of the student's income. Since income tends to increase with experience, the school is likely to earn more.

Advantages of this scheme:

- It will result in strong employer-university cooperation and career development programs. Colleges talk directly with employers, work toward placing their students at internships to better prepare them for the job market, and teach them both the hard and soft skills necessary for them to succeed.

- Demand and supply of graduates would be equal or close to equal, strengthening the value of a college degree. Colleges would discontinue courses for which their graduates cannot find jobs, and reopen them as the job market changes.

- With colleges being the financier of students, they are more likely to invest heavily in student instruction and be extremely selective of students they admit. No other proposal can make colleges improve their instruction. This selectiveness would not reduce the number of students they admit, as they need a lot of students to be in business. Furthermore, this arrangement would make colleges recruit more high quality tenured professors and it would change the relationship between colleges and students from customer or client to partners.

- The scheme covers almost all the students' expenses. Students can then study in peace without worrying about debt.

- Colleges that cannot compete would simply die out, while those that produce the best graduates that can fill the jobs or invent new money-making enterprises would thrive. The government wouldn't have to worry about punishing schools like for-profit universities because of their low student loan repayment rates. Colleges will simply go out of business if their graduates cannot satisfy the job market and repay what they have borrowed.

- During the admissions process, colleges provide an initial estimated percentage of pay to be deducted for the working life of the student. Students will then be more aware or conscious of the financial cost to them, unlike the current third-party arrangement which makes many students unaware of the implications of how much they must repay. This awareness is likely to make many students choose to go to colleges where costs are lower. Over time this would reduce the cost of college, as those that are too expensive will be compelled to bring their prices down to compete.

- Loans are dischargeable if the student dies, or if it is proven that the student has a condition that hampers his or her ability to work. This would reduce the extraordinary burden that student debt has on disabled students. This of course would only be feasible with many students enrolled in the program.

The amount to be repaid would vary depending on the course or major. To get a sense of how much could be hypothetically charged, a close look at the recent survey conducted by the National Association of Colleges and Employers found that 2016 graduates are projected to have an average salary of $50,556. The survey, which looked at the first-year income of more than 45,000 graduates, found big differences in pay depending on the new hires' college majors. Graduates from the sciences, or STEM (Science, Technology, Engineering, Math) majors, consistently earn more than their humanities peers. The average salary for bachelor's degree graduates earning engineering degrees is projected to be the highest at $64,891 while the lowest was education at $34,891 (NACE Staff, 2016).

Calculations.

Since the cost of college varies between majors and colleges, the percentage of income to be charged would also vary with the major and college. To calculate the percentage of income to be paid after graduation for a bachelor's program, the college would use the prevailing average salary for recent graduates of that major in their state or nationally and how much the student owes the school plus a fixed interest rate between 4 to 6.5 percent. The calculated percentage is then set, and this set percentage is permanent.

The calculations below illustrate how this approach would work, and how much the student would repay as a percentage of income after graduating from a four-year bachelor's program. The calculations assume that the graduate is 24 and will work until the retirement age of 65.

According to the College Board, the average cost of tuition and fees for the 2015–2016 school year was $32,405 at private colleges, $9,410 for state residents at public colleges, and $23,893 for out-of-state residents attending public universities. The average cost of room and board in 2015–2016 ranged from $10,138 at four-year public schools to $11,522 at private schools. The average cost for books and supplies for the 2015–2016 school year was $1,298 at public colleges and $1,249 at private colleges. The College Board reports that average cost of Personal and Transportation Expenses for 2015–2016 ran from $2,661 at private colleges to $3,215 at public universities. Since tuition for engineering is more expensive, $2,000 is added annually for four years to make an additional $8,000. Also, the calculation uses a fixed interest rate set at 4.5%.

Below are the calculations for in-state college.

1. Average cost of in-state college tuition and fees ($9,410 x 4 years), plus average cost of room and board ($10,138 x 4 years), plus average cost of books and supplies ($1,298 x 4 years), plus average cost of personal and transportation expenses ($3,215 x 4 years) = $96,244

   Fixed interest rate = 96,244(1 + (0.045 × 41)) = 273,814.18

   Total = **$273,814.18**

   With an average 2016 education salary of $34,891, the student's gross pay would be $2,907.58. To offset the loans, the percentage to pay back for the 41years would be set at 19.1%. For the first year, this is about $566.5 monthly. Assuming the graduate receives a 1% pay rise annually till 65, the college would end up making $319,056. If the graduate receives a 2% pay rise annually, the college makes $372,566, and at 5% pay rise annually, the total is $532,857.

2. Tuition for engineering in many colleges is on average about $2,000 more expensive than many other majors. So, adding an extra $2,000 per year in tuition would give us $104,244. At a fixed interest of 4.5% it would be

   A = 104244(1 + (0.045 × 41)) = 296,574.18

   Total= **$296,574.18**

   With an average 2016 engineering salary $64,891, Gross Pay =$5,407.58, To offset the loans, the percentage to pay back for the 41years would be set at 11.1% For the first year, this is about $603 monthly. Assuming the graduate gets a 1% pay rise annually, the college would end up making $344,848. If the student gets a 2% pay rise annually, the college makes $402,684 and at 5% pay rise annually, it comes down to $582,918.

Figure 6-1: Table Showing the Breakdown of Cost and Profit.

	In-State		Out-of-State		Private Colleges	
	Engineering	Education	Engineering	Education	Engineering	Education
Average National Salary.	$64,891	$34,891	$64,891	$34,891	$64,891	$34,891
Cost of four-year college with 4.5% fixed interest rate.	$296,574.18	$273,814.18	$461,356.58	$438,596.58	$567,133.68.	$544,373.68
1% pay raise per year.	$344,848.	$319,056	$537,465	$511,158.	$661,735	$635,606
2% pay raise per year.	$402,684	$372,566	$627,607	$596,887	$772,718	$742,207
5% pay raise per year.	$582,918	$532,857	$908,512.	$853,687	$1,118,573	$ 1,061,529.
Profit at 1% pay raise.	$48,273.82 ↑16.3	$45,241.82 ↑16.5	$76,108.42 ↑16.5	$72,561.42 ↑16.5	$94,601.32 ↑16.7	$91,232.32 ↑16.7
Profit at 2% pay raise.	$106,109.82 ↑36	$98,751.82 ↑36	$166,250.42 ↑36	$158,290.42 ↑36	$205,584.42 ↑36.2	$197,833.32 ↑36.3
Profit at 5% pay raise.	$286,341.82 ↑96.5	$259,038.82 ↑94.6	$447,155.42 ↑97	$415,090.42 ↑94.6	$551,439.32 ↑97.2	$517,155.32 ↑95

A slight annual pay raise of 1% produces a 17% profit on average, a 2% pay raise produces a 37% profit on average, and a 5% produces a 97% profit on average. Importantly, since pay rises with experience, the graduate would be expected to make more as they gain experience which translates into higher earning power.

If a student wants to go for a master's or doctorate, the same prevailing state or national average salary for recent graduates with similar qualifications, along with the costs incurred, would be used to set the percentage of monthly wages needed to service the loans. With this approach, pursuing a college degree wouldn't be taken lightly as students would be more conscious of the cost of college before they enter. This would balance the demand for a college education and make colleges reduce costs. A student who understands that 30% of their pay for their entire working lives will be taken to pay their college debt will be unlikely to attend that school. Universities will therefore have to offer deals in pay percentage to entice students to study with them until masters or doctorate level. One college could offer 15% of pay to study till master's degree level and another offer students this same percentage for studies till doctorate degree level. This inevitably would bring cost down.

This approach works well for everyone, regardless of age. However, the younger the student, and the cheaper the costs incurred during studies, the less will be the set monthly percentage of income to be paid for the rest of his or her working life. Overall, the scheme works perfectly for both colleges and students. Most importantly, it would significantly improve the quality of education.

II. Approach 2

This approach is similar to approach one, except that colleges would only cover the cost of tuition. Students or their parents would pay for room and board, books, transportation, and living expenses. Like approach one, a set percentage of the student's income would be paid for the rest of the working life of the student. However, students would be borrowing less compared to approach one, and would, therefore, be paying back a much smaller percentage of their income to service the loans for the rest of their working life.

III. Approach 3

With this approach, the college remains the financier of the student's education. However, unlike approaches one and two, repayment is not tied to a set percentage of income for the rest of the working life of the student. Instead, it is paid within a fixed period, and the loan comes with higher interest rates. With this approach, the college only covers tuition because it would be too expensive and burdensome for the graduate to pay back within a fixed period if they covered the total cost of college, like in approach one. Importantly, under this approach, the loan would not be dischargeable under any circumstances, even in fatal illness, unlike approaches one and two. Also, with this approach students would be submitting a collateral, or require a cosigner who would pay the loans if they fail to meet their obligations.

2. Negative Consequences Must Always Be Equal to The Severity of Wrongdoing.

To make this scheme work, students would be obligated to work so that the colleges can recoup their investments. Any graduate who absconds, or chooses not to work (without proof of sufficient disability) would be subject to severe financial, civil and criminal penalties. This would have to be clearly stated in the contract between the university and the student before admissions.

Figure 6-2: Summary Differences Between Approaches 1, 2 and 3.

Approach 1 and 2	Approach 3
Tied to fixed percentage of income which is set at graduation.	Not tied to percentage of income.
Interest rate is fixed between 4 and 6.5. percent.	Interest rate is fixed but higher.
Dischargeable if the student is sick such that they cannot work or they die. This, of course, would need many students to enroll in it.	Not dischargeable under any circumstances.
Paid for the entire working life of the student.	Paid for a fixed period of years. Preferably 10-15 years.
Co-signer not needed.	Co-signer or collateral needed.
Severe financial and criminal penalties for absconding or failing to pay back.	Collateral is confiscated, co-signer pays or faces criminal prosecution if student absconds or fails to pay.
Covers everything from tuition, room, and board, transportation, and books (approach one), or tuition only (approach two).	Covers only tuition.
Universities could make a lot of money if students do very well over their working life, or lose money if students cannot secure good jobs.	Universities make money but cannot gain anything more if student is financially successful.
Interest does not accrue during the period of study; an interest rate of between 4-6% is only added to the principal at graduation.	Interest accrues per year during studies.

Students would be free to choose any approach that works for them. Ultimately, approach one and two would be most ideal for colleges and universities if they can produce students who go on to make a lot of money. Although private colleges are not compelled to participate, in the absence of federal dollars for students to borrow, they may have no other choice than to use one of these approaches. Students who wish to pay out of pocket and directly for their college cost remain free to do so.

3. Principles of General Homogeneity: Homogenization to help those in the negative homogenous group.

The Federal Pell Grant Program which helps to provides need-based grants to low-income students is an effort to help students from families in the negative homogenous group to move to the positive homogenous group. It is a commendable effort, and it should be continued. However, it should only be given to low-income students who gain admission to colleges with 95 to 100 percent employment rate. This way the funds are spent on colleges with good records and the grants are given to low-income students who are most qualified to go to college.

Alternative Solution.

Using these same principles, an alternative solution in which the government uses its position as a powerful third party to control cost could be envisioned.

A. Benefits Should Never Exceed or Go Beyond Contribution.

As already discussed, in the current system, benefits and contribution are not equal. One way to equalize them is for the government to raise the qualification or eligibility for any college or university to receive federal dollars. In this scenario, no college or university employment rate for recent graduates for a particular major should fall below 15 percent of the best college employment rate for that major for three consecutive years. For example, if Yale University has the highest employment rate for recent graduates of mechanical engineering at 98%, no other college whether public, private or for-profit, receiving federal dollars should fall below an employment rate of 83 percent for recent mechanical engineer graduates for three consecutive years. This number is adjusted every three years using the college with the highest employment rate for that particular major. This would equalize benefits and contribution.

B. Negative Consequences Should Be Equal to The Severity of Wrongdoing.

To ensure that negative consequences are equal to the severity of wrongdoing, any college or university that fails to meet the required employment rate for three consecutive years would be cut off from the federal loan program for a minimum of five years for that particular major. In other words, federal loans will not be available to students who gain admissions to blacklisted colleges or universities for such a major for five years. This would make colleges and universities to devote their attention to majors for which their graduates are doing best on the job market and eliminate those in which they are doing poorly. Also, this would make colleges to teach their graduates soft and hard skills needed for the job market and increase investment in instructions.

Furthermore, to curb the constant rise in tuition costs, students who go to colleges that are less expensive should be eligible for lower interest rates on their loans. This means students who attend colleges and universities whose total tuition costs for a major is greater than 15 percent of the least expensive college for the same major will face higher interest rates on their loans. For example, if the total four-year cost of mechanical engineering at Duke University is $10,000 and this is the least expensive in the country, students who attend colleges where the total cost for mechanical engineering is not greater than $11,500 will be eligible for significantly lower interest rates on their loans. In contrast, students who go to colleges where the cost of mechanical engineering is higher than this amount will face higher interest rates on their loans. This approach would serve as a penalty to colleges whose programs are exorbitantly expensive and curb the constant jacking up of tuition rates. In addition, it will increase student's attraction for less expensive colleges and put pressure on more expensive ones to cut cost.

Conclusions.

There are two main problems with the higher educational system: quality and cost. The best way to overcome these problems is to make colleges have a stake in what becomes of their students. If their students fail, they fail; if students do well, then they reap the benefits. This approach would eliminate the student loan debt problem, get colleges to focus on improving the quality of their instruction, and most importantly, get the economy and the educational sector to work hand in hand.

The higher education sector must be the destination for the best of the best if it is to keep its promise as the place where great things are achieved. Reforms are badly needed, and these reforms must start in the middle school and high school sectors. The problems with unqualified students in the higher education sector are in part due to problems in the lower education sectors. So, until serious reforms are instituted to improve the quality of education for middle school and high school education, the number of students that can succeed through the rigors of a college education will remain low. The entire education system is dependent on the quality of high school graduates it produces, and when that part fails the entire system fails.

Finally, this proposal could be applied to community colleges and technical and trade colleges. Those that can produce graduates who can get jobs will thrive, while those that offer nothing to students and the economy simply fold. The government has no reason to entangle itself in subsiding unqualified students or colleges that cannot produce graduates who are employable.

Chapter 7

Tax Policies, Inequality and Economic Growth

Wealth and income inequality in America are at near record levels. According to Pew Research Center, American middle class which has been the nation's economic majority is now tied in number by those in the economic tiers above and below it; 120.8 million adults in middle-income households, and 121.3 million in lower and upper-income households combined in early 2015. From 16% in 1971, American adults in the lowest-income tier have risen to 20% as of 2015. In contrast, the highest-income tier has risen more than twice from 4% in 1971 to 9%, in 2015 (Pew Research Center, 2015).

A research report by Emmanuel Saez and Gabriel Zucman found that since the 1970s, the share of household wealth owned by the top 1%—1.6 million families with net assets above $4 million— has increased to about 42% of total wealth. The top 0.1%— 160,700 families with net assets above $20 million in 2012 has increased from 7% to 22%. However, for the bottom 90% of families, household wealth fell from 35% in the mid-1980s to 22.8% in 2012. In other words, today the top 0.1% has almost the same amount of wealth as the bottom 90% combined. Importantly, almost all the increase in the top 1% shares over the last three decades is due to the astronomical rise in the top 0.1% share of wealth (Saez and Zucman, 2016).

According to a 2011 Congressional Research report, income inequality increased between 1996 and 2006 as measured by the Gini coefficient. During this period, inflation-adjusted average after-tax income grew by 25%, and the poorest 20% of tax filers, saw a 6% reduction in income while the top 0.1% of tax filers, saw an almost doubling of their income (Hungerford, 2011). From 2009 to 2012, average real income per family grew by 6.0%. During this time, income for the top 1%, grew by 31.4% while the bottom 99% incomes grew only by 0.4%. In other words, in the first three years of the recovery from the 2008 recession, the top 1% received 95% of the income gains. In 2012, the top 1% incomes increased by almost 20% while those at the bottom 99% incomes grew only by a mere one percent. Put simply, the top one percent incomes are close to full recovery from the recession, but the bottom 99% incomes have hardly started to recover (Saez, 2013).

With such massive disparity in wealth and income, the pressing question then becomes what happened, and how did income and wealth levels become so unequal in America? From globalization to a stagnating median wage, technological change, market segmentation, to tax policies, many factors drive inequality. There are arguments that tax policies have little or no effect on income disparities, but they can play an important role in mitigating income inequality, especially in the short- to medium-term (Burman, 2014).

Debate on the use of tax policies to combat inequality centers on the argument for a more progressive tax system, and on the other side, the argument is for slashing the top tax rates to increase investment and the production of goods and services. Close examination of both arguments shows that both are opposites that fail to tackle income disparities and at the same time achieve sustainable and equitable economic growth.

In 1981, President Ronald Reagan slashed the top tax rate to 28% from 70%, and this came with generous business deductions. There was a break in this policy during the George H. W. Bush and Bill Clinton presidency, but tax cuts for the rich returned in 2001 in the George W. Bush presidency. Clinton raised the top rate to 39.6 per cent and George W. Bush reduced the top rate to 35 percent and on capital gains tax rate to 15 percent. To this day, tax cuts, or supply-side economics, is the default way of thinking for many on the political right to spur economic growth. Proponents of supply-side economics, or trickle-down economics as it also known, argue that tax cuts will unleash a torrent of new investment that will lead to economic growth, boost job creation, and result in a broadly shared prosperity. Furthermore, they argue that there will be no loss of revenue from the tax cuts, as growth would be very strong that the tax cuts would ultimately pay for themselves.

On first thought, supply-side economics seem reasonable. However, the evidence for its viability as a tool to move the economy forward and tackle inequality is sketchy, at best. Proponents often credit President Reagan's huge 1981 deregulation and tax cut with spurring robust growth in the ensuing years. It must be noted, however, that President Reagan raised taxes several times to deal with budget deficits and led a massive increase in defense spending, from $325.1 billion and $339.6 million in 1981 to as much $456.5 billion in 1987 (Schneider and Merle, 2004). This increased defense spending must have contributed to the economic growth. Furthermore, though the standard of living rose during the Reagan years, its growth was no faster than during 1950-1980 and his tax policy contributed to an increase in the level of inequality (Plotnick, 1993).

A report by the nonpartisan Congressional Research Service that analyzed the top tax rates since 1945 found that reduction in the top tax rates has had little association with saving, investment, or productivity growth. It concluded that tax rate change limited to a small group of taxpayers at the top of the income distribution has a negligible effect on economic growth and may be associated with increased concentration of income at the top (Hungerford, 2012).

Moreover, a 2015 report by the International Monetary Fund (IMF) adds to growing evidence that supply-side economics does not do what its proponents claim. IMF researchers found that a higher net Gini coefficient is associated with lower output growth over the medium term. This simply means that income inequality is associated with lower output growth. Also, the researchers found an inverse relationship between the income share concentration to the top 20 percent and economic growth. According to the report, when the richest 20% of society increase their income by one percentage point, annual economic growth rate shrinks by nearly 0.10% in the following five years. In contrast, the rate of economic growth increases by nearly 0.4% over the same period when the income of the lowest 20% of earners grows by a one percentage point. This shows that there exists a positive relationship between higher middle-class disposable income shares and higher growth. Also, it suggests that benefits do not trickle down (Dabla-Norris, et al. 2015).

Also, a study that investigated how tax changes for different income groups affect macroeconomic activity found that at both the state and federal level, the effect of tax cuts for the top 10% on employment growth is negligible and statistically insignificant. In contrast, it found that tax cuts for lower-income groups have a positive relationship with employment growth (Zidar, 2013).

Perhaps the most glaring failure of supply-side economics is found in the state of Kansas where it was fully put to the test. Governor Sam Brownback of Kansas enacted the largest tax cuts in the state's history in 2012 and 2013, reducing the top tax bracket by 25% and eliminating all taxes on business profits that are reported on individual income, with promises of huge economic returns. In the end, the state reported it was $338 million short of funds expected in the 2014 fiscal year. Unemployment increased because the rich and wealthy simply kept the money gained from tax cuts and didn't invest as envisioned. A 2016 study found that, at both extensive and intensive margins, the behavioral responses towards the government's tax policies have been tax avoidance rather than real supply side responses (DeBacker et al., 2016).

The Congressional Joint Economic Committee reported that Kansas had only 9,400 new private sector jobs in 2015, an average of 780 jobs per month (out of 2.6 million nationwide). A study found that two years post-enactment of the tax changes, it failed to yield a net increase in private-sector employment (Turner and Blagg, 2017). Per-pupil state aid declined from $4,400 to $3,800, forcing cutbacks in staffing, classes, and school days in certain districts. The state Supreme Court had to issue orders requiring Kansas to come up with enough money to pay for K-12 education. In March 2016, Governor Brown-back cut $17 million from the state's six public universities in response to revenue shortfalls, and had to delay a $93 million contribution to the state pension fund. His tax policies even got Moody's Investors Services to down-grade Kansas' outlook from stable to negative for the first time in over a dec-ade (New York Times Editorial Board, 2014; Zorn 2016).

Aside from the problems with economic growth job creation and inequality, there is little evidence to back the claims that tax cuts to the those at the top would eventually pay for themselves. A report by the nonpartisan Congres-sional Research Service that examined the relationship between tax rates and economic growth found no evidence that the cost of tax reductions is signifi-cantly reduced by feedback effects. According to the report, the feedback effects are in the range of 3% to 10% and can, in some cases, be negative (Gravelle and Marples, 2014). Unsurprisingly, the 2003 tax cuts, by President Bush did not improve economic growth or pay for themselves, but instead increased the deficits and debt and contributed to a rise in income inequality (Horton, 2017).

So, the role of supply-side economics to spur economic growth especially in the long term that is beneficial to all is grossly overstated, to say the least, but many on the political right still push it as the default way to make the econo-my grow. Perhaps it is because it just seems intuitively correct in a way that empirical data cannot disprove unequivocally, or perhaps there are ideologi-cal reasons for pushing it.

On the other side of the argument is the push for a more progressive tax sys-tem. According to a research study by the National Bureau of Economic Re-search, increasing top marginal tax rates on ordinary income and capital gains would decrease after-tax income inequality (Fieldhouse, 2013). A 2007 paper by Piketty and Saez found that since the 1960s, U.S. federal tax system has become less progressive at the top of the income distribution and this is due primarily to a drop in corporate taxes and to a lesser extent on capital income. In a 2011 article, they argued for the elimination of loopholes to eliminate most tax avoidance opportunities and then increase top tax rates to as much as 80% and higher (Piketty, Saez, and Stantcheva, 2011). In a 2013 paper, Piketty and Saez argued that optimal inheritance tax rate might be as large as 50%–60%—or even higher. Economist Joseph E. Stiglitz has also called for an increase in the top marginal income tax rates to achieve sustainable and equi-table economic development (Stiglitz, 2014).

The evidence that a more progressive tax system will combat income ine-quality without compromising economic growth is sketchy at best. An analy-sis by experts at the Brookings Institute found that raising the top individual tax rate up to 50 percent and redistributing all new revenue to households in the bottom 20 percent of the income distribution would have a trivial or very modest effect on overall income inequality (Gale, Kearney and Orszag, 2015).

Proponents of higher taxes point to the 1950s, during the Eisenhower administration, and the 1990s, during the Clinton administration, during which high marginal tax rates coexisted with economic growth and low income inequality. However, the underlying reasons are complicated. Most of the growth in the Clinton era was fueled significantly by a tech boom or Internet-driven growth that boosted business productivity. As for Eisenhower's administration in the 1950s, this 91% applied to earnings over $3 million when adjusted for inflation, and they were tax breaks and deductions just like today that lowered effective tax rate (Syrios, 2015).

The biggest problem with high taxes is that it is perceived as unfair. This causes people and corporations to adjust their tax affairs to receive more of their returns in less heavily taxed forms and take greater advantage of loopholes in the tax code to avoid paying it. Research shows that a one percentage point increase in the tax rate is associated with a 3 percent increase in evasion (Fisman and Wei, 2004). Many especially the wealthy and large corporation end up moving their money overseas, stashing it in tax havens outside the reach of the state. There has been a tenfold increase since the 1980s of US companies shifting profits to the Caribbean, Luxembourg, and similar countries. About 20 percent of all US corporate profits are stashed in such havens and its typically done within the letter of the law to avoid paying taxes (Zucman, 2014). Holdings in tax havens which are unrecorded are more than double the net foreign debt of many countries, and evidence suggests that they mostly belong to residents of rich countries where taxes are quite high (Zucman, 2013).

Many proponents of higher taxes argue that blocking of tax loopholes and increased negative consequences will increase compliance but the evidence that this would work is debatable. Research shows that tax evasion rises sharply with wealth because people naturally want to keep more of their money for themselves. In Scandinavia, on average about 3% of personal taxes are evaded, but this rises to almost 30% for those in the top 0.01%; households with more than $40 million in net wealth (Alstadsæter, Johannesen and Zucman, 2017). Also, research shows that evaders respond to higher tax rates by increasing their evasion activity (Crane and Nourzad, 1990).

Furthermore, extremely high taxes can hamper the competitive advantage and damage the investment reputation of a state or nation. France's effort to cut down its public deficit by imposing a 75% rate on earnings above €1m ($1,118,400) is a good example. The super high tax rate in France caused several high-profile French citizens to leave the country and it damaged France's reputation and competitiveness. Money generated from the tax was €260 million ($271.6m) in its first year and €160 million ($167.1m) in the second—a small amount when compared with its budget deficit. In the end, the high tax was deemed counterproductive and dropped (Penketh, 2014).

Also, higher taxes discourage work, saving, and entrepreneurship (Carroll, 2009). This could also lead to the stagnation of the entrepreneurial sector, which is a key sector for economic growth and tax revenue. A large percentage of all business taxes are paid by owners of sole proprietorships, partnerships, and corporations that are often small. These businesses are the bedrock of innovation. Higher taxes can quickly take the life out of this sector. This would stagnate the economy, as innovation from small business is one of the drivers of investment in the economy.

Importantly, many factors, like energy prices, war or crisis, global competition, lack of oversight or regulatory failure, interest rates, and government spending, among others, affect what happens in the economy, regardless of tax policies. This makes it hard to draw firm conclusions on the exact economic impact of tax cuts or high taxes. That said, taxation can play a key role in spurring or depressing economy growth and fighting inequality.

De-entropification Solution.

Taxes are important to help pay for social and public services. High taxes are unfair, and low taxes result in reduced government revenues with far-reaching negative repercussions. The goal, therefore, of a good tax code must be to

1. encourage people to work more and invest more,

2. reduce poverty and income inequality, and

3. ensure that the state can collect enough tax revenues to meet its obligations.

Achieving all this is hard. As previously discussed, at the heart of supply-side economics is for the wealthy to get generous tax cuts and then invest in the economy. This investment, it is argued, spurs economic growth and those at the bottom benefit from the jobs that are created. However, if those at the bottom do not have enough money to spend, the rich who are supposed to invest will hold out on investing, increasing the income and wealth inequality. On the other hand, high taxes discourage entrepreneurship and investment, reduces the tax base due to evasion which in turn could adversely affect economic growth. So, both arguments fail to overcome either the problem of inequality, or that of more investment. A middle ground approach is needed that overcomes the problem of inequality, tax evasion and creates a climate of investment. This can be achieved by applying three principles to the system.

1. Benefit of Any Contributor in The System Should Never Exceed Their Contribution.

High taxation, or tax cuts for some people, both violate this principle. High taxes take too much of a person's contribution (their sweat and hard work), while the benefits they enjoy are no different from those enjoyed by people who pay less. This is grossly unfair, and it is why people look for ways to avoid paying taxes, or stay away from investing. No one wants to work and not keep a significant part of the fruits of their labor. On the other hand, tax cuts give excessive benefits to those at the top. It works with the hope that this benefit would be matched with the contribution of investment, but all too often this contribution is never realized.

To match benefit with contribution, a system that applies a 99.9% rule would do the trick. The 99.9%, or "spend it all," rule allows a business or individual to spend a percentage of their earnings that is supposed to be taken away in taxes, either for themselves or their business. For corporations and businesses, this simply means they would be mandated to spend some of the money that was supposed to be taken away from them in taxation on their products and services or on new investment.

For example, if the statutory corporate tax rate is 40% and a tax cut of 20% is given to a corporation, they would have to spend this money to lower the prices of their products and services such that consumers enjoy the benefits of these low prices. This would increase the purchasing power of consumers and spur them to buy more. As demand increases, businesses would expand and hire more people. This would spur investment, since businesses know that a decent portion of their taxable profit would be returned to them to reinvest in their business. The multiplier effect of this approach means the government would make up the money over time in taxes as businesses expand.

Companies could be creative about how they spend this money toward their consumers. A department store, for example, could say that if a consumer spends a specific amount with them in the first three months of the year, he or she would get a certain discount for the remainder of the year. Car dealerships could apply their tax cuts by paying for the gas for every new car bought for a couple of months to spur buying. Real estate companies could pay the property taxes for those who buy from them for a certain period. Businesses could develop different smart ideas and strategies to pass the money back to their customers. This approach would increase a company's sales and build a loyal customer base. Everybody wins in this scenario: the consumer enjoys the price reduction in products and services, and the company increases its sales. Many businesses are likely to exceed the 99.9% rule spending because the benefits to their business warrant such a move.

Also, the government could direct businesses to invest this tax cuts in economically disadvantaged areas so as to improve the economic situation.

For estate and inheritance taxes, the same 99.9 percent rule can be applied. If the inheritance or estate tax is 30 percent, the government could freeze it at 15 percent and apply the 99.9 percent rule on the other 15 percent. The individual then spends this money during the fiscal year. It can also be applied to capital gains tax. The fact that people are keeping a substantial part of their money that should have been taken away in taxes to reinvest in themselves or their businesses will increase investment and growth that would benefit everyone.

To apply the 99.9% rule on individuals' income taxes, there are three possible approaches.

A. Approach one

For this approach, the 99.9% rule will be exclusively for those in the highest marginal tax rates; 24 percent marginal tax rate and above. Using the 2018 tax rate, the marginal tax rate could be frozen at say 12%, and the 99.9% rule would be applied to the balance. This means those in the 24 percent tax bracket would face a 12% marginal tax rate and the balance would be subject to the 99.9 percent rule. The same applies to those in the 32%, 35%, and 37% tax brackets.

Tax rate	For Unmarried Individuals, Taxable Income Over	For Married Individuals Filing Joint Returns, Taxable Income Over	For Heads of Households, Taxable Income Over
High group froze at 12%			
24%	$82,501 to $157,500	$165,001 to $315,000	$82,501 to $157,500
32%	$157,501 to $200,000	$315,001 to $400,000	$157,501 to $200,000
35%	$200,001 to $500,000	$400,001 to $600,000	$200,001 to $500,000
37%	over $500,000	over $600,000	over $500,000

Figure 7-1: Approach One Breakdown.

People could invest this money in stocks, bonds, real estate, furniture, cars, or donate the money to towards research, and so on. The government could determine allowable investment opportunities to maximally impact the economy. However, this should be as broad as possible lest the entire system loses its appeal.

With this arrangement, people are likely to spend more than the required 99.9% as this would benefit them. They would be quite simply pursuing their self-interest while at the same time they would help the entire economy. This approach would reduce tax evasion, encourage people to invest and work harder, since their future success would not simply be taken away by the government in taxes. As they spend, businesses would expand and more jobs would be created, which would benefit people at the middle and bottom. In the end, the entire economy would benefit from the proposal, and the government would make more money from the increased spending. It would also reduce the problem of income inequality, as money wouldn't be hoarded without any real investment or spending, as is the case with tax cuts.

B. Approach Two.

This approach would include everyone in the economy. People would be divided into a low and a high group, based on tax bracket. Like approach one above, the high group starts at the 24% marginal tax rate, and the lower group includes the remaining tax brackets. The marginal tax rate is frozen at 12% for the high group and 5% for the lower group and the 99.9 percent rule is applied to the balance.

Tax rate	For Unmarried Individuals, Taxable Income Over	For Married Individuals Filing Joint Returns, Taxable Income Over	For Heads of Households, Taxable Income Over
High group froze at 12%			
24%	$82,501 to $157,500	$165,001 to $315,000	$82,501 to $157,500
32%	$157,501 to $200,000	$315,001 to $400,000	$157,501 to $200,000
35%	$200,001 to $500,000	$400,001 to $600,000	$200,001 to $500,000
37%	over $500,000	over $600,000	over $500,000
Low group froze at 5%			
10%	Up to $9,525	$0 to $19,050	$0 to $13,600
12%	$9,526 to $38,700	19,051 to $77,400	$13,601 to $51,800
22%	$38,701 to $82,500	$77,401 to $165,000	$51,801 to $82,500

Figure 7-2: Approach Two Breakdown.

Most people in America fall into the lower group. Giving them back the money they have worked hard for, that was supposed to be taken away in taxes, would reduce the financial burden many families face. It would allow them to spend the extra money on basics, and on household amenities they need. Also, since this spending involves everyone in the economy, its effect on the economy would also include the purchase of high-end goods. Ultimately, the government would recoup all the lost money through increased investment and business expansion.

C. Approach three.

This approach would focus solely on those in the lower tax brackets. It would be frozen at the 5% marginal tax rate, and any additional earning would be subject to the 99.9% rule. This would spur economic growth, as most people in this tax bracket do a lot of spending and with their spending, investment confidence would increase. Also, with this approach, the government would keep all the money from those at the top in taxes. This approach would fight the problem of inequality while at the same time spurring investment and economic growth.

Low group froze at 5%			
10%	Up to $9,525	$0 to $19,050	$0 to $13,600
12%	$9,526 to $38,700	19,051 to $77,400	$13,601 to $51,800
22%	$38,701 to $82,500	$77,401 to $165,000	$51,801 to $82,500

Figure 7-3: Approach Three Breakdown.

Approach two is the best because it affects every tax payer. However, the government can choose the approach that best suits the circumstances of the economy.

2. Negative Consequences Must Always Be Equal to Severity of Wrongdoing.

To make this approach successful, negative consequences must be matched with the severity of failing to meet the 99.9% requirement. If a person fails to spend at least 99.9% of this money on qualifying goods and services, they would face a penalty of paying the full statutory marginal tax rate they were supposed to pay, plus 50%. In other words, they would pay back 150%. This severe penalty would make people fulfill the requirement and even spend more, to be on the safe side. Also, this negative consequence or penalty means the government can be certain, not hopeful, that this money would be spent on the economy.

3. Rule or Laws Must Be Simple, Clear and Consistent.

There are too many loopholes, deductibles, and exemptions in the current US tax code. This complexity means the effective tax rate of people, in the same tax bracket are often different. Thus, the amount of money people in the same tax bracket would receive to spend as part of the 99.9% rule could be vastly different. Some could receive a lot, while others, due to qualification or lack of qualification for one or more exemption, rule, or deductible, receive close to nothing. Making the tax code simpler, unambiguous, and consistent by eliminating some of the loopholes, deductibles, and exemptions would be vital to the success of the whole approach.

Conclusions.

The tax system needs reform so that it can effectively combat inequality, provide the government with revenues and encourage investment. Supply-side economics and high taxation are unsuccessful approaches to spur economic growth and fight income inequality and tax evasion at the same time.

The 99.9% rule that allows people to keep a certain percentage of their taxable income and spend it on themselves is a good way to keep the economy rolling. People spending money they have earned that should have been confiscated by the state makes them happy and increases the fairness in the tax code. This would spur people to work harder and it would reduce tax invasion. Furthermore, the negative consequences and benefits enshrined in the 99.9% rule increases the certainty that this money would be spent, and not simply hoarded. Businesses would benefit enormously from this spending and investment confidence would soar. In the end, this would have a ripple effect on the economy and everyone would benefit. The government would make back all the money returned to taxpayers in investment and hiring increases.

However, to achieve the maximum effect, this 99.9% rule must be applied to different types of taxes at the same time. That means it should be applied to capital gains, income, corporate, estate, inheritance, etc. for maximum positive effect on the economy. Finally, although the 99.9% rule would work well at any time in the economy, the benefits from its application would probably be greatest during an economic downturn rather than during boom periods when unemployment is low and spending is quite good. The possibility of increased inflation and low savings also adds to concerns about its application and usefulness.

Chapter 8

The Political System and Government

Peaceful human cooperation is vital for the sustenance of civilization, but this is not possible without a government—a social apparatus of coercion and compulsion. Ironically, this apparatus that was invented to uphold the rule of law and fight crime and violence whenever necessary can employ the same violence it was created to eliminate. In recognition of this fact, many people have called government an evil, although a necessary one. Government is perhaps the most necessary and beneficial institution, as without it, social cooperation, prosperity, and civilization cannot be developed and preserved. However, there lies a danger in entrusting too much authority to implement the use of violence in the hands of men. All too often, the men who are selected to protect the community against aggression easily turn into the most dangerous aggressors. They transgress their mandate and misuse the power given to them for the oppression of those whom they were supposed to defend.

To overcome this tendency, humans have tried to create the perfect government; one that is responsive and answerable to the people. So far, all attempts to create this perfect government have failed. This is evident in the sense of despair and disgust people around the world feel about politicians and the political system.

In the United States, many citizens are distrustful of government and unhappy with the political system. According to Gallup's 2014 survey, three in four Americans (75%) perceived corruption as widespread in the US government. Also, according to Gallup's annual Mood of the Nation poll, conducted January 5-8, 2014, 65% of Americans are dissatisfied with the nation's political system and how it works (McCarthy, 2014). Another poll conducted by the Associated Press in April of 2016 found that almost eight in ten Americans say they're dissatisfied or angry with the way the federal government is working. Many Americans held sharp disdain for the political system and expressed anger with both parties, career politicians, and Washington insiders (Webber and Swanson, 2016).

This dissatisfaction is not unique to America. Around the world, from Britain to Venezuela, dissatisfaction for politicians and the political system is very high. Many pundits and political experts have attributed the anger and dissatisfaction to rising inequality, mass immigration, globalization, corruption, stagnant wages, and student debts, among other ills. What they fail to see is that within the structure of all existing political systems or government is a deep flaw in the way power is distributed, and this flaw is at the heart of why it never works satisfactorily for all citizens.

To get a good sense of this, it is important to understand that the nation-state is unique among other human inventions. Unlike a private enterprise, where the founder, owner, or largest shareholder decides what becomes of the corporation, the nation-state belongs equally and collectively to all citizens. For this reason, a government with power concentrated at the top is not right for a nation-state. Interestingly, governments around the world, from those that practice communism, monarchy, authoritarianism, and totalitarianism to the liberal democracies, all use this structure: a top-down representational system where a select few, either by birthright or inheritance, as in a monarchy, party selection in Communism, or elections in democracies, decide for the rest of the people.

The first problem with this top-down structure is that it inevitably results in the emergence of elitism. This simply means that it divides the political system into two distinct groups: an elite or establishment ruling class, and the hoi polloi. The elites in a monarchy are the king, queen, their family, advisers, and ministers. In other forms of government, they are the senior party officials, ministers, presidents, members of congress, governors, etc. In a monarchy, the elites retain and control power by birthright, and in liberal democracies, the elites control the structures of the political system. Many politicians attend exclusive private schools and are from wealthy upper-class families with extensive political connections. Dynasticism, which is a product of elitism, is common in all forms of government, even in so-called democracies. In democracies, although elections are constantly held to give a veneer of involvement, the system tends to recycle the rich and powerful.

Elitism results in the need for control. In the United States, the elites retain control of the system through money. A House of Representatives candidate must raise an average of almost $2,000 every day of their two-year cycle to run a winning campaign and candidates for the U.S. Senate must raise an average of $3,300 every day for six years (Lioz and Shanton, 2015). The cost of a campaign for president runs to well over a billion dollars. This makes running for office a privilege only afforded to the wealthy, the well-connected, or those anointed by the elites. Even if a person is successful in the presidential primaries with their money or small donations, such a feat is impossible to repeat in the general elections. Those who are making large donations are not simply doing it out of the kindness of their hearts; they are paying for access. With access, the economic elites can push for policies that are favorable to them that may not necessarily be favorable to citizens at the bottom, who comprise the bulk of the nation. So, the system fosters corruption, nepotism, cronyism, and plutocracy.

Politicians are influenced by the company they keep. By constantly attending intimate gatherings with the richest citizens, over time they naturally become divorced from the agenda of the majority and adopt the perspectives and agendas of the rich. Even so-called populist or honest politicians soon lose their way in the system. They adopt policies that protect the interests of their rich friends to keep the donations and support coming. As reward for their contributions, after the election, the richest donors are the ones who receive the one-on-one meetings and telephone calls (Pennington, 2016).

This skewed elitist system is at the heart of the socioeconomic and other forms of inequality in the United States and around the world. Many people are very quick to blame capitalism for income and wealth inequality, but the true driving force behind income or wealth inequality is the top-down elitist political system that makes it easy for those with wealth and power to manipulate it to their favor. A recent study by Princeton University Professor Martin Gilens and Northwestern University Professor Benjamin found that "economic elites and organized groups representing business interests have substantial independent impacts on US governmental policy." On the other hand, average citizens and mass-based interest groups have little or no independent influence. Their study found that even when most Americans disagree with economic elites and/or with organized interests, they generally lose (Page and Gilens, 2014).

In very developed democracies, although the elites have an advantage over ordinary citizens, they do not always get what they want. In less-developed democracies, the situation is worse. The political and economic elites can literally buy the political process and steal the country dry. Politicians misappropriate and embezzle state funds and then stash them in faraway tax havens where they are untraceable, while many citizens live in abject poverty with no access to basic amenities. Pay-to-play is a very common occurrence in many countries, and outright theft of state funds or kleptocracy is normal. Special favors to cronies, resulting in monopolies and other forms of nepotism, are standard practice.

An interesting example is the story of Chris Ngige, a governor of the state of Anambra in Nigeria whose political godfather, Mr. Chris Oba, had installed in office. In 2003, Ngige was abducted from the government house by hoodlums for failing to abide by the reward agreement reached before the elections. Gangs believed to be conniving with the police set fire to the governor's office and other buildings. According to a BBC article titled "Tensions High in Nigeria State," published November 12, 2004, Ngige was forced to write a resignation letter at gunpoint. While the rule of law could have prevented this from

happening, the structure of government, where so much power is concentrated at the top, contributed to its happening.

In the Philippines, Ferdinand Marcos, his wife Imelda, and a small circle of
close associates stole the country dry. Estimates of Marcos' wealth ran from a
low of US$5 billion to a high of US$15 billion. In Zaire, now the Republic of
Congo, Mobutu Sese Seko stole almost half of the $12 billion in aid money
that his country received from the International Monetary Fund during his
reign. Mohammed Suharto of Indonesia stole as much as $35 billion during
his three decades in power, before being deposed. Sani Abacha of Nigeria is
estimated to have stolen between $2 billion to $5 billion and Slobodan Milosevic of Serbia about $1 billion. Jean-Claude Duvalier of Haiti stole between
$300 million and $500 million, Alberto Fujimori of Chile about $600 million,
Pavlo Lazarenko of Ukraine between $114 million and $200 million, Arnoldo
Alemán of Nicaragua about a $100 million, and Joseph Estrada about a $100
million (Denny, 2004; Sandbrook, 2016). The list goes on.

Developed nations are not immune from this problem. In the United States,
because of the rule of the law, political office is not a means to get rich directly, but it is a platform or springboard to get rich, as life after politics is very
attractive for many politicians. Former politicians are highly sought after in
the private sector. They earn big bucks making speeches and working as lob-
byists for big corporations and special interest groups.

Another flaw with this top-down structure is that it makes the nation-state
vulnerable to dictatorship or autocracy. This tendency is quite common in the
developing world where democratic institutions are weak. However, in more
developed democracies, even with checks and balances governments can use
threats, whether imagined or real, to overreach and violate the rights of citizens. The case of Germany, a democratic country where Hitler and his party
took over the nation democratically and crushed the opposition, shows unequivocally that this threat remains strong in developed democracies. The
current anti-immigration and nationalistic atmosphere in Europe and the
United States show that the nation-state will never be free of such dangers as
long as this top-down power structure remains in place. Even today, there are
still many countries around the world that are run by dictators who pillage
resources, violate the rights of citizens, and treat the country as their personal
property.

Take the case of the president of Equatorial Guinea, Teodoro Obiang Ngue-
ma Mbasogo, who has been in power since 1979 and who has no intention of
stepping down. His regime violates the basic rights and freedoms of citizens.
Although Equatorial Guinea is one of Africa's biggest oil producers, few ordinary people are benefiting from the economic boom (Basong, 2005). In Zim-
babwe, President Robert Mugabe is the only leader many Zimbabweans have

ever known since the country gained independence in 1980. He employs state power to terrorize and intimidate his opponents. The rights of his opponents are routinely violated, and his shortsighted policies have pushed the country's economy to the precipice.

In Eritrea, the regime of Isaias Afewerki has taken over the country and associated it with the unenviable title of having one of the worse human rights records on the planet. Rights of citizens are trampled upon with impunity, and basic freedoms do not exist. Pervasive corruption and nepotism are the order of the day. Arbitrary arrests and forced disappearances have turned the country into a penitentiary state with countless underground prisons (Zere, 2016). From Belarus to North Korea, the list of dictatorships goes on.

Another flaw with the top-down power structure is that the leader at the top creates a winner-take-all feeling that divides society. This problem is particularly evident in multicultural or multiethnic countries. In a country like Nigeria, with well over 200 ethnic groups, the presidency means so much to everyone. When one ethnic group dominates the political sphere, other citizens feel marginalized. All too often the president or governor spends state resources to develop the areas dominated by his ethnic group while neglecting other parts of the country or state. This weakens trust in the government, the political system, and state institutions. Kenya's election violence of 2007 is another good example of the divisiveness inherent in this top-down power structure. Ethnically diverse Kenya was thrown into chaos because President Mwai Kibaki, a Kikuyu, was declared the winner in an election fraught with irregularities while many others believed Mr. Odinga, a Luo, had won fair and square. The elections tapped into the tribal tensions that lay beneath the surface, in Kenya, and only an extraordinary arrangement to accommodate Mr. Odinga with the position of Prime Minister calmed the situation (Gettleman, 2007). Rwanda, Burundi, the Republic of Congo, and South Sudan are multiethnic countries that have also suffered from this divisive system.

This same problem can be seen in the United States, which is ideologically divided. The 2016 election of Donald Trump brought to the fore the deep ideological and racial divides in the country. Peaceful protests and riots broke out across the country, with many rejecting the president-elect, claiming him not to be their president. Thousands of angry protesters surrounded Trump's buildings in New York and Chicago, and in some areas, they clashed with his supporters. One-half of the country is happy and feeling victorious at the electoral success of Donald Trump, while the other half is unhappy and frightened. This divide is likely to worsen with subsequent elections. So, this top-down power structure, with a powerful leader at its helm, doesn't bring people together—especially in multiethnic or multicultural societies. It tears people apart.

Another flaw with the top-down power structure is its vulnerability to coups d'état. Whether it is a presidential coup, a palace coup, or a putsch, all forms of coup d'état shortchange the people from the governance of the state. Many coups have led to the emergence of terrible leaders who unleashed the state apparatus to terrorize and perpetrate some of the worst human rights abuses on fellow citizens. The case of Alberto Fujimori is a good example of this problem. In 1990, Alberto Fujimori of Peru came to power but failed to secure control over the Peruvian Congress. As relations between him and Congress deteriorated, he overstepped his authority, closed Congress, suspended the constitution, fired judges, and declared an emergency rule. The Peruvian military offered Fujimori institutional support, and he held onto power (Sims, 1997). While some would argue that the weak democratic institutions in Peru at that time allowed Fujimori to act the way he did, the deeper reason it happened comes down to excessive power at the top.

The same problem of coups has been observed in Russia, in 1993 when Boris Yeltsin expanded executive powers; in Kazakhstan in 1994, when President Nursultan Nazarbaev dissolved Parliament and drafted a new constitution that expanded his executive powers; in the Philippines in 1973, when Ferdinand Marcos transformed his elected government into a dictatorship. Also, in Nigeria in 1975 which saw the overthrow of General Yakubu Gowon; in 1983 that saw the emergence of Buhari; in 1985 by Babangida; and in again in 1994 that led to the emergence of General Sani Abacha. In Chile in1973, leading to the emergence of the Pinochet regime; and in Mauritania, which led to the overthrow of President Taya and the emergence of a military council headed by Colonel Ely Ould Mohammed Vall (Basong, 2005). The list goes on. Postcolonial countries in Africa have particularly suffered and has been held back from development by coups d'état, whose existence is only possible because of the structure of power concentrated at the top.

Another flaw with this top-down power structure is that it makes the nation-state vulnerable to foreign interference or meddling. Ukraine, a country of more than 45 million people, is a victim of geography. The country's soul is being fought over by foreign powers meddling in her internal affairs. The country is currently torn apart and at war with every possibility of never reuniting. All this meddling is only possible because of the structure that concentrates power at the top. With power at the top, foreign powers just need to install someone sympathetic to their interests to control the destiny of the country.

In the Republic of Congo, it was foreign meddling that led to the untimely death of Patrice Lumumba, the first democratically elected leader of the Democratic Republic of Congo. The death of Lumumba changed the destiny of the Congo in ways that can perhaps never be ascertained. Lumumba was a fiercely independent and nationalistic Congolese leader who wanted to take full control over Congo's resources. His rhetoric and independence were perceived as a threat that needed to be eliminated to protect western interests. To fight him, the US and Belgium bought the support of Lumumba's Congolese rivals and hired killers. In the end, Lumumba was toppled and assassinated. Mobutu, a stooge for Western powers, was installed to safeguard their interests (Nzongola-Ntalaja, 2011). This travesty was only possible because of the structure of government with concentrated power at the top.

The coup d'état that led to the ouster of Salvador Allende of Chile is another classic example of the vulnerability of the nation-state to foreign interference. Lebanon, Syria, Yemen, and many other weak states suffer from this problem. The problem of foreign interference continues today in many developing countries, especially in Africa in the form of neocolonialism. Many multinational corporations and their governments can influence the leaders of weak states to get favorable deals for their companies by lining the pockets of the leaders. All too often, such an arrangement allows these multinationals to act with impunity and reckless abandon, damaging the environment that ordinary people are dependent on for their livelihood and survival.

In the United States, foreign governments can meddle in the decision making of the state through lobbying. While legal, with power concentrated at the top, the foreign policy of the country could be redirected or hijacked to further the interest of a foreign power. In other words, it creates a situation in which US foreign policy is in the interest of a few or a foreign entity, and does not satisfy the wishes and needs of the vast majority of Americans.

The nation-state is the collective property of all citizens, but the current political system doesn't fully look after the interest of all citizens. It is a system that is structurally defective. For this reason, all efforts to reform it through campaign finance reforms will ultimately fail to eliminate its flaws. Such efforts are palliative. The system must be discarded for something else that is unique to the nation-state.

De-entropification Solution.

There are two very important principles to consider in fixing the system.

1. The Power or Authority of Any Contributor in The System Should Never Exceed Their Contribution.

This principle is being violated in the current political system because the distribution of power is not in line with contribution. In the current system, burden and power are not equal. All citizens in a nation-state are equal owners of the state. Therefore, if a few at the top wield more power than those at

the bottom who make the bulk of the system, then power is unfairly distributed.

In a corporation, owners have the largest share of power because of the burden of risking their savings and livelihood, toiling day and night to make the
company a success. This burden or input entitles them to the profits of the
company and gives them the power to fire and hire anyone. They could hire a
CEO and delegate some of their authority to this person. For a nation-state,
the citizens collectively share the burden of preserving and sustaining the
entity they call their nation. They all must pay taxes, defend the state when it
is at war, obey when called upon to take on difficult or sensitive tasks that are
vital to the interest of the state, represent it in international events, etc. No
citizen is more equal than another because the nation only exists and owes its
continuous existence to the burden that all citizens carry equally.

Some argue that it is not completely unfair that the rich or members of the
elites should have more political power than the ordinary citizen; after all,
they pay more in taxes and provide jobs for the common people. But this is a
flawed argument because many ordinary people die fighting wars on behalf of
the state, many ordinary citizens sacrifice their lives every day in ways that
cannot be measured financially, and they do this because they understand
that the state belongs to them as much as to any other citizen. So, no matter
how much an individual pay in taxes, no matter how many houses they own,
or the size of the contribution of their family to the establishment of the state,
their stakes or shares in the state remain equal to that of any other citizen.

Therefore, a political system that entrusts one individual with the power to
veto bills that could become law, and to decide with a few advisers the foreign
policy of a nation is not one in which power is equally distributed. A system in
which only a few people in Congress can make laws for more than 300 million
other citizens is not one in which power is equally shared. A system in which
only a few people can decide that the nation goes to war and commit thousands of young lives to fighting in foreign lands is a system where power is
unfairly distributed. A system in which only nine people can interpret the laws
of the land is not one that distributes power fairly. A system in which a few
people can decide to borrow money, resulting in massive deficits that all citizens would have to pay for in taxes and that could bankrupt the state, is not a
system in which power is equally shared.

To elucidate further on the absurdity of the current political system, it is important to see political office holders as lawyers who are supposed to be
fighting on behalf of the people they represent, consulting with them and
giving them sound advice. In a normal situation, lawyers cannot reach a decision on any issue or make a deal without the approval and consent of their
clients. However, the way the system works, political office holders, for the

most part, do not need the consent or approval of their clients in whatever they decide. They often vote against their promises and act in the interest of their cronies rather than the people they were elected to represent. Trade deals like The North American Free Trade Agreement (NAFTA), The Transatlantic Trade and Investment Partnership (TTIP), and The Trans-Pacific Partnership (TPP) that affect the lives of millions of citizens are simply written and signed by a few elites without the consent, understanding, and approval of their employer, the people. The Iraq War, in which thousands of US soldiers lost their lives, resulting in irreparable trauma to their families, was simply decided by a few citizens at the top. Such an important decision that commits a nation to war, and one for which the country could suffer existential reprisal attacks, is too serious to be decided by a few in a nation of more than 300 million people who are supposed to be equal.

To make the system adhere to this principle, there are several significant changes that must be made in the current political structure. The most important of these changes is the addition of the people not just as mere voters who elect representatives, but as a functioning arm of government. The government would, therefore, have four branches: The Executive, Judiciary, Congress or Parliament, and the People.

i. The People.

Of all nations, Switzerland is the only one that practices some level of direct democracy. The Swiss system allows citizens to vote directly on many issues, but it still doesn't go far enough to match contribution and power. To match contribution with power, the people must be the only ones who can approve any bill before it becomes law. In other words, only the people can sign off or veto a bill from Congress, approve all trade deals, international agreements, the national budget, supplemental appropriations, raise the debt ceiling, declare war on a foreign country, and impeach leaders including the President, Prime Minister, Governor or Mayor.

In addition, legislative work shouldn't be the exclusive job of a few in Congress. Any citizen should be able to write a bill and submit it to Congress. A bill written by a citizen or group would have to meet at least a 30% population approval to be sent to the Speaker of the lower house, who then sends it to the appropriate committee for any necessary amendments so that it is in line with existing laws before being put to a vote. Furthermore, any citizen could move to repeal an existing law by writing a bill to that effect. If it gets the required votes, it would be moved to Congress for debates and final approval.

The logistics of making this work would be enormous. An average of 758 bills pass each session in Congress and when the 112th Congress ended in 2015, it passed 561 out of over 6,000 bills introduced according to the Brookings vital statistics on Congress. To require people to go to the polls 561 times to approve or disapprove bills would be an impossible task. Therefore, to make this work, a secured Intranet system would have to be created. It would not in any way be connected to the World Wide Web, and it would have to be totally secure.

All citizens who are at least 18 years of age and older would have an account in the portal where they can sign in from the convenience of their computers to vote on bills and post their written bills to be voted on by other citizens. Bills that successfully come through Congress would be uploaded in electronic form into the portal for the people to approve or veto it. A simple majority would be enough for bills to pass. Voting periods would have to be timed so that the job of governance would not be delayed or slowed. Voting for a bill could be performed in the afternoons within at least a two-hour period, after which the results would designate the bill as approved or disapproved by the people.

The technology to build such a secure portal is currently available and should work just fine. Unlike current technology, this secured portal should be a quick and efficient way to run a true government of the people.

ii. The Congress or Parliament.

Members of Congress would serve as consultants for their constituency, advising them on how to vote. Congress remains the law-making body of the country or state. In this approach, their main function is to make sure that bills, whether emanating from Congress or the people, are in line with existing laws before sending them out to the secure portal for a vote. So, unless a bill is approved by Congress, it cannot be sent to the people. Also, Congress would continue to have oversight over all branches of government and can open investigations or hearings on any issue. They would remain in charge of approving all appointments from the Executive. For transparency, Congress would have a tracking system on the secured portal so that citizens could see the status of bills, their progress, and could push their representatives to help facilitate their approval in Congress.

iii. The Executive branch.

Too much power in the hands of one individual—the main characteristic of presidential or prime ministerial systems—is counterproductive. It creates more division than unity. So instead of having an elected president as head of the Executive, a better approach could take the form of an elected cabinet. This simply means the different secretaries or ministers are elected directly to the executive branch. Candidates would stand for election for cabinet positions, like Secretary of State, Secretary of Defense, Secretary of Education, and so on. Their election campaigns would be focused on the issues facing the department, and voters would elect a candidate based on their platform and policies for the department. The cabinet members would then select one among them to be the president. This position would be rotated annually or every two years among the cabinet members. If a cabinet member is not reelected, and that department is supposed to take its turn with the presidency, the newly elected member to that department simply assumes the presidency.

The role of the president would be largely ceremonial. He or she would represent the country in international affairs but would hold no more power than any other member of the cabinet. All cabinet members would be equal, and decisions would be reached by consensus. The cabinet would develop federal policies and prepare national budgets which would be approved by Congress and then by the people. They would enforce federal laws and appoint federal officials. The cabinet would discuss foreign treaties and make initial agreements. However, these treaties could only become law after being approved by the Congress and the people. The cabinet would be responsible for keeping the country safe and strong, both in wartime and during peaceful periods. The cabinet would command the armed forces daily to keep the country safe, but they would have no authority to send the armed forces to war or armed conflict without the explicit approval of the people. However, in the case of an emergency attack, they would assume the full authority to order a reprisal attack or war without the approval of the people.

Another way to constitute the Executive is for the most successful political parties which in the US would be the democratic and republican parties, to be allotted cabinet positions in the Executive branch. These cabinet members could then select a president who represents the country in international affairs and meets with foreign leaders. The position would rotate annually or every two years between cabinet members, and the role of the president would be largely ceremonial. All cabinet members would be equal, and all decisions reached by consensus. This is another good approach for multiethnic or multicultural countries where an all-powerful president can be divisive. Switzerland has a government that employs such an arrangement, and it works well. Any of these approaches—a directly elected cabinet or a party-constituted cabinet—could work well for the US.

iv. The Judiciary.

The Judiciary, on all levels of government, should be nominated by the Executive and approved by the Congress and the people. This would give the people some say in how the justices are selected who interpret the laws and pass judgment on issues that affect their everyday lives. For Justices of the Supreme

Court, the Executive would nominate two candidates to Congress for approval. After all the hearings and Congressional approval, the candidates would face an election, and one would be elected by the people to the Supreme Court. This would secure the legitimacy of the Supreme Court as a body that is truly representative of the people.

Also, the size of the Supreme Court needs to be expanded from the current nine to fifty-one, representing the 50 states plus Washington DC. This size would allow for a variety of opinions and ideas that would make it truly representative of the changing demographics of the US population. In addition, justices should be rotated to the lower courts every three years for a short stint so that they can see the effect of their judgments on people's lives. Remaining too long at the top leads to stagnation and decline. Therefore, this rotation to lower courts would keep justices informed or up to date. It would bring them closer to the people and make them better at their jobs in the top court.

2. All Contributors Must Act Within the Established Rules or Laws, And Everyone Must Be Equal Before Them (Rule of Law).

No American should be above the law, regardless of place or authority. The current structure where the Federal Bureau of Investigation (FBI) is under the Justice Department, a department under the executive branch headed by the President, raises serious doubts about its ability to function independently and impartially. The firing of former FBI Director James Comey by President Donald Trump who was investigating allegations of Russian collusion with the Trump campaign in the 2016 presidential elections is a clear sign that the current system is broken. A better structure is clearly needed to ensure the rule of law and equality of all before the law.

The best way to achieve this is to split the office of the US Attorney General from the Justice Department to become an independent entity with the FBI under it. A Secretary of Justice appointed by the government would be in the Executive branch and would be responsible for the Justice portfolio and developing policy. An Attorney General, independent of all branches of government, would be responsible for providing legal advice to all branches of government, and for representing the government in all legal proceedings. He or she would act completely independently in the public interest, without reference to partisan politics, and would be the defender of the rule of law or the watch person of the system. In other words, he or she would be charged with seeing that the administration of public affairs is in accordance with the law.

To make sure this position is completely independent of partisan politics, a public commission, constituted by the Supreme Court, would interview and select candidates for this position. This commission would comprise technocrats of the highest standing with no connection to political office. Candidates for the position of Attorney General could be from academia, the legal profession, or any other background. They would be required to have a track record of the highest integrity, and a career spent working for the public good. The commission would recommend at least two candidates to the Supreme Court, who would then vote to select one for the position. The Attorney General would operate for a term of 10 years and could be renewed for one additional term by the Supreme Court. The Attorney General would be answerable only to the Supreme Court or the people for only those two branches can remove the Attorney General from office. Allegations of wrongdoing would be investigated by an independent commission set up by the Supreme Court, and if he or she is indicted, a majority vote by the Supreme Court will result in their dismissal.

Conclusion.

The problem with political systems in the United States and around the world is the concentration of power at the top. This system favors the elites, and it is not right for a nation-state. A nation-state is the equal and collective property of all its citizens, and only a system that takes this fact into account will eliminate vices like corruption, cronyism, foreign interferences and dictatorship that currently bedevils the current system.

The separation of the office of the attorney general from that of the justice department is another important reform to ensure that everyone including the president is equal before the law. The biggest concern with the proposed system is its vulnerability to hacking. Unless a way is found to build it such that it is impossible to hack, it will not be feasible to use. Also, the system needs an informed citizenry that understands the complexities of the law and current affairs. This would need the reintroduction of the fairness doctrine to both mainstream and alternative news media.

Chapter 9

The United Nations and the Security Council

The League of Nations, created by the Treaty of Versailles following World War I, was the first attempt to create a truly international organization for the promotion of diplomacy, cooperation between nations, and the achievement of international peace and security. It had four specific functions: international disarmament, arbitration of international disputes, implementation of economic sanctions against aggression, and treaty revision. The League had some successes. In 1920, it helped take home about half a million prisoners of war captured during World War I. In 1921, it helped arbitrate between Sweden and Finland, which led to Sweden giving the Aaland Islands to Finland. It stopped the invasion of Bulgaria by Greece in 1925. Also, in 1922, the League helped set up camps and fed Turkish refugees. In 1923, the League sent economics experts to help Austria when its government went bankrupt. In 1926, it approved the Slavery Convention and helped free about 200,000 slaves. In 1926, 26 League nations signed an international convention to combat the drug trade, a law that is still in force. In the 1920s, the League Health Committee worked to prevent malaria and leprosy.

However, the League had some serious failures that ultimately led to its demise. The need for unanimity for all decisions in both the Council and the Assembly was a structural flaw that led to regular paralysis. The absence of the United States in the league was a blow to the League's prestige and undermined efforts to create a workable system of collective security (Wilkinson and O'Sullivan, 2004). Furthermore, in 1921, Poland invaded Vilnius, the capital of Lithuania, and the League could do nothing. The League couldn't deter the aggressive behavior of powerful nations. In 1931, Japan moved its army into Manchuria, China, and although the League found Japan guilty of aggression, it was unable to do anything to reverse Japan's behavior. When France invaded the Ruhr, and when Italy invaded Corfu in 1923, the League could do nothing. In 1935, Italy invaded Abyssinia (Eritrea and Ethiopia), and all appeals for help by Emperor Haile Selassie to the League resulted in nothing that could reverse the Italian invasion. Furthermore, between 1923 and 1932, disarmament talks failed because Germany demanded as many weapons as everyone else. When Hitler violated the Treaty of Versailles and moved troops into the Rhineland in March 1936, the League talked but failed to act. Additionally, nothing was done to block Hitler's Anschluss with Austria in 1938 and his many other transgressions. Finally, when Hitler invaded Poland in the fall of the 1939 which led to the start of World War II, the League was all but dead.

Following the end of the Second World War, the United Nations (UN) was formed in an attempt once again to create a collective security system between nations. The UN Charter was signed on June 26, 1945, by representatives of 50 countries. After the Charter had been ratified by several important countries, it came into existence on October 24, 1945. A powerful security council was designed into the UN by the victors of the Second World War, to be primarily responsible for the maintenance of international peace and security. The Security Council consists of fifteen nations, five of whom are permanent: France, Russia, (formerly the Soviet Union), China, the United States, and the United Kingdom. These permanent members wield veto power over any resolution of the Council, regardless of international support, and it was designed like this to overcome some of the failings of the League.

The UN began with much optimism and hope that the world had moved into a new era in international relations. Such hopes turned out to be hasty because of the emergence of the Cold War, which evolved simultaneously with the creation of the UN. The Cold War, which divided the world into blocs, increased tension, brought the world into many conflicts and created fear of even greater conflict. During the Cold War, the Security Council, which was supposed to maintain international peace and security, found itself in a state of quagmire. There was a constant stalemate with permanent members unable to make decisions on any issue on which their national interest was threatened. During this period, the United States blocked the admission of numerous states it perceived as Soviet vassals such as Albania, Bulgaria, Hungary, and Romania, while the Soviet Union blocked pro-Western states such as Austria, Ireland, Japan, and Italy.

On other occasions, the UN was sidelined. The UN found itself on the periphery of events in Hungary in 1956, the Berlin crisis of 1961, the Vietnam War, and the Soviet invasion of Afghanistan in 1979. Brutal proxy wars, such as in Korea, the Congo, and Vietnam, were prolonged by superpower divisions in the Security Council. Many peacekeeping missions failed, and genocides such as in Cambodia and Guatemala failed to be prevented by the UN (Heiss, 2015).

However, even with all its failings, the UN had some success during this time. It came to the defense of South Korea in the Korean War and provided a framework that allowed the flow of communication between the great powers to resolve crises and tensions. The UN provided a forum for negotiation and the airing of grievances in several Cold War crisis such as Korea, Iran, the Cuban Missile Crisis, the Vietnam War, and the Soviet invasion of Afghanistan. It also helped to bring temporary peace, notably in the Middle East, where resolutions helped to enshrine the terms of ceasefires in 1967 and again in 1973. Furthermore, there were significant achievements outside the immediate domain of peace and security, including; the adoption of the Universal Declaration of Human Rights in 1948, establishment of several UN programs like UNESCO, the World Food Program to fight famine, hunger and poverty, the protection of the Galapagos Islands and more than 1,000 other World Heritage sites. The UN also helped with decolonization efforts which resulted in the independence of many new states, all of which ultimately joined the world body (Mortimer, 2015).

The demise of the Soviet Union and the end of the Cold War, which had cast a shadow over the United Nations throughout its first four decades, brought renewed optimism that the paralysis that had plagued the Security Council would disappear. During the 1990s, the UN did an extraordinary job liberating Kuwait from the tyranny of the Saddam regime during the first Gulf War. Peacekeeping missions soared and were expanded to maintain peace and order all around the world. The UN intervened in the Balkans, some countries in Africa, and former Soviet republics where conflict erupted. The UN Peacekeeping Force helped implement a peace agreement in Sierra Leone from 1999 to 2005 after the country's devastating civil war. More than 75,000 ex-fighters were disarmed, including hundreds of child soldiers, and more than 42,000 weapons were destroyed as well as 1.2 million rounds of ammunition. Burundi was the site of another UN peacekeeping operation, which can be considered for the most part to be a success.

Efforts at denuclearization and the prevention of weapons of mass destruction resulted in several countries giving up such weapons voluntarily. South Africa, at the end of Apartheid, gave up such weapons, as did several former Soviet republics. Several other countries committed to ending nuclear weapon research programs and submit to inspections by the UN International Atomic Energy Agency. Other successes include the prosecution of Laurent Gbagbo, Slobodan Milosevic, and Charles Taylor for war crimes, as well as the 2011 Libyan campaign that toppled the Gadhafi regime. Successful negotiations with Iran culminated in the so-called Iranian nuclear deal, another success that can be ascribed to the UN.

However, the UN has experienced serious failures since the end of the Cold War. On July 11, 1995, toward the end of Bosnia's 1992-95 war, Bosnian Serb forces executed 8,000 Muslim men and boys and dumped their bodies into pits (Sito-Sucic and Katana, 2015). The Dutch peacekeepers stationed there were unable to act because of their mandate and could only watch as the killings took place. Furthermore, the catastrophic failure of UN peacekeeping efforts in Somalia cannot be forgotten. Several peacekeepers were killed, and the bodies of dead US soldiers were paraded through the streets of Mogadishu. In the end, the US withdrew its troops and in 1995 the UN withdrew all peacekeeping troops (Richburg, 1993). Also, the UN failed to prevent the 1994 genocide in Rwanda that left over 800,000 people dead (Maritz 2012). Findings from a 1999 inquiry determined that the UN as a whole failed in the Rwandan episode.

Rape and child sex abuse in the Democratic Republic of Congo in early 2005 also put the UN in a bad light. UN peacekeepers were involved in paying women and teenage girls for sex, and sometimes raping them. Similar allegations were reported in Cambodia, Bosnia, and Haiti. This reinforced the view that the UN lacked discipline in its peacekeeping operations. Another low point was the inadvertent spread of cholera by the Nepali peacekeeping force in Haiti, resulting in the infection of more than 700,000 people, of whom about 8,000 died. Iraq's Oil-For-Food Program embroiled the UN in allegations of corruption and tarnished its reputation, perhaps forever. Vast sums of money were channeled into private hands, with some even being used to acquire influence at the UN. The Oil-For-Food Program reinforced the view that the world body is riddled with corruption, misappropriation, and mismanagement (Spencer, 2015).

Another major failure occurred in Sudan, where the UN failed to protect and prevent the death of civilians who were slaughtered indiscriminately, due to the veto power of some permanent members. In Sri Lanka, the United Nations failed in its mandate to protect Tamil civilians caught up in the final phases of the island's bloody war. A 2011 UN probe estimated that about 40,000 people were killed in the final phases of that war (Bhalla, 2014).

In 2006, during the second Lebanon war between Israel and Hezbollah, the UN failed to reach a cease-fire on time that could have saved the lives of many civilians. In the 2014 Israeli-Gaza conflict, the UN also failed to act decisively to get a cease-fire on time that would have saved the lives of many civilians caught up in the violence.

The invasion of Iraq in March 2003 by the United States and her allies, without the imprimatur of the Security Council, is arguably one of the biggest failures of the UN since the end of Cold War. It further reinforced the prevailing notion that the UN is a toothless tiger that is incapable of managing international affairs when powerful nations' interests are at stake. The Russian annexation of Crimea is another major failure. Once again, the UN was sidelined and the European Union (EU), in concert with the United States, acted outside of the world body to place sanctions on Russia for its actions. In Syria, the failure of the UN is even more glaring, resulting in extraordinary loss of lives and mass migration not seen in decades. Profound splits between the permanent members, with Russia and China in one corner and the US, UK, and France in the other, have led to inaction. There have been endless conferences and meetings to resolve the conflict with little result to show.

There are other problems brewing in different parts of the world that the UN seems unable to resolve. The problem in the South China Sea between China and several neighboring nations may result in grave danger to the international order. It could disrupt the entire world order and even result in a major conflict. Another serious problem that the UN doesn't seem to have a solution for is the perpetual state of tension between nuclear-armed Pakistan and India. The belligerent North Korean regime engages in nuclear saber rattling, and the UN has no clear means to hold it accountable. Around the world, arms sales are at an all-time high since the end of cold war (Fleurant, Wezeman, Wezeman, and Tian, 2017). The threat of a major conflict looms, but the UN seems always to be on the sidelines, unable to act. The fact that the UN is powerless to resolve these problems shows that it is an ineffective body stuck in the past, and unfit to manage the complex problems of the 21st century.

Studying many of the successes and failures of the UN since its inception, it becomes apparent that there are several reasons for the body's ineffectiveness, and one of the main reasons is its power structure. The same five countries, victors of the Second World War, hold permanent seats in the Security Council. Each can use its veto power to override and hold the entire world hostage to their national interests.

Aside from the veto, another reason for the ineffectiveness of the UN is the significant differences or dissimilarities between member-states. It is an organization of nations with little shared values, interests, and ideals. In many of its member states, human rights violations are still routine, the rule of law isn't respected, and democracy is still non-existent. Non-interference in the internal affairs of a country is a principle strongly held by some members, regardless of the atrocities being perpetrated by the authorities. On the other hand, for some other member-states, intervention is necessary when human rights and the rule of law are being flagrantly violated. Such significant dissimilarities result in the formation of blocs, endless bickering, inaction and increases the tendency for powerful states to bypass the body in pursuit of their interests.

Also, the UN faces funding problems. With endless crises around the world, the world body is constrained by funds to meet its ever-increasing obligations. The UN also suffers from a lack of transparency and accountability, which is the gold standard of governance in the 21st century. There is widespread backdoor jockeying for top jobs in the UN Secretariat and UN agencies, and in key bodies like the Human Rights Council and the Security Council. Many decisions are made behind closed doors and are reached in an opaque manner. Member-state contributions to peacekeeping missions present another problem. Although there have been some improvements, the UN is still unable to meet the peacekeeping challenges it faces. Refugee crises and mass migrations, which have been quite common in the past few years amid a growing humanitarian crisis, add to the challenges the world body faces.

There have been calls for reform of the UN's institutions and its methods of conducting business so that it can become a more representative and effective body. Unfortunately, these calls have so far been resisted. Calls by Japan, India, Brazil, and Germany to be added to the Security Council have met significant resistance from rival countries. France floated the idea of limiting veto power in cases of mass atrocities, but this has been met by resistance from some permanent members (Charbonneau and Irish, 2015).

Clearly, the UN and its many agencies need significant reforms so that all member nations feel a sense of belonging. The excessive power entrusted in the hands of a few powerful nations is not the structure that the UN needs to tackle today's problems. A Security Council in which most permanent members are European states is not in any way reflective of the world today. Ultimately, unless the world body reforms itself to truly represent all nations, its legitimacy will erode over time, with irrelevance all but certain to become its future just like the League. Saudi Arabia's recent rejection of a seat on the UN Security Council, while accusing the UN body of double standards over the Syrian War, is an unprecedented diplomatic assault on the UN, and a sign of the deep frustration that many nations have with how the UN operates (Worth, 2013). The recent withdrawal of Russia, South Africa, and Burundi from the International Criminal Court is a testament to the erosion of trust and legitimacy of international institutions. The need for change at the UN and its many agencies has never been more urgent.

De-entropification Solution.

Four important principles can be applied to the United Nations to make it more inclusive, truly representative of all member states and effective.

1. Principle of General Homogeneity, and

2. Power of Any Contributor in The System Should Never Exceed Their Contribution.

The UN consists of 193 member states, and each contributes to the international system. Some nations contribute more due to the size of their population, the strength of their culture, economy and military power. This must be taken into consideration.

To create a fair system, where contribution and power are matched, all nations must be represented in the power structure. The current Security Council fails in this regard, and must therefore, be reformed. Adding a few nations to the Council is not the solution to its problems. The opposition to the addition of Japan, Germany, Brazil, and India to the Security Council shows that national representation is an outdated approach because it results in winners and losers. A regional approach, instead of national representation, would be the best way to go because it would allow small states to have a say in the Security Council without marginalizing more powerful states.

Using the principle of general homogeneity, we can split the globe based on economics, geography, military, culture, and interest into nine regions or blocs: North America, Latin America and The Caribbean, Africa (Sub-Sahara), Eurasia, East Asia, Asia Pacific, South Asia, Middle East and North Africa (MENA), and Europe.

1. **North America**

   USA, Canada, Mexico, **Israel**

2. **Latin America and The Caribbean**

   All countries in Latin America and the Caribbean

3. **Eurasia**

   Russia, Kyrgyzstan, Armenia, Kazakhstan, Belarus, Turkmenistan, Uzbekistan, Tajikistan, Georgia, **Azerbaijan, Moldova, Ukraine, Serbia, Iran**

4. **Africa (Sub-Sahara)**

   All countries in Sub Saharan Africa, **Libya, Morocco, Sudan, Djibouti, Egypt, Tunisia, Algeria, Haiti.**

5. **East Asia**

   China, Mongolia, North Korea, **South Korea, Pakistan.**

6. **Asia Pacific**

   Japan, Australia, Myanmar, Fiji, Kiribati, Marshall Islands, Micronesia, **Mongolia, South Korea,** Nauru, New Zealand, Palau, Papua New Guinea, Samoa, Solomon Islands, Timor-Leste, Tonga, Tuvalu, Vanuatu.

7. **South Asia**

   Afghanistan, India, **Pakistan**, Bangladesh, Sri Lanka, Nepal, Bhutan, Maldives, Brunei, Myanmar, Cambodia, East Timor, Indonesia, Laos, Malaysia, The Philippines, Singapore, Thailand, Vietnam.

8. **The Middle East and North Africa (MENA)**

Bahrain, Djibouti, Iraq, Jordan, Kuwait, Lebanon, Oman, Qatar, Saudi Arabia, Syria, Tunisia, United Arab Emirates, Yemen, Palestine, **Israel, Turkey, Pakistan, Algeria, Egypt, Iran, Libya, Morocco, Sudan, Tunisia, Mauritania.**

9.   **Europe.**

European Union Countries, Norway, Iceland, Liechtenstein, Albania, Switzerland, United Kingdom, Bosnia and Herzegovina, Kosovo, Macedonia and Montenegro, **Serbia, Turkey, Georgia, Moldova, Ukraine, Azerbaijan, Israel.**

Countries highlighted in bold are those that may not necessarily fit in a group for several reasons and could, therefore, be placed in another group. For the Russian and Central Asian group, countries like Ukraine, Azerbaijan, Georgia and Moldova could remain there or be placed in the European group. For the East Asian group, South Korea and Mongolia could remain there or be moved to the Asian Pacific group. For the South Asian group, Pakistan could remain there or be placed with the MENA group or East Asian group. Countries located in Africa like, Algeria, Egypt, Djibouti, Libya, Morocco, Tunisia, Mauritania, Sudan could remain in the MENA group or join the African group. Also, Iran could remain in the MENA group or join the Eurasian or East Asian group. A Caribbean nation like Haiti could remain there or join the Sub-Saharan African group. Israel could remain in the MENA group or join the North American or European group. Also, Serbia could join the Eurasian group or stay in the European Group.

Countries are not permanently fixed in any group and remain free to move to any group that aligns with their national interest and values as far as the group wishes to have them as members. This flexibility of freedom of movement along homogenous lines allows a country to move to a group that best represents their interest and values from one it believes doesn't.

These nine regions would all be represented in the Security Council. A member nation from each region would represent the region on the Council on a rotational basis. This way all members, whether big or small, will be involved in decision making for their region. Positions to be taken on resolutions will be discussed by the region before the representing member votes. If they are to introduce a resolution, all members of the region would have deliberated on its content and agreed on it. Each region would have a veto over any resolution, so agreements would need to be reached by all regions— which in this case is the whole world—before a resolution can pass. This arrangement will increase diplomatic efforts to woo all regions of the world rather than just five nations to reach consensus on issues. Importantly, this would reduce, if not eliminate, the sense of alienation and frustration that many member states currently feel about the UN.

Furthermore, to ensure that power and contribution are matched, all nine regions, whether rich or poor, must contribute equally financially, to peace-keeping efforts and all other efforts of the UN. The current situation, where the United States and to an extent Japan foot most of the bill, is not a fair arrangement. The UN needs the commitments of its members for it to be a viable organization, and this commitment must be taken very seriously. When nations are not well-represented, as in the current structure of the UN, it is not unreasonable for them to be reluctant to commit much to the organization. However, an expansion of the Security Council using this regional approach should eliminate such feelings.

3. Homogenization: To Reduce the Differences Between Member Nations of the UN.

One of the biggest problems plaguing the UN is the lack of common values and interests between member states and more must be done to reduce these differences. One way to achieve this is through increased investment in international cultural exchanges and education, especially amongst the youths. There are presently many student exchanges, sports exchanges, and scholarly or professional exchanges, and many of these are funded by governments, and private-sector organizations. At the level of the UN, the United Nations Alliance of Civilizations (UNAOC) is the organization that promotes cultural and academic exchanges. More funding should be provided to this organization so that it can expand on its work and complement existing cultural exchanges. Such contacts will help to create a trans-racial and ethnic world and less divided United Nations.

4. All Contributors Must Act Within the Established Rules or Laws, And Everyone Must Be Equal Before Them (Rule of Law).

One of the problems with the current international system is the culture of acting outside international law with impunity by powerful nations who are shielded from UN sanctions because of their veto in the Security Council. This threatens the legitimacy of the UN and makes the organization look weak. Most worryingly, it creates a sense of double standards, and a tendency for other nations to see the rules as expendable. Even with the regional approach, which allows veto power to be spread evenly across all regions, a member state could still act outside the law because of the veto that their region wields in the Security Council. So, to make all nations subject to the rule of law, a mechanism must be put in place to override the veto. This is where a UN Parliament becomes extremely important.

The United Nation needs a parliament to bring it into the 21st century. This parliament would have representatives from all member nations that would be directly elected every five years by universal suffrage. Like the European Parliament, these UN parliamentarians will not be merely selected by their national governments but by popular vote from their constituency, and from political parties that may be different from that of the national government. The seats in the parliament would be distributed based on national population. This means a country like India, for example, would have more seats than Cuba or Luxembourg. This would make it truly representative of the world population, and the number of seats would be adjusted as population changes.

The parliament would be the law body of the UN. It would be the body that truly represents the heart and conscience of the citizens of the world. It would have a president whose job is to coordinate its activities. It would have supervisory and budgetary responsibilities over all UN agencies. Furthermore, it would also be tasked with holding hearings on any issues, whether national or international, including potential nominees for UN appointment and approving the appointment of the heads of all UN agencies. Also, it would be tasked with the admission of new members to the UN. The Parliament would work hand in hand with the Secretary-General and the Security Council. It would be tasked with creating committees to investigate any issues, member states, or persons, including the Secretary-General.

Importantly, the Parliament would be able to overturn the veto of a region. So, if a region were to use its veto to block the Security Council from intervening in a crisis or sanctioning an erring member state, the Secretary-General could send the failed resolution to the parliament to vote on it. A two-thirds majority vote would overturn the veto, thus allowing the Security Council to move forward with the resolution. This would allow the veto to remain useful, but not to be used to hold the world hostage during a crisis where the UN needs to act. It would allow the conscience of the world to override the national interest of a powerful member state that doesn't want the world to act, which has paralyzed the world body for a long time. It would strengthen the world body's credibility.

The Security Council would remain the organ of the UN tasked with security and international peace. It would remain the only organ that can pass binding resolutions on any member state and further actions to enforce these resolutions. It would be the only body that could sanction a member state for wrongdoing. So, on matters of peace and security, the parliament could investigate but must send its recommendations to the Security Council to act. The Security Council would remain the body that nominates the Secretary-General, but this nominee must be approved by the parliament. The current selection process for the Secretary-General lacks transparency and occurs behind closed doors. Under this new structure, a potential nominee must face a hearing in parliament and proper scrutiny before being given the job. If he or she is not approved, then the Council sends a new person to the parliament. Such scrutiny is needed to strengthen the UN and hold the Secretary-General, who is the face of the organization, to the highest standards. This same approach should be the standard for all appointments to top UN agencies. This would strengthen the rule of law in the UN.

The Secretary-General is the person who facilitates exchanges between the Security Council and the parliament. He or she works as a political intermediary to help foster cooperation in the Security Council and in resolving conflicts around the world through special missions, observers, envoys, and mediators to promote compromise and conciliation.

The General Assembly remains an important arm of the UN, where heads of national government come to deliberate and air their concerns or grievances. However, it must remain a body with no authority other than to pass nonbinding resolutions or communiqués about their thoughts and concerns.

5. Negative Consequences Must Always Be Equal to the Severity of Wrongdoing.

In the Security Council, a mechanism must be developed so that any region that fails to meet their financial, peacekeeping, etc. obligations to the UN would have their veto power suspended. This negative consequence for failure to meet agreed obligations to the UN will ensure that all regions and member states take their commitments to the world body seriously.

Also, western support for Kosovo's independence without the agreement of Serbia opened a Pandora's box. Russia has pointed to these precedents in her annexation of Crimea, and recognition of South Ossetia and Abkhazia. It is conceivable that other powerful nations will use the same precedent to try something similar. When the rules are shredded, or simply replaced by powerful nations to suit their interests, other nations will take inspiration from those actions. Also, NATO's bombardment of Yugoslavia, and the war in Iraq, which were undertaken without the imprimatur of the UN Security Council, makes other nations see international rules or laws as expendable. For the international system to work effectively, strong deterrents are needed so that potential bad actors are swayed from bad behavior, and a culture of acting within the law or rules is fostered.

Unless the UN can apply sanctions or other forms of negative consequences that are commensurate with the wrongdoing of any member-state or individual, regardless of power or place, it will never be an effective organization.

Even with a parliament to overturn the veto, there are still powerful member-states that the UN cannot punish because it just doesn't have the means to do so. Right now, many so-called global institutions like the International Monetary Fund and World Bank, world trade organizations, and the SWIFT money system are dominated by western nations and this makes it impossible for the UN to bring sanctions on them, even if they act outside international law. Only when major global bodies are under the UN structure, such that punishment from the UN results in a lack of access to vital institutions, will the rule of law be respected. In other words, only when the UN wields a big stick that can hurt any nation, regardless of economic or military power if they act outside international law, will stability and a culture of obeying rules between nations flourish.

While the United States is unarguably the most powerful country on the planet, it cannot replace the UN. Efforts by the US and her allies to achieve hegemony militarily or economically will always be resisted or counteracted by other nations, especially powerful ones. This results in the formation of parallel power structures that end up weakening previous ones. The current western domination of many important international bodies only weakens their legitimacy and pushes emerging powers to pursue alternatives. The launch of the Asian Infrastructural Investment Bank (AIIB), led by the Chinese, shows that old structures can give way to new ones when dissatisfaction and marginalization thrive. The same motivation lies behind the New Development Bank established by BRICS (Brazil, Russia, India, China and South Africa).

Also, the past few decades have seen the establishment of an International Criminal Court (ICC) in The Hague, which has successfully brought several bad actors to justice for war crimes. The ICC, unfortunately, is not a part of the UN, and has been unable to prosecute the leaders of powerful nations for crimes that are arguably just as serious as the ones it has taken upon itself to prosecute when it comes to weaker nations. This has eroded its legitimacy. For many small nations, especially those in Africa, the ICC is perceived as a tool of witch-hunt, and its legitimacy is openly questioned. However, the ICC is a great organization and should be strengthened. It should be incorporated into the United Nations as a body that can prosecute any individual or country that goes to war or breaks any UN charter without the imprimatur of the Security Council. Judges in the ICC must be representative of the different regions of the world. This full representation would give the court the credibility and legitimacy it currently lacks. It must be free to pursue any case without fear or favor, and any decision reached would be binding on the international community since it would carry the full weight of the Security Council. The war in Iraq, as well as Russian annexation of Crimea, would perhaps not have happened if the UN had a mechanism to overcome the veto and the ICC had the teeth to prosecute individual leaders for wrongdoing. So, the importance of the expanding the powers of the ICC is very important to create a stable international system where rules are supreme.

Moreover, the International Court of Justice and the Court of Arbitration need to be reformed and strengthened. They should follow the nine-region representation so that their decisions are not seen as biased. In a case of arbitration like that between the Philippines and China in the South China Sea dispute, the fact that the court's decision could not sway Beijing is a very unfortunate situation. Unfortunately, this is a result of the inadequacies of the current international system. The status of all international courts should be strengthened, and their decisions must be binding. They must carry the authority of the Security Council and the world. Nations could decide to enter negotiations after the court decisions, and that's entirely up to them. However, all nations must accept the verdict of the courts; if not, the Security Council could sanction them for defying the court.

Unless the UN has the power and means to apply the right amount of deterrence that matches the wrongdoing of any nation that acts outside the law, regardless of power or wealth, it will always remain ineffective. A strong and powerful UN is the only way international peace and security can be guaranteed.

Conclusions.

The biggest challenges facing the United Nations includes unequal power structure, undemocratic institutions, lack of fair representation and its inability to punish powerful members and their vassals. These challenges must be overcome, if not, the UN will lose whatever its left of its credibility and go the way of the League of Nations.

The Security Council must be reformed so that the UN becomes a more powerful and representative body. The creation of a parliament that can override the veto of each region is necessary; the parliament would make the UN a 21st century organization and a more accountable body. Furthermore, the UN must be the global center of power. Blocs formed to gain superiority only lead to the creation of alternatives by nations who feel excluded. This only perpetuates the power politics that have dominated the world. If the world is to be a place where civility and rules are supreme, mechanisms must be created so that all nations can be punished by the world body. Only when this is achieved will international security and peace be guaranteed.

Also, the UN needs its own standing military force to deal with Security Council resolutions. The lack of discipline seen in many peacekeepers is due to a lack of standards in different national armies. The North Atlantic Treaty Organization (NATO) has taken over the job of the UN on different occasions, and this has created resentment in some quarters with allegations that the organization is pursuing a different agenda from what the Security Council resolution mandated. A UN standing military force, consisting of all nations that train together to standardize their tactics and behavior, and that can deploy peacekeepers when called upon, would strengthen the world body, eliminate such resentments or confusions, and make the world a much better place.

Chapter 10

Final Conclusions

There are several key points to keep in mind when trying to employ de-entropification.

A. The first thing to think about is what to do with the high entropic contributors. Reforming, expelling, or putting them in a special group must be considered.

B. In a large social system, the number one goal of De-entropification must be to reduce the negative homogenous group and increase the positive homogenous group.

C. If a system employs a third party, all efforts must be explored to see if it can work optimally without this third party. However, if a third party is necessary, it must be included in the system.

D. Third parties employed in a system must be competent, adequately empowered, impartial and objective.

E. If the application of a principle would result in the violation of another principle, this approach must be abandoned. However, it should be applied, if it will result in a significant benefit to the system and will not in any way compromise its optimal functioning.

F. Application of De-entropification requires creativity, flexibility of thinking and intimate knowledge of a system.

G. De-entropification solutions must be applied without any bias or prejudice to address all the problems in a system.

H. In a situation where more than one principle could be applied to fix the problems in a system, the most appropriate principle should be applied.

I. A system is held together by the interaction of multiple principles and all must be in place to effectively counteract the forces of social entropy. For example, a system in positive homogeneity could face the breakdown of professionalism and system checks and balances in the absence of the principle of the rule of law, inequality of negative consequences and severity of wrongdoing or the absence of a competent third party to provide oversight.

J. Commonality could be positive or negative. When negative traits are common in a system than positive traits, such a system is in negative homogeneity and vice versa.

K. Homogenization should only be employed when its benefits outweigh keeping the system in its current state.

L. Homogenization must never be done at the expense of any other group. If its goal is to pull people from the negative to the positive homogenous group, then everyone regardless of race or ethnicity, religion, gender, sexual orientation etc. in the negative homogenous group should be included in this effort.

M. Homogenization to make a system more reflective or representative (in terms of gender, ethnicity or race, religion, etc.) must only be applied in relation to primary contributors that are in direct interaction within a system or between primary contributors and the larger community/society.

N. Making a system representative or reflective of its contributors or the community is not always essential to achieving positive homogeneity. In many cases, positive traits of contributors and cultural competency are sufficient for a system to achieve positive homogeneity.

O. Before homogenizing a system to make it more representative, there should be evidence that its current state is suboptimal or dysfunctional and consideration should first be given towards cultural competency training and other efforts. Only when making it representative will overcome the dysfunction in the system or will result in a significant benefit to it and the larger society, should this approach be employed.

P. Most importantly, contributors must always be thought of as human beings and not merely numbers. This means, the pursuit of system improvements, cost savings and efficiency should always be married as much as possible with the wellbeing or satisfaction of all contributors.

Social systems need to be constantly de-entropified, because emerging events and human actions are always moving the system toward greater social entropy. Around the world, it is quite clear that social systems are being overwhelmed by emerging problems and challenges. This makes it all the more important to understand the concept of De-entropification.

Today, immigration is a big issue that has brought with it increased social tensions between the different groups in America and Europe. Increases in

Islamophobia, terrorism, cultural tensions, and the rise of the "alt-right" are all byproducts of a non-ideal immigration policy. Actions like the banning of burkinis in France and the veil in Belgium and other European countries are all reactionary response to this policy. The primary purpose of immigration must be to bring in people who can join the positive homogenous group, and this must be done in a controlled way.

Efforts and laws must be put in place to homogenize the system in the case of a non- ideal immigration policy. Such homogenization effort takes time to bear fruit because a nation-state is a large social system with many contributors. Also, non-ideal immigration is perceived as threatening by natives and this adds to why it must be avoided. Politicians and policy makers who support mass migration or pay lip service to immigration reforms because of votes, idealism, or lobbying efforts from big business are playing a very dangerous game. At the end of the day, human beings are merely advanced mammals with atavistic fears and proclivities. To ignore these tendencies, to make light of them and brush them aside as silly or old-fashioned, is to play an even more dangerous game. There is no utopia in this world and those who have sought to create one either intentionally or inadvertently have ended up creating dystopia and those who try in the future will ultimately end up with the same results.

Increasingly expensive technological advances in medicine, rapid population growth, and a large aging population have changed the face of healthcare such that new ways of thinking are needed. Obamacare and government-run, single-payer systems are solutions of the past. They just cannot meet the emerging challenges of healthcare. Healthcare cooperatives that control hospitals and facilities will bring down costs. Competition among these cooperatives would keep quality high while keeping costs down. Furthermore, healthcare in different countries faces different challenges, and they complement each other. The future of healthcare is outside of national borders, with healthcare cooperatives the best solution to fully exploit it. Healthcare that is affordable and accessible to all is impossible with the current solutions, and all efforts to stay the course with these solutions will either fail to bring costs down or fail to achieve quality access for all.

Amadou Diallo, Jr., Kendra James, Sean Bell, Eric Garner, Dylan Noble, Michael Brown, and Alton Sterling represent a few unarmed people killed at the hands of the police since 1999 also. The death of several law enforcement officers by civilians shows that the US criminal justice system needs reform. Positive homogeneity between the police and the communities they serve must be established. The bail system needs to be reformed so that it does not serve as extra punishment for the indigent. The use of homogenous courts, like veteran's courts and drug court, should be expanded to other at-risk groups to create a fairer and smarter justice system. Police training and continued education should be expanded to keep police abreast of the latest techniques and to communicate ideas of how to be better at their jobs. Furthermore, recruitment standards in the police should be raised and made more rigorous so that the best of the best are selected to serve. Third-party special prosecutors should be used to consider allegations of wrongdoing by police officers so that officers that act outside the law are swiftly brought to justice when the evidence indicates that there is a case to be answered. Barriers to reentry should also be dismantled where necessary.

In terms of higher education, the cost of college is skyrocketing and the quality of education is going down. Many students are faced with crippling debt and an economy that is unable to provide them with the kind of well-paying jobs they envisioned they would get after graduation. Put simply, the return on investment for many is bad. One of the reasons for this can be traced to well-intentioned government policies to provide funds to anyone who wants to go to college. The notion that everyone must have a four-year degree from college, and the government must do something to help everyone achieve this, is very problematic. The best way forward for higher education is to make colleges responsible for their product (students) and rid the system of all third parties providing loans—including the government. This approach will solve the problem of quality and bring costs down. If the government values education because it considers an informed citizenry to be essential, then it could focus on cost-effective online solutions. A massive, free, online school available to any citizen who has finished high school is a better way for the government to use it resources effectively. Students can enroll and learn history, biology and other subjects in an advanced level, take exams, and earn a national certificate of education.

Supply-side economics—which has been one of the leading doctrines for several decades to grow the economy—does not bring prosperity for all. Higher taxes, on the other hand, also fails to bring prosperity for all and grow the economy. The 99.9% or "spend it all" rule is a better approach. Instead of simply giving people tax breaks in the hope that they will spend it, they will be given this money with the certainty that they will spend it lest they face a penalty of paying it back. This approach would better fight the problem of inequality while stimulating economic growth.

Social Security needs serious reform. Both the OASI and the SSDI need complete overhauls in their benefit structures because they are unsustainable. Many people receive benefits even when they didn't pay a cent into these programs. Put simply, the benefit structure for both programs is not just haphazard, it's incomprehensible. Solutions like moving funds between them, raising payroll taxes, eliminating tax caps, and increasing the retirement age are palliative and do not address the structural problems with these programs. Individual accounts with focus on the last 35 years of life are the best way to structure the OASI. The same individual account should be applied to the SSDI with employees paying additional payroll taxes to enroll any of their dependents they want to enjoy SSDI benefits.

The current political system uses a flawed power structure that favors the elites. The nation-state is the equal and collective property of all citizens and the proposed system discussed in Chapter 8 will eliminate many of the vices of the current political system. The biggest concern with having this proposed system is that it needs a highly educated and well-informed citizenry to work. Hopefully, this would be achieved as citizens become more aware of the workings of government over time. Also, a secured portal system, although disconnected from the Internet, may still be vulnerable to attacks and hackings. Unless a way is found to build the system such that it cannot be hacked, or for nations to sign an agreement not to hack such systems, this would be a big obstacle to its success. With this understanding, it is fair to say that perhaps this is a system for the future and not one that is immediately feasible. However, this is the way government and the political system should operate.

The world faces serious threats like terrorism, climate change, and the possibility of pandemics that it can only overcome with quick and effective collective international response. Threat of war looms, and great power politics is back after a period of absence since the end of the Cold War. The need for serious reforms at the UN has never been more urgent. The ongoing war in Syria, the war in Iraq, the annexation of Crimea and the problems in the South China Sea are all evidence that the United Nations is unsuited to meet the emerging challenges of the 21st century. The UN Security Council needs to include all nations in a regional arrangement to give it the legitimacy and clout that it needs. Also, the UN needs a parliament to make it a beacon of democracy, transparency, and the rule of law. Failure to make these needed reforms could see the UN become increasingly irrelevant in the future.

However, it is important to note that, the creation of a parliament might be impossible in the near term because democracy is still a distant dream in many parts of the world. Also, powerful nations like the United States and its allies are unlikely to give up the advantages they enjoy in many global institutions. National interest, for many countries, always comes before global interest. This unfortunately means that for the foreseeable future, the UN will continue to be a weak organization that can only punish small, weak nations while powerful ones and their vassals act with impunity when it serves their interests.

The solutions proffered in this book using these principles are not the only possible solutions for the social systems discussed here. Anyone could use the same principles to creatively come up with solutions that are equally good but different. This is the beauty of de-entropification. It allows for exciting and creative solutions to how a social system should work better, and with the different solutions people could agree on the one that is most feasible and cost-effective. Also, the nine principles used to analyze and restructure the systems discussed in this book can be greatly improved upon. It is quite possible that there are other principles missed in this book. Using these principles as a starting point, perhaps others can one day expand on them and improve them. Someday, hopefully, social gravity and de-entropification might become an important field that people use to understand, correct problems and critique social systems.

Bibliography

ACLU. "Stop and Frisk in Chicago." 2015. http://www.aclu-il.org/wp-content/uploads/2015/03/ACLU_StopandFrisk_6.pdf.

-------. "Annual Stop-and-Frisk Numbers." https://www.nyclu.org/en/stop-and-frisk-data. (Accessed May 6, 2017).

-------. 2009. "The Persistence of Racial and Ethnic Profiling in the United States: A Follow-Up Report to the U.N. Committee on the Elimination of Racial Discrimination." August. https://www.aclu.org/files/pdfs/humanrights/cerd_finalreport.pdf.

-------. 2011. Combating Mass Incarceration - The Facts. June 17. https://www.aclu.org/infographic-combating-mass-incarceration-facts?redirect=combating-mass-incarceration-facts-0.

-------. ACLU Policy Priorities for Prison Reform. https://www.aclu.org/other/aclu-policy-priorities-prison-reform (accessed May 14, 2017).

-------. Inadequate Representation. https://www.aclu.org/other/inadequate-representation. (accessed May 14, 2017).

Adida Claire L., David D. Laitin and Marie-Anne Valfort. 2010. "Identifying barriers to Muslim integration in France." *National Academy of Sciences*, Volume 107 (52) 22384-22390, doi:10.1073/pnas.1015550107.

Administration on Aging. A Profile of Older Americans: 2015. https://aoa.acl.gov/aging_statistics/profile/2015/docs/2015-profile.pdf.

Al Jazeera. 2016. "El Cajon crowds protest police killing of Alfred Olango." September 28.

Alesina Alberto & Eliana La Ferrara. 2005. 'Ethnic Diversity and Economic Performance', *Journal of Economic Literature* 43, 762–800.

-------. 2000. "Participation in Heterogeneous Communities', *Quarterly Journal of Economics* 115, 847–904.

Alesina, Alberto, Reza Baqir and William Easterly. 1999. 'Public Goods and Ethnic Divisions', *Quarterly Journal of Economics* 114, 1243–84. https://doi.org/10.1162/003355399556269.

Allen Reniqua. 2013. Our 21st-century segregation: we're still divided by race. *The Guardian*, April 3.

Allport, Gordon. 1954. "*The Nature of Prejudice*". Reading, MA: Addison-Wesley.

Alstadsæter Annette, Johannesen Niels and Zucman Gabriel. 2017. "Tax Evasion and Inequality". May 28. http://gabriel-zucman.eu/files/AJZ2017.pdf.

American Academy of Actuaries. 2002. "Raising the Retirement Age for Social Security." October. https://www.actuary.org/pdf/socialsecurity/age_oct02.pdf.

American Association of University Professors. "Background Facts on Contingent Faculty." https://www.aaup.org/issues/contingency/background-facts. (Accessed May 24, 2017).

American Student Assistance. "Life Delayed: The Impact of Student Debt on the Daily Lives of Young Americans." http://www.asa.org/site/assets/files/3793/life_delayed.pdf. (Accessed May 23, 2017).

Anderson, Christopher J. & Aida Paskeviciute. 2006. 'How Ethnic and Linguistic Heterogeneity Influence the Prospects for Civil Society: A Comparative Study of Citizenship Behavior', *Journal of Politics* 68, 783–802. DOI:10.1111/j.1468-2508.2006.00470.x.

Annett, Anthony. 1999. "Ethnic and religious division, political instability, and government consumption', *International Monetary Fund*, mimeo, March.

Anwar Shamena, Patrick Bayer, Randi Hjalmarsson. 2012. The Impact of Jury Race in Criminal Trials. The Quarterly Journal of Economics; 127 (2): 1017-1055. doi: https://doi.org/10.1093/qje/qjs014.

Aondoakaa Tion Patrick, and Orluchukwu Godwin. 2015. "Federal Character Principles in Nigerian Constitution and Its Applicability: Issues and Challenges". IOSR *Journal of Humanities and Social Science* (IOSR-JHSS) Volume 20, Issue 12, Ver. V (Dec.) PP 51-57.

Arum Richard and Josipa Roksa. 2011. "Your So-Called Education." *New York Times*, May 14.

Ashkenas Jeremy and Haeyoun Park. 2015. "The Race Gap in America's Police Departments." *New York Times*, Updated April 8.

Associated Press. 2015. "California Governor Signs Bill to Fight Racial Profiling.

Association of American Medical Colleges. 2016. The Complexities of Physician Supply and Demand: Projections from 2014 to 2025." *IHS Inc.* April 5. https://www.aamc.org/download/458082/data/2016_complexities_of_supply_and_demand_projections.pdf

Autor David H. and Mark G. Duggan. 2006. "The Growth in the Social Security Disability Rolls: A Fiscal Crisis Unfolding." Journal of Economic Perspectives. Volume 20, Number 3, Pages 71–96, August.

Avik Roy. 2013. "How Americans Game the $200 Billion-a-Year 'Disability-Industrial Complex." *Forbes*, April 8.

Bailey Kenneth D.1990. *Social Entropy Theory.* Albany, New York: State University of New York (SUNY) Press. ISSN 1094-429X

Balko Radley. 2015. "Chicago's police review agency fires investigator for not exonerating cops." *Washington Post*, July 21.

Bartsch Matthias, Andrea Brandt and Daniel Steinvorth. 2010 "Turkish Immigration to Germany: A Sorry History of Self-Deception and Wasted Opportunities." *Der Spiegel*, September 07.

Barua Bacchus, Milagros Palacios, and Joel Ames. 2017."The Sustainability of Health Care Spending in Canada." *Fraser Institute*. March 14, 2017.

Basong, B. Valery. 2005. "Coup d'etats in Africa: The Emergence, Prevalence and Eradication." *Stanford University*.

BBC. "Aims, Organization and Powers of The League Of Nations". http://www.bbc.co.uk/schools/gcsebitesize/history/mwh/irl/aimsrev1.shtml. (Accessed 6 October 2016).

--------. 2004."Tensions high' in Nigeria state". BBC, November 12.

Bell Brian, Stephen J. Machin and Francesco Fasani. 2013. "Crime and Immigration: Evidence from Large Immigrant Waves." *Review of Economics and Statistics,* Volume 95 (4), October.

Bell, Brian. 2014. "Crime and immigration: Do poor labor market opportunities lead to migrant crime? *IZA World of Labor,* doi: 10.15185/izawol.33.

Benokraitis Nijole. 1982. Racial Exclusion in Juries. *The Journal of Applied Behavioral Science,* Vol 18, Issue 1, pp. 29 – 47. March 1, doi: 10.1177/002188638201800105.

Berman Yonatan, Eshel Ben-Jacob, and Yoash Shapira. 2016. "The Dynamics of Wealth Inequality and the Effect of Income Distribution". *PLoS ONE* 11(4): e0154196. https://doi.org/10.1371/journal.pone.0154196.

Bernie Sanders Education Plan. "Summary of Sen. Sanders' College for All Act." https://www.sanders.senate.gov/download/collegeforallsummary/?inline=file. (Accessed May 25, 2017).

Bhalla Nita. 2014. "U.N. failed to protect civilians during Sri Lanka's bloody war end, says report". *Reuters,* September 5.

Blalock, Hubert M. Jr. 1967. *Toward a Theory of Minority-group Relations.* New York: John Wiley & Sons.

Blumer, Herbert. 1958. "Race Prejudice as a Sense of Group Position." *The Pacific Sociological Review,* Vol. 1, No. 1, pp. 3-7.

Bobo, Lawrence D. & Mia Tuan. 2006. *Prejudice in Politics: Group Position, Public Opinion and the Wisconsin Treaty Rights Dispute.* Cambridge, MA: Harvard University Press.

Bobo, Lawrence D. 1999. "Prejudice as Group Position: Micro foundations of a Sociological Approach to Racism and Race Relations." *Journal of Social Issues* 55, 445–72. DOI: 10.1111/0022-4537.00127.

Boccia Romina and Rachel Greszler. 2013. "Social Security Benefits and the Impact of the Chained CPI." *Heritage Foundation,* May 21.

Boccia Romina and Virginia Reno. 2015. "Updating Social Security for the 21st Century: 12 Proposals You Should Know About." *AARP Public Policy Institute,* Updated October 2015. http://www.aarp.org/work/social-security/info-05-2012/future-of-social-security-proposals.html.

Bonczar, Thomas P. 2003. Prevalence of Imprisonment in the U.S. Population, 1974–2001." Washington, D.C.: *Bureau of Justice Statistics,* August, NCJ 197976. https://www.bjs.gov/content/pub/pdf/piusp01.pdf.

Bonk Lawrence. 2015. "San Diego Police Outfitted 600 Officers with Body Cameras and Saw a Drastic Reduction in Complaints." *Independent Journal Review.*

Borger Julian and Bastien Inzaurralde. 2017. "Russian Vetoes Are Putting UN Security Council's Legitimacy at Risk, Says U.S". *The Guardian,* last modified on April 12.

Borjas George J. 2013. "Immigration and the American Worker: A Review of the Academic Literature." *Center for Immigration Studies,* April. https://www.hks.harvard.edu/fs/gborjas/publications/popular/CIS2013.pdf.

--------. 2016. "Yes, Immigration Hurts American Workers." *Politico*, September/October.

--------. 2017. "The Wage Impact of the Marielitos: A Reappraisal." *ILR Review*, February 13, doi:10.1177/0019793917692945.

Bosman Julie and Tamar Lewin. 2015. "With $350 Billion Plan, Hillary Clinton Prods Rivals on Student Debt." *New York Times*, August 13.

Bowcott Owen. 2005. "Report Reveals Shame of UN Peacekeepers". *The Guardian*, March 24.

Braun Aurelian. 2013. "Out of 5,000 Bills in Every Congress, Guess How Many Become Law? *Mic*, August 10.

Brewer, M. B. & Brown, R. J. 1998. *"Intergroup Relations."* in Gilbert, D. T., Fiske, S. T. & Lindzey, G., eds, Handbook of Social Psychology, 4th edn. New York: Oxford University Press.

Brook Yaron. 2008. "The Government Did It." *Forbes*, July 18.

Brookings. 2017 "Vital Statistics on Congress". *Brookings Institute*, January 9. https://www.brookings.edu/multi-chapter-report/vital-statistics-on-congress/.

Brooks, Rosa. 2016. America's Police Problem Isn't Just About Police." Foreign Policy, January 5.

Brown Meta, Andrew Haughwout, Donghoon Lee, Maricar Mabutas, and Wilbert van der Klaauw. 2012. "Grading Student Loans." *Federal Reserve Bank of New York*, March 05.

Brown, Randall T. 2010. "Systematic Review of the Impact of Adult Drug Treatment Courts." *Translational research: the journal of laboratory and clinical medicine* 155.6 (2010): 263–274. http://doi.org/10.1016/j.trsl.2010.03.001.

Brutel Chantal. 2017. "Being Born in France Of an Immigrant Parent: A Diverse Population Reflecting the History of Migratory Flows." *National Institute of Statistics and Economic Studies*, February 8.

Buff, Maureen J. and Timothy D. Terrell. 2014. "The role of third-party payers in medical cost increases." *Journal of American Physicians and Surgeons*, v.19, no.3, 2014 Fall, p.75(5) (ISSN: 1543-4826).

Bureau of Federal Prisons. "Inmate Race." Last updated 29 April 2017. https://www.bop.gov/about/statistics/statistics_inmate_race.jsp. (Accessed May 5, 2017).

Bureau of Justice Statistics. 2012. Survey of State Criminal History Information Systems. *U.S. Department of Justice, Office of Justice Programs.* https://www.ncjrs.gov/pdffiles1/bjs/grants/244563.pdf.

Burman Leonard E. 2014. "Taxes and Inequality". *The Urban Institute*, March 20. http://www.urban.org/sites/default/files/publication/22421/413067-Taxes-and-Inequality.PDF.

Canadian institute of Actuaries. 2013. "Canada's Current Health Care System is Not Sustainable; Action Needed to Maintain the System's Survival." September 17. https://www.cia-ica.ca/docs/default-source/2013/213076e.pdf?sfvrsn=0.

Capecchi Christina and Mitch Smith. 2016. "Officer Who Shot Philando Castile Is Charged with Manslaughter." *New York Times*, November 16.

Card, David, Christian Dustmann and Ian Preston. 2012. "Immigration, Wages, And Compositional Amenities." Journal of the European Economic Volume 10 (1), February, Pages 78–119, DOI: 10.1111/j.1542-4774.2011.01051.x.

Card, David. "The Impact of the Mariel Boatlift on the Miami Labor Market." *Industrial and Labor Relations Review*, 43, no. 2 (1990): 245-57. doi:10.2307/2523702.

Carnevale Anthony P., Martin Van der Werf and Cary Lou. 2016. "The Enrollment Effects of Clinton's Free College Proposal." *Georgetown University Center on Education and The Workforce, McCourt School of Public Policy.*

Carnevale Anthony, Nicole Smith and Jeff Strohl. 2013. "Recovery: job growth and education requirements through 2020." *Georgetown University, Center of Education and the Workforce.* June.

Carson E. Ann and Elizabeth Anderson. 2016. Prisoners in 2015." *Bureau of Justice Statistics*, December, NCJ 250229. https://www.bjs.gov/content/pub/pdf/p15.pdf.

Carson, E. Anne. 2015. "Prisoners in 2014." Washington, DC: Bureau of Justice Statistics. September, NCJ 248955. https://www.bjs.gov/content/pub/pdf/p14.pdf.

Casey Dame Louise. 2016. "The Casey Review: A review into opportunity and integration." December 5. https://www.gov.uk/government/uploads/system/uploads/attachment_dat a/file/575973/The_Casey_Review_Report.pdf.

CBO Cost Estimate. 2017. "H.R. 1628, American Health Care Act of 2017, as passed by the House of Representatives on May 4, 2017". May 24. https://www.cbo.gov/system/files/115th-congress-2017-2018/costestimate/hr1628aspassed.pdf.

------- Cost Estimate. 2017. "H.R. 1628 Better Care Reconciliation Act of 2017, as posted on the Website of the Senate Committee on the Budget on June 26, 2017". June 26. https://www.cbo.gov/system/files/115th-congress-2017-2018/costestimate/52849-hr1628senate.pdf.

-------. 2016. "Expand Social Security Coverage to Include Newly Hired State and Local Government Employees." Joint Committee on Taxation, December 8. https://www.cbo.gov/budget-options/2016/52267.

-------. 2016. "Increase the Maximum Taxable Earnings for the Social Security Payroll Tax." December 8. *Joint Committee on Taxation*, https://www.cbo.gov/budget-options/2016/52266.

-------. 2016. "The 2016 Long-Term Budget Outlook." July, https://www.cbo.gov/sites/default/files/114th-congress-2015-2016/reports/51580-ltbo-one-col-2.pdf.

------- Cost Estimate. 2017. American Health Care Act. March 13. https://www.cbo.gov/system/files/115th-congress-2017-2018/costestimate/americanhealthcareact.pdf.

-------. "The 2015 Long-Term Budget Outlook, June 2015, http://www.cbo.gov/publication/50250. (accessed May 5, 2017).

Center for Medicare and Medicaid Services. 2017. "National Health Expenditure Fact Sheet." last Modified: March 21. https://www.cms.gov/research-statistics-data-and-systems/statistics-trends-and-reports/nationalhealthexpenddata/nhe-fact-sheet.html.

Center on Prison Studies. http://www.prisonstudies.org/country/united-states-america. (Accessed May 13, 2017).

Centers for Medicare and Medicaid Services. 2015. "2015 Annual Report of the Boards of Trustees of the Federal Hospital Insurance and Federal Supplementary Medical Insurance Trust Funds." July 22. https://www.cms.gov/research-statistics-data-and-systems/statistics-trends-and-reports/reportstrustfunds/downloads/tr2015.pdf.

Centers for Medicare and Medicaid Services. 2016. "2016 Annual Report of The Boards of Trustees Of The Federal Hospital Insurance And Federal Supplementary Medical Insurance Trust Funds." June 22, 2016. https://www.cms.gov/research-statistics-data-and-systems/statistics-trends-and-reports/reportstrustfunds/downloads/tr2016.pdf.

Charbonneau Louis and John Irish. 2015. "Dozens of Nations Back French Appeal to Limit Use of U.N. Veto". *Reuters*, September 30.

Charles Kerwin. & Patrick Kline. 2006. 'Relational Costs and the Production of Social Capital: Evidence from Carpooling', *The Economic Journal*, Vol. 116, No. 511 (Apr. 2006), pp. 581-604. DOI: 10.1111/j.1468-0297.2006.01093. x.

Chicago Tribune. "Chicago shooting victims." http://crime.chicagotribune.com/chicago/shootings/. (accessed December 31, 2016).

Christensen Kaare, Gabriele Doblhammer, Roland Rau, James W Vaupel. 2009. Ageing populations: the challenges ahead." *The Lancet.* 2009;374(9696):1196-1208. doi:10.1016/S0140-6736(09)61460-4.

Chronicle of Higher Education. 2012. "The Role of Higher Education in Career Development: Employer Perceptions." December. http://www.chronicle.com/items/biz/pdf/Employers%20Survey.pdf.

Cillizza Chris. 2013. "The Least Productive Congress Ever". *Washington Post*, July 17.

Clark Kim. 2016. "Now You Can Sell Shares in Yourself to Pay for College." *Times*, November 16.

Claxton Gary, Cynthia Cox, Anthony Damico, Larry Levitt   and Karen Pollitz. 2016. Pre-existing Conditions and Medical Underwriting in the Individual Insurance Market Prior to the ACA. *Kaiser Family Foundation*, December 12.

Codespote Suzanne. 2015. "Medicare Unfunded Obligation for the 2015 Trustees Report." July 22. *Office of the Actuary, Center for Medicare and Medicaid Services. http://morningconsult.com/wp-content/uploads/2014/07/CMS-Actuary-memo-on-Medicare-75yr-unfunded-obligation-2014-Trustees-Report-1.pdf.

Coffe, Hilde, and Benny Geys. 2006. 'Community Heterogeneity: A Burden for the Creation of Social Capital?', *Social Science Quarterly*, Vol. 87, No. 5: 1053-72. Doi. 10.1111/j.1540-6237.2006.00415.x

Cohen Andrew. 2013. "How Americans Lost the Right to Counsel, 50 Years After 'Gideon." *The Atlantic*, March 13.

Cohen Patricia. 2015. For-Profit Colleges Accused of Fraud Still Receive US Funds." *New York Times*, October 12.

-------. 2017. "Crackdown on For-Profit Colleges May Free Students and Trap Taxpayers." *New York Times*, August 28.

Cohen, Robin A, Michael Martinez E and Emily Zammitti P. 2016, "Health Insurance Coverage: Early Release of Estimates from the National Health Interview Survey". CDC, January–March. https://www.cdc.gov/nchs/data/nhis/earlyrelease/insur201609.pdf.

Cohen, Susan G. & Dane. E. Bailey. 1997. 'What Makes Teams Work: Group Effectiveness Research from the Shop Floor to the Executive Suite', *Journal of Management* 23, 239–90.

Cohn D'vera. 2015. "Future immigration will change the face of America by 2065." *Pew Research Center*, October 5.

Coleman, David. 2010. "Projections of the Ethnic Minority Populations of the United Kingdom 2006–2056." *Population and Development Review,* VL – 36 (3).

Committee of Public Accounts. 2014. "Government likely underestimating value of student loans never paid back." *Commons Select Committee*, February 14. http://www.parliament.uk/business/committees/committees-a-z/commons-select/public-accounts-committee/news/student-loans-report-publication/.

Complete College America. "Four-Year MYTH." http://completecollege.org/wp-content/uploads/2014/11/4-Year-Myth.pdf. (Accessed May 23, 2017).

Consumer Financial Protection Bureau. 2015. Student loan servicing: Analysis of public input and recommendations for reform. September. http://files.consumerfinance.gov/f/201509_cfpb_student-loan-servicing-report.pdf.

Cooper Alexia and Erica L. Smith. "Homicide Trends in the United States, 1980-2008: Annual Rates for 2009 and 2010." Bureau of Justice Statistics. November 2011, NCJ 23601. https://www.bjs.gov/content/pub/pdf/htus8008.pdf.

Costa, Dora L. & Matthew E. Kahn. 2003. 'Cowards and Heroes: Group Loyalty in the American Civil War', *Quarterly Journal of Economics* 118, 519–48. DOI: https://doi.org/10.1162/003355303321675446.

Coughlin Teresa A., John Holahan, Kyle Caswell, and Megan McGrath. 2014. "Uncompensated Care for the Uninsured in 2013: A Detailed Examination." *Kaiser Family Foundation*, May 30.

Cox Cynthia and Ashley Semanskee. 2016. Preliminary Data on Insurer Exits and Entrants in 2017 Affordable Care Act Marketplaces. *The Henry J Kaiser Family Foundation*, Aug 28.

CQ Press. "City Crime Rankings 2013." http://os.cqpress.com/citycrime/2012/CityCrime2013_CityCrimeRankingsFactSheet.pdf. (Accessed May 20, 2017).

Crane Steven E. and Farrokh Nourzad. 1990 "Tax Rates and Tax Evasion: Evidence from California Amnesty Data". *National Tax Journal,* Vol 43, No 2, page 189-99, June.

Daalder Ivo H. 1998. Decision to Intervene: How the War in Bosnia Ended. *Brookings Institute*, December 1.

Dabla-Norris Era, Kalpana Kochhar, Nujin Suphaphiphat, Frantisek Ricka, Evridiki Tsounta. 2015. "Causes and Consequences of Income Inequality: A Global Perspective". June, *International Monetary Fund, Strategy, Policy, And Review Department*.

Davies Nick. The $10bn question: what happened to the Marcos millions? The Guardian. https://www.theguardian.com/world/2016/may/07/10bn-dollar-question-marcos-millions-nick-davies. (Accessed June 9, 2017).

Davis, James A., & Tom William Smith. (1991). General social surveys, 1972-1991; Cumulative codebook, Chicago: *National Opinion Research Center*.

Davis, Lois M., Jennifer L. Steele, Robert Bozick, Malcolm V. Williams, Susan Turner, Jeremy N. V. Miles, Jessica Saunders, and Paul S. Steinberg. 2014. How Effective Is Correctional Education, and Where Do We Go from Here? The Results of a Comprehensive Evaluation. *RAND Corporation*. http://www.jstor.org/stable/10.7249/j.ctt6wq8mt.

de Klerk F.W. 2013. "South Africa, The Nation That Gave Up Its Nukes". *L.A Times*, December 22.

De la Maisonneuve Christine and Joaquim Oliveira Martins. 2013. Public spending on health and long-term care: a new set of projections." *OECD Economic Policy Paper* No. 06. June. https://www.oecd.org/eco/growth/Health%20FINAL.pdf.

DeBacker Jason Matthew, Bradley Heim, Shanthi Ramnath and Justin M. Ross. 2016. "The Impact of State Taxes on Pass-Through Businesses: Evidence from the 2012 Kansas Income Tax Reform." July. Available at SSRN: https://ssrn.com/abstract=2958353

Deloitte. "2015 health care outlook: China." https://www2.deloitte.com/content/dam/Deloitte/global/Documents/Life-Sciences-Health-Care/gx-lshc-2015-health-care-outlook-china.pdf (accessed May 12, 2017).

-------. 2015 Healthcare Outlook: Japan. https://www2.deloitte.com/content/dam/Deloitte/global/Documents/Life-Sciences-Health-Care/gx-lshc-2015-health-care-outlook-japan.pdf (accessed May 12, 2017).

-------. 2015 Healthcare Outlook: Middle East. https://www2.deloitte.com/content/dam/Deloitte/global/Documents/Life-Sciences-Health-Care/gx-lshc-2015-health-care-outlook-middle-east.pdf. (accessed May 12, 2017).

-------. 2015 Healthcare Outlook: Southeast Asia. https://www2.deloitte.com/content/dam/Deloitte/global/Documents/Life-Sciences-Health-Care/gx-lshc-2015-health-care-outlook-se-asia.pdf. (accessed May 12, 2017).

Denny Charlotte. 2004. "Suharto, Marcos and Mobutu head corruption table with $50bn scams". *The Guardian*, March 26.

Department of Human and Health Services. 2016. "About 2.5 Million People Who Currently Buy Coverage Off-Marketplace May Be Eligible for ACA Subsidies." October 4.

https://aspe.hhs.gov/system/files/pdf/208306/OffMarketplaceSubsidyeligib
le.pdf

Department of Justice. 2014. "Re: Albuquerque Police Department." April 10.
https://www.justice.gov/sites/default/files/crt/legacy/2014/04/10/apd_find
ings_4-10-14.pdf.

-------. 2015. Justice Department Announces Findings of Two Civil Rights
Investigations in Ferguson, Missouri. *Department of Justice, Office of Public
Affairs*, March 4. https://www.justice.gov/opa/pr/justice-department-
announces-findings-two-civil-rights-investigations-ferguson-missouri.

-------. 2015. Justice Department Reaches Agreement with City of Cleveland to
Reform Cleveland Division of Police Following the Finding of a Pattern or
Practice of Excessive Force. *Department of Justice, Office of Public Affairs.*
May 26. https://www.justice.gov/opa/pr/justice-department-reaches-
agreement-city-cleveland-reform-cleveland-division-police.

-------. 2016. "Phasing Out Our Use of Private Prisons." August 18.
https://www.justice.gov/archives/opa/blog/phasing-out-our-use-private-
prisons.

-------. 2016. Justice Department Announces Findings of Investigation into
Baltimore Police Department. *Department of Justice, Office of Public Affairs*,
August 10. https://www.justice.gov/opa/pr/justice-department-announces-
findings-investigation-baltimore-police-department.

-------. 2017. Justice Department Announces Findings of Investigation into
Chicago Police Department. *Department of Justice, Office of Public Affairs.*
January 13. https://www.justice.gov/opa/pr/justice-department-
announces-findings-investigation-chicago-police-department.

-------. 2017. Justice Department Reaches Agreement with City of Baltimore to
Reform Police Department's Unconstitutional Practices. *Department of Justice, Office of Public Affairs*, January 12,
https://www.justice.gov/opa/pr/justice-department-reaches-agreement-
city-baltimore-reform-police-department-s.

DePillis Lydia. 2014. "Do diverse police forces treat their communities more
fairly than almost-all-white ones like Ferguson's? *Washington Post*, August
22.

Desrochers Donna M. and Steven Hurlburt. 2014. "Trends in College Spending: 2001–2011." *Delta Cost Project*, July.

Dewan Shaila and Andrew W. Lehren. 2016. "After a Crime, the Price of a Second Chance." *New York Times*. December 12.

Diamond Jeremy, "Trump details student loan policies, but doesn't mention
cost." *CNN*, October 13, 2016.

Donovan Daniel. 2012. "International Criminal Court: Successes and Failures". *International Policy Digest*, March 23.

Drake, Bruce. 2015. Divide between blacks and whites on police runs deep.
Pew Research Center, April 28.

Drouin Jean P., Viktor Hediger, and Nicolaus Henke. 2008. "Health care costs: A
market-based view." *The Mckinsey Quarterly*. September.

Drug Policy Alliance. 2016."The Drug War, Mass Incarceration and Race."
February

https://www.drugpolicy.org/sites/default/files/DPA%20Fact%20Sheet_Drug %20War%20Mass%20Incarceration%20and%20Race_(Feb.%202016).pdf.

Duguet Emmanuel, Noam Leandri, Yannick L'Horty and Pascale Petit. 2008. "Are Young French Jobseekers of Ethnic Immigrant Origin Discriminated Against? A Controlled Experiment in the Paris Area" May. http://dx.doi.org/10.2139/ssrn.1138244.

Duwe Grant and Valerie Clark. 2013. The Effects of Private Prison Confinement on Offender Recidivism: Evidence from Minnesota. *Criminal Justice Review*, Vol 38, Issue 3, pp. 375 – 394. doi: 10.1177/0734016813478823.

--------. 2014. The Effects of Prison-Based Educational Programming on Recidivism and Employment. *The Prison Journal*, Vol 94, Issue 4, pp. 454 – 478, September 4. doi: 10.1177/0032885514548009.

Eber Gabriel and Margaret Winter. 2012. "Private Prisons Are the Problem, Not the Solution." *ACLU*, April 30.

Ed Financial Services. "Revised Pay as You Earn (REPAYE)." https://edfinancial.com/HelpCenter/LowerPaymentOptions/Income-Driven-Repayment-Information-Center/REPAYE. (Accessed May 23, 2017).

Eddy Melissa and Gardiner Harris. 2016. "Obama and E.U. Leaders Agree to Keep Sanctions on Russia". *New York Times,* November 18.

Eisenberg, Avigail. 2007. "Equality, trust, and multiculturalism." *Social Capital and Social Diversity, ed. Fiona Kay and Richard Johnston*: 67-94.

Elinson Zusha and Dan Frosch. 2015. Cost of Police-Misconduct Cases Soars in Big U.S. Cities. *Wall Street Journal*, July 15.

Elmendorf, Douglas. 2012. Letter to the Honorable John Boehner providing an estimate for H.R. 6079, the Repeal of Obamacare Act. Cost Estimate, July 24. https://www.cbo.gov/sites/default/files/43471-hr6079_0.pdf.

Engfer Anette, Klaus A. Schneewind. 1982. "Causes and Consequences of Harsh Parental Punishment. An Empirical Investigation in A Representative Sample Of 570 German Families." *Child Abuse & Neglect*, Volume 6, Issue 2, Pages 129-139, ISSN 0145-2134, http://dx.doi.org/10.1016/0145-2134(82)90005-9.

Etehad Melissa. 2016. "After Nice, Newt Gingrich wants to 'test' every Muslim in the U.S. and deport sharia believers." *Washington Post*, July 15.

Ewing Walter, Daniel E. Martínez, and Rubén G. Rumbaut. 2015. "The Criminalization of Immigration in the United States." *American Immigration Council*, July 13.

FBI. "Arrest by Race 2013." https://ucr.fbi.gov/crime-in-the-u.s/2013/crime-in-the-u.s.-2013/tables/table-43.

Fieldhouse Andrew. 2013. "Rising Income Inequality and the Role of Shifting Market-Income Distribution, Tax Burdens, and Tax Rates". *Economic Policy Institute*, June 14.

Fielding Jonathan E, Grace Tye, Patrick L Ogawa, Iraj J Imam, Anna M Long. 2002. "Los Angeles County drug court programs: initial results.*" Journal of Substance Abuse Treatment*, Volume 23, Issue 3, 217 – 224. DOI: http://dx.doi.org/10.1016/S0740-5472(02)00262-3.

FinAid. "History of Student Financial Aid." http://www.finaid.org/educators/history.phtml. (Accessed May 23, 2017).

Fischer Karin. 2013. "The Employment Mismatch." *The Chronicle of Higher Education*, March 04.

Fisman Raymond and Shang-Jin Wei. 2004. "Tax Rates and Tax Evasion: Evidence from "Missing Imports" in China". *Journal of Political Economy*, 2004, vol. 112, no. 2, 471-496.

Fleurant Aude, Pieter D. Wezeman, Siemon T. Wezeman and Nan Tian. 2017. "Trends in International Arms Transfers, 2016". *Stockholm International Peace Research Institute (SIPRI)*, February. https://www.sipri.org/sites/default/files/Trends-in-international-arms-transfers-2016.pdf.

Ford Matt. 2017. "When Your Judge Isn't a Lawyer". *The Atlantic*, February 5.

Förster Michael and Horacio Levy. 2014. United States: Tackling High Inequalities Creating Opportunities for All. *OECD publications*, June. https://www.oecd.org/unitedstates/Tackling-high-inequalities.pdf.

France24. 2015. "Rising number of wealthy French fleeing abroad". *France24*, Last updated August 8.

Friedman Zack. 2017. "Student Loan Debt In 2017: A $1.3 Trillion Crisis". *Forbes*, February 21.

Frost & Sullivan. 2016. Malaysia – The 20 by 2020 Inevitability". January 27. https://ww2.frost.com/news/press-releases/frost-sullivan-malaysia-20-2020-inevitability/.(accessed May 12, 2017).

Frum David. 2016. "The Great Immigration-Data Debate." *The Atlantic*, January 19.

Full Facts. 2012. "Are wages going down because of immigration? December 17, https://fullfact.org/economy/are-wages-going-down-because-immigration/.

Funke Daniel and Tina Susman. 2016. "From Ferguson to Baton Rouge: Deaths of black men and women at the hands of police". *LA Times*, July 12.

Gale William G., Melissa S. Kearney and Peter R. Orszag. 2015. "Would a significant increase in the top income tax rate substantially alter income inequality". *Economic Studies at Brookings*, September.

Gallup. 2015. "75% in U.S. See Widespread Government Corruption." *Gallup*, September 19.

GAO 2008 and the Congressional Budget Office. Testimony before the Committee on Homeland Security and Governmental Affairs Statement of Gene L. Dodaro. Available at http://www.gao.gov/new.items/d09453t.pdf.

Gauthier-Villars David and Charles Forelle. 2010. "French Parliament Passes Law Banning Burqas." *Wall Street Journal*, Last Updated Sept. 15.

Gautney Heather. "What is Occupy Wall Street? The History of Leaderless Movements". *Washington Post*, October 10, 2011.

Gettleman Jeffrey. 2007. "Disputed Vote Plunges Kenya into Bloodshed". *New York Times*, December 31.

Giles, Michael W. & Arthur Evans. 1986. "The Power Approach to Intergroup Hostility." *Journal of Conflict Resolution* 30, 469–85.

Giovanni Thomas. 2012. "Community-Oriented Defense: Start Now." *Brennan Center for Justice*, July 20.

Glaeser Edward & Alberto Alesina. 2004. *Fighting Poverty in the US and Europe: A World of Difference.* Oxford: Oxford University Press.

Glanton Dahleen. 2016. "With 500 homicides in Chicago, time for African-Americans to get tough on crime". *Chicago Tribune,* September 7.

Goff Phillip Atiba, Tracey Lloyd, Amanda Geller, Steven Raphael, and Jack Glaser. 2016. The Science of Justice: Race, Arrests, and Use of Force. *Center for Policing Equity,* July. http://policingequity.org/wp-content/uploads/2016/07/CPE_SoJ_Race-Arrests-UoF_2016-07-08-1130.pdf.

Gold Matea, Mark Berman and Renae Merle. 2016. "Not My President': Thousands Protest Trump in Rallies Across The U.S." *Washington Post,* November 11.

Goldstein, Amy. 2017. Aetna exiting all ACA insurance marketplaces in 2018. *Washington Post,* May 10.

Governor of New York. 2014. Governor Cuomo Launches Initiative to Provide College Classes in New York Prison. February 16. https://www.governor.ny.gov/news/governor-cuomo-launches-initiative-provide-college-classes-new-york-prison.

Grant Harriet. 2017. "UN Agencies 'Broke and Failing' In Face of Ever-Growing Refugee Crisis". *The Guardian,* last modified on April 28.

Gravelle Jane G. and Donald J. Marples. 2014. "Tax Rates and Economic Growth". *Congressional Research Service,* January 2.

Greg Ip. 2016. "What Really Drives Anti-Immigration Feelings." *Wall Street Journal,* June 29.

Greszler Rachel. 2014. "Raising the Social Security Payroll Tax Cap: Solving Nothing, Harming Much." *The Heritage Foundation,* August 1. http://thf_media.s3.amazonaws.com/2014/pdf/BG2923.pdf.

--------. 2015. "Private Disability Insurance Option Could Help Save SSDI and Improve Individual Well-being." *The Heritage Foundation,* July 20.

Grimsley, Edwin. 2012. What Wrongful Convictions Teach Us About Racial Inequality." September 26. *The Innocence Project,* https://www.innocenceproject.org/what-wrongful-convictions-teach-us-about-racial-inequality/.

Grono Nick. 2008. "The International Criminal Court: success or failure? Open Democracy, June 9.

Hager Eli. 2015. "Job Opening: No Training, Low Pay, High Turnover." *The Marshall Project,* June 5. https://www.themarshallproject.org/2015/06/05/job-opening-no-training-low-pay-high-turnover#.NimXAxbGk.

Hainmueller Jens and Daniel J. Hopkins. 2014. "Public Attitudes Toward Immigration." Annual Review of Political Science Vol. 17:225-249. May, DOI: 10.1146/annurev-polisci-102512-194818.

-------. 2015. "The Hidden American Immigration Consensus: A Conjoint Analysis of Attitudes toward Immigrants." *American Journal of Political Science* Volume 59, Volume 59 (3), July, DOI: 10.1111/ajps.12138.

Haislmaier Edmund and Alyene Senger. 2017. The 2017 Health Insurance Exchanges: Major Decrease in Competition and Choice. *Heritage Foundation.* January 30.

Hamilton Matt. 2016. "Dylan Noble, fatally shot by Fresno police, was drunk and had traces of cocaine in his body, autopsy shows". *LA Times*, August 2.

Harlow Caroline W. 2003. Education and Correctional Populations. NCJ 195670. Washington, D.C.: U.S. Department of Justice, Bureau of Justice Statistics. bjs.ojp.usdoj.gov/content/pub/pdf/ecp.pdf.

Haughwout Andrew, Donghoon Lee, Joelle Scally, Wilbert van der Klaauw. 2015. "Student Loan Borrowing and Repayment Trends, 2015." *Federal Reserve Bank of New York*, April 16.

Heiss Mary Ann. 2015. "Exposing "Red Colonialism": U.S. Propaganda at the United Nations, 1953–1963". *Journal of Cold War Studies*, Volume 17, Issue 3, July, p.82-115.

Henderson Barney. 2015. "What have been the successes and failures of UN peacekeeping missions? *The Telegraph,* September 28.

Hessick Andrew F. & Reshma Saujani. 2002. Plea Bargaining and Convicting the Innocent: The Role of the Prosecutor, the Defense Counsel, and the Judge. *Brigham Young University Journal of Public Law*, Vol. 16, p. 189.

Hesson Ted. 2015. "Why American Cities Are Fighting to Attract Immigrants." *The Atlantic,* July 21.

Hiler Tamara, Lanae Erickson Hatalsky, and Megan John. 2016. "Incomplete: The Quality Crisis at America's Private, Non-Profit Colleges." The Third way, May 26.

Hillary Clinton. "Making college debt-free and taking on student debt." https://www.hillaryclinton.com/issues/college/. (Accessed May 25, 2017).

Hoeve Machteld, Judith Semon Dubas, Veroni I. Eichelsheim, Peter H. van der Laan, Wilma Smeenk, and Jan R. M. Gerris. 2009. "The Relationship Between Parenting and Delinquency: A Meta-analysis". *Journal of Abnormal Child Psychology*, 37(6), 749–775. http://doi.org/10.1007/s10802-009-9310-8.

Holahan John, Matthew Buettgens, Lisa Clemans-Cope, Melissa M. Favreault, Linda J. Blumberg, Siyabonga Ndwandwe. 2016."The Sanders Single-Payer HealthCare Plan: The Effect on National Health Expenditures and Federal and Private Spending." *Urban Institute,* May.

Holzer Harry J., Steven Raphael & Michael Stoll. 2003. Employment Barriers Facing Ex-Offenders. Washington, D.C.: *The Urban Institute.* www.urban.org/UploadedPDF/410855_holzer.pdf

Horton Emily. 2017. "The Legacy of the 2001 and 2003 "Bush" Tax Cuts". Center on Budget and Policy Priority, March 31.

Hough Mike, Jonathan Jackson, Ben Bradford, Andy Myhill and Paul Quinton. 2010. "Procedural Justice, Trust, and Institutional Legitimacy." *Policing: A Journal of Policy and Practice*, August 1, 4(3):203, VI - 4. https://doi.org/10.1093/police/paq027.

Hudson, Redditt. 2014. "Being a cop showed me just how racist and violent the police are. There's only one fix." *Washington Post,* December 6.

Human Right Watch. "No Escape Male Rape n US Prisons." https://www.hrw.org/reports/2001/prison/report.html.

--------. 1995. The Fall of Srebrenica and the Failure of UN Peacekeeping: Bosnia and Herzegovina". *Human Right Watch*, Volume 7, No. 13, October. https://www.hrw.org/sites/default/files/reports/bosnia1095web.pdf.

-------. 2010. "The Price of Freedom: Bail and Pretrial Detention of Low Income Nonfelony Defendants in New York City." December 2. https://www.hrw.org/report/2010/12/02/price-freedom/bail-and-pretrial-detention-low-income-nonfelony-defendants-new-york.

Hungerford Thomas L. 2011. "Changes in the Distribution of Income Among Tax Filers Between 1996 and 2006: The Role of Labor Income, Capital Income, and Tax Policy". *Congressional Research Service*, December 29.

Hungerford Thomas L. 2012. "Taxes and the Economy: An Economic Analysis of the Top Tax Rates Since 1945 (Updated)". *Congressional Research Service*, December 12.

Iyengar Radha. 2007. "An Analysis of The Performance of Federal Indigent Defense Counsel." *National Bureau of Economic Research*, Working Paper 13187, June. Available at SSRN: https://ssrn.com/abstract=994235

Jackson Jonathan, Ben Bradford, Betsy Stanko, and Katrin Hohl. 2012. *Just Authority? Trust in the Police in England and Wales*. ISBN-10: 1843928485, ISBN-13: 978-1843928485 *Routledge*, July 27. Willan; 1 edition.

Jacobson Louis. 2013. "CNN's Don Lemon says more than 72 percent of African-American births are out of wedlock." *Politifact*, July 29.

Jaitman Laura and Stephen Machin. 2013. "Crime and immigration: new evidence from England and Wales." *IZA Journal of Migration*, October 25. DOI: 10.1186/2193-9039-2-19.

James, Nathan. 2016. The Federal Prison Population Buildup: Options for Congress. Congressional Research Service, May 20. https://fas.org/sgp/crs/misc/R42937.pdf.

Jennings Wesley G., Mathew D. Lynch, Lorie A. Fridell "Evaluating the Impact of Police Officer Body-Worn Cameras (BWCs): The Orlando Police Department (OPD) Experience." 2015. October 6, http://media.cmgdigital.com/shared/news/documents/2015/10/09/OPD-Final-Report-Executive-Summary-10-6-15.pdf.

Jick Hershel, Andrew Wilson, Peter Wiggins and Douglas P. Chamberlin. 2012. Comparison of Prescription Drug Costs in the United States and the United Kingdom, Part 1, 2 and 3. *The Journal of Human Pharmacology and Drug Therapy*, volume 32. http://dx.doi.org/10.1002/phar.1141.

Joffe-Walt Chana. 2013. "Unfit for Work: The startling rise of disability in America." *NPR*.

John David and Virginia Reno. The Future of Social Security:12 Proposals You Should Know About." http://www.aarp.org/content/dam/aarp/work-and-retirement/social-security/2012-06/The-Future-Of-Social-Security.pdf. (Accessed October 22, 2016).

Johnson Anne, Tobin Van Ostern, and Abraham White. 2012. "The Student Debt Crisis." *Center for American Progress*, October 25.

Jordahl Henrik. & Magnus Gustavsson. *2008*. Inequality and Trust in Sweden: Some Inequalities are More Harmful than Others. *Journal of Public Econom-*

ics, Volume 92, Issues 1–2, February, Pages 348-365.
https://doi.org/10.1016/j.jpubeco.2007.06.010.

Kaiser Family Foundation. 2010. "Survey of Detroit Area Residents." *The Washington Post/Kaiser Family Foundation/Harvard University.* January 06. https://kaiserfamilyfoundation.files.wordpress.com/2013/01/8039.pdf.

-------. 2015. "Average Individual Mandate Penalty to Rise 47 Percent to $969 in 2016 for Uninsured People Eligible for ACA Plans." December 09.

-------. 2016. "Key Facts about the Uninsured Population." September 29.

-------. 2016. "Key Facts about the Uninsured Population." September 29. http://kff.org/uninsured/fact-sheet/key-facts-about-the-uninsured-population.

-------. 2017. "Premiums and Tax Credits Under the Affordable Care Act vs. the American Health Care Act: Interactive Maps." April 27.

Kaplan Robert D. 2011. "The South China Sea Is the Future of Conflict". *Foreign Affairs,* August 15.

Karlan, Dean S. 2007. 'Social Capital and Group Banking'. *The Economic Journal,* Volume 117 (517). http://karlan.yale.edu/sites/default/files/ecoj_463.pdf.

Kim E. Tammy. 2015. "Poor clients pay just to apply for a public defender" *Al Jazeera America,* January 9.

Kim Victoria and Frank Shyong. 2015. Maternity tourism' raids target California operations catering to Chinese. March 3, *LA Times.*

King Shaun. 2016. "To help fix police brutality, cops can no longer have less training than the average cosmetologist." *NY Daily News,* July 26.

Kipgen Nehginpao. 2013."Conflict in Rakhine State in Myanmar: Rohingya Muslims' Conundrum." *Journal of Muslim Minority Affairs* Vol. 33(2), February. http://dx.doi.org/10.1080/13602004.2013.810117.

Knack Stephen and Philip Keefer. 1997. Does Social Capital Have an Economic Payoff? A Cross Country Investigation". *The Quarterly Journal of Economics,* Vol. 112, No. 4, pp. 1251-1288, November.

Koigi Bob. 2016. "Future of ICC in doubt after African countries withdraw". *Euractiv,* Last Updated Nov 11.

Koopmans Ruud. "Trade-Offs between Equality and Difference: Immigrant Integration, Multiculturalism and the Welfare State in Cross-National Perspective." *Journal of Ethnic and Migration Studies,* Vol. 36, Issue 1, 2010.

Kotlikoff Laurence. 2014. "America's Ponzi scheme: Why Social Security needs to retire." PBS, April 7.

Krebs Christopher P., Christine H. Lindquist, Willem Koetse, and Pamela K. Lattimore. 2007. "Assessing the Long-Term Impact of Drug Court Participation on Recidivism with Generalized Estimating Equations." *Drug and alcohol dependence.* 2007;91(1):57-68. doi: 10.1016/j.drugalcdep.2007.05.011.

Krippendorff, Klaus. 1986. A dictionary of cybernetics. Norfolk VA: *The American Society for Cybernetics.* Retrieved from http://repository.upenn.edu/asc_papers/224.

Krogstad Jens Manuel, Jeffrey S. Passel and D'vera Cohn. 2017. "5 facts about illegal immigration in the U.S." *Pew Research Center,* April 27.

Kulish Nicholas and Fernanda Santos. 2017. "Illegal Border Crossings Appear to Drop Under Trump." *New York Times,* March 8.

Lantigua-Williams Juleyka. 2016. "How Much Can Better Training Do to Improve Policing? *The Atlantic,* July 13.

Le Deu Franck, Rajesh Parekh, Fangning Zhang, and Gaobo Zhou. 2012. "Health care in China: Entering 'uncharted waters." *McKinsey & Company,* November.

Leigh, A. 2006. 'Trust, Inequality and Ethnic Heterogeneity', *Economic Record* 82, 268–80.

Leinfelt, Fredrik. H. 2006. Racial Influences on the Likelihood of Police Searches and Search Hits: A Longitudinal Analysis from an American Midwestern City". *The Police Journal* Vol 79, Issue 3, pp. 238 – 257, September 1.

Levert Stéphane. 2013. Sustainability of the Canadian Health Care System and Impact of the 2014 Revision to the Canada Health Transfer. *Society of Actuaries.*

Levitt Larry, Anthony Damico, Gary Claxton, Cynthia Cox and Karen Pollitz. 2017. "Gaps in Coverage Among People with Pre-Existing Conditions." *Kaiser Family Foundation,* May 17.

Levy Clifford J. 2008. "Russia Backs Independence of Georgian Enclaves". *New York Times,* August. 26.

Lioz Adam and Karen Shanton. 2015. "The Money Chase: Moving from Big Money Dominance in the 2014 Midterms to A Small Donor Democracy". *Demos,* January 14.

Liptak Adam. 2007. "Public Defenders Get Better Marks on Salary." *New York Times,* July 14.

-------. 2015. Exclusion of Blacks from Juries Raises Renewed Scrutiny. *New York Times.* August 15.

-------. 2010. "Justices, 5-4, Reject Corporate Spending Limit." *New York Times,* January 21.

Lisenkova Katerina and Miguel Sanchez-Martinez. 2016. "The Long-Term Macroeconomic Effects of Lower Migration to the UK." *National Institute of Economic and Social Research,* May 24.

Lobosco Katie. 2016. "6 Things to Know About Tuition-Free College." CNN, April 26.

Louis Jacobson. 2013. "Medicare and Social Security: What you paid compared with what you get." Politifact, February 1.

Lucca David O., Taylor Nadauld, and Karen Shen. 2017. "Credit Supply and the Rise in College Tuition: Evidence from the Expansion in Federal Student Aid Programs." *Federal Reserve Bank of New York Staff Reports,* no. 733. July 2015; revised February.

Marcus Jon. 2016. "Germany proves tuition-free college is not a silver bullet for America's education woes." *Quartz,* October 18.

Maritz Dominique. 2012. "Rwandan Genocide: Failure of the International Community? *E-International Relations,* April 7.

Martin Anne B, Micah Hartman, Benjamin Washington, Aaron Catlin, the National Health Expenditure Accounts Team. 2017. "National Health Spending: Faster Growth In 2015 As Coverage Expands and Utilization Increases." *Health Affairs*, January vol. 36 no. 1 166-176.

Martin Joyce A., Brady E. Hamilton, Stephanie J. Ventura, Michelle J.K. Osterman, Elizabeth C. Wilson, and T.J. Mathews. 2012. "Births: Final Data for 2010." National Center for Health Statistics, Centers for Disease Control and Prevention, Volume 61, Number 1, August 28. https://www.cdc.gov/nchs/data/nvsr/nvsr61/nvsr61_01.pdf.

Mauro, Paolo. 1995. Corruption and Growth', *Quarterly Journal of Economics*, Vol 110 (3): 681-712. https://doi.org/10.2307/2946696.

McCabe Kristen, Doris Meissner. 2010. "Immigration and the United States: Recession Affects Flows, Prospects for Reform." Migration Policy Institute, January 20.

McCarthy Justin. 2014. "In U.S., 65% Dissatisfied with How Gov't System Works". *Gallup*, January 22.

McCurry Justin. 2017. "North Korea warns 'thermonuclear war could break out at any moment". *The Guardian*, April 18.

McDonough, John E. 2015. "The Demise of Vermont's Single-Payer Plan." *New England Journal of Medicine*; 372:1584-1585. April 23, 2015. DOI: 10.1056/NEJMp1501050.

McGreevy Patrick. 2015. "Brown Signs Legislation to Protect Minorities from Racial Profiling and Excessive Force." *LA Times*, October 4.

McMorrow Stacey and John Holahan. 2016. The Widespread Slowdown in Health Spending Growth Implications for Future Spending Projections and the Cost of the Affordable Care Act. *Urban Institute*, June.

McNiel Dale E. and Renée L. Binder. 2007. "Effectiveness of a Mental Health Court in Reducing Criminal Recidivism and Violence." *American Journal of Psychiatry* 164:9, pp. 1395-1403. https://doi.org/10.1176/appi.ajp.2007.06101664.

Migration Advisory Committee. 2012. "Analysis of the Impacts of Migration." January 2012. https://www.gov.uk/government/uploads/system/uploads/attachment_data/file/257235/analysis-of-the-impacts.pdf.

Miguel, E. & Gugerty, M. K. 2005. 'Ethnic Diversity, Social Sanctions and Public Goods in Kenya', Journal of Public Economics 89, 2325–68.

Mitchell Josh. 2016. "Student Debt Is About to Set Another Record, But the Picture Isn't All Bad." *Wall Street Journal*, May 2.

Moehling Carolyn, and Anne Morrison Piehl. "Immigration, Crime, and Incarceration in Early Twentieth-Century America." *Demography* 46.4 (2009): 739–763. https://www.ncbi.nlm.nih.gov/pmc/articles/PMC2831353/.

Moore Marlee E. and Virginia Aldige Hiday. "Mental Health Court Outcomes: A Comparison of Re-Arrest and Re-Arrest Severity Between Mental Health Court and Traditional Court Participants." *Law and Human Behavior*, Vol 30: 659. DOI: 10.1007/s10979-006-9061-9.

Mortimer Edward. 2015. "The First 70 Years of the United Nations: Achievements and Challenges". *UN Chronicle*, September.

Mourshed Mona, Viktor Hediger and Toby Lambert. "Gulf Cooperation Council Health Care: Challenges and Opportunities."

http://middleeasthospital.com/GCC%20HEALTHCARE%20CHALLENGE.pd
f (accessed May 12, 2017).

NACE Staff. 2016. "Stem Grads Projected to Earn Class Of 2016's Highest Average Starting Salaries". *National Association of Colleges and Employers*, January 27.

National Center for Education Statistics. "FAST FACTS."
https://nces.ed.gov/fastfacts/display.asp?id=40. (Accessed May 24, 2017).

National Registry of Exonerations. 2017. "Exonerations In 2016." March 7.
https://www.law.umich.edu/special/exoneration/Documents/Exonerations
_in_2016.pdf.

National Registry of Exonerations.
https://www.law.umich.edu/special/exoneration/Pages/Exonerations-in-
the-United-States-Map.aspx.

Netter Lorraine. "Dependent and Spouse Benefits Under Social Security Disability." http://www.disabilitysecrets.com/resources/social-security-
disability/social-security-disability-coverage/dependent-benefits.htm. (Accessed December 5, 2016).

New York Times Editorial Board. 2014. "Kansas Ruinous Tax Cuts". New York Times, July 13.

Newman Brian. 2016. "National Poll Indicates Strong Support for Making College Tuition Free." Campaign for Free College Tuition, August 24.

Newport, Frank. 2014. Gallup Review: Black and White Attitudes Toward Police." *Gallup*, August 20. http://www.gallup.com/poll/175088/gallup-
review-black-white-attitudes-toward-police.aspx.

Newton, K. & Delhey, J. 2005. 'Predicting Cross-national Levels of Social Trust: Global Pattern or Nordic Exceptionalism?', *European Sociological Review* 21, 311–27.

Nicholson-Crotty Sean, Nicholson-Crotty Jill and Fernandez, Sergio. 2017. "Will More Black Cops Matter? Officer Race and Police-Involved Homicides of Black Citizen." *Public Administration Review*, Volume 77. Wiley Subscription Services.

Noah, Timothy. 2012. The Mobility Myth. *New Republic*, February 7.

Norm Stamper. 2016. *To Protect and Serve: How to Fix America's Police.* June 7, Nation Books, Hardcover: 336 pages. ISBN-10: 1568585403, ISBN-13: 978-1568585406

Noye, Ursula. 2015. Black strikes, A Study of the Racially Disparate Use of Peremptory Challenges by the Caddo Parish District Attorney's office" August, *Reprieve Australia.*
https://blackstrikes.com/resources/Blackstrikes_Caddo_Parish_August_201
5.pdf.

Nzongola-Ntalaja Georges. 2011. "Patrice Lumumba: the most important assassination of the 20th century". *The Guardian*, January 17.

OECD. "Education at a Glance 2016: OECD Indicators." OECD Publishing Paris, http://.10.1787/eag-2016-en.

-------. 2016. "Education at a Glance 2016: OECD Indicators." *OECD Publishing, Paris.* September 15. DOI: http://dx.doi.org/10.1787/eag-2016-en

Office of National Statistics. 2015. "Overview of the UK Population." November 5,
http://webarchive.nationalarchives.gov.uk/20160105160709/http://www.ons.gov.uk/ons/dcp171776_422383.pdf.

Oltermann Philip. 2016. "Germany axed tuition fees – but is it working out? *The Guardian*, last modified on June 5.

Ontario Ministry of Finance. 2005. Toward 2025: assessing Ontario's long-term outlook. Toronto: The Ministry. Available: www.fin.gov.on.ca/english/economy/ltr/2005/05_ltr.pdf

Packman David. 2011. "2010 NPMSRP Police Misconduct Statistical Report." *The Cato Institute's National Police Misconduct Reporting Project*. April 5. http://www.leg.state.nv.us/Session/77th2013/Exhibits/Assembly/JUD/AJUD338L.pdf.

Page Benjamin I. and Martin Gilens. 2014. "Testing Theories of American Politics: Elites, Interest Groups, and Average Citizens". *Perspectives on Politics* 12(3):564-581, September.

Pan Ké Shon Jean-Louis. 2011. "Residential segregation of immigrants in France: an over view." *Population and Societies*, April.

Passel Jeffrey S. and D'vera Cohn. 2016. "Number of babies born to unauthorized immigrants in U.S. continues to decline." *Pew Research Center*, October 26.

Patterson Orlando. 2015. "The Real Problem with America's Inner Cities." *New York Times*, May 9.

Peng Ito. 2016. "Japan and its immigration policies are growing old." *East Asia Forum*, June 7.

Penketh Anne. 2014. "France forced to drop 75% supertax after meagre returns". *The Guardian*, December 31.

Pennant, R. 2005. Diversity, Trust and Community Participation in England. Home Office Findings 253, *Research, Development and Statistics Directorate*.

Pennington Kenneth. 2017. "We Need Small Donors to Halt the March to Plutocracy". *The Guardian*, Last modified January 31.

Perlez Jane. 2016. "Tribunal Rejects Beijing's Claims in South China Sea". *New York Times*, July 12.

Perry Tony. 2015. "San Diego police body camera report: Fewer complaints, less use of force." *LA Times*. March 18.

Pew Center on the States. 2011. State of Recidivism the Revolving Door of America's Prisons. *Pew Center*, April 11. http://www.pewtrusts.org/~/media/legacy/uploadedfiles/wwwpewtrustsorg/reports/sentencing_and_corrections/staterecidivismrevolvingdooramericaprisons20pdf.pdf.

Pew Research Center. 2015. "Modern Immigration Wave Brings 59 Million to U.S., Driving Population Growth and Change Through 2065." September 28.

-------. 2015. "The American Middle Class Is Losing Ground". *Pew Research Center Social & Demographic Trends*, December 9.

--------. 2015. Modern Immigration Wave Brings 59 Million to U.S., Driving Population Growth and Change Through 2065. September 28.

--------. 2016. "America's Shrinking Middle Class: A Close Look at Changes Within Metropolitan Areas". *Pew Research Center Social & Demographic Trends*, May 11.

Phillips Tom, Oliver Holmes and Owen Bowcott. 2016. "Beijing Rejects Tribunal's Ruling in South China Sea Case". *The Guardian*, July 12.

Pidd Helen and Josh Halliday. 2015. "One City, Two Cultures: Bradford's Communities Lead Parallel Lives." June 15, *The Guardian*.

Piketty Thomas and Emmanuel Saez. 2013. "A Theory of Optimal Inheritance Taxation." *Econometrica*, Vol. 81, No. 5 (September 2013), 1851–1886.

Piketty Thomas and Saez Emmanuel. 2007. "How Progressive is the U.S. Federal Tax System? A Historical and International Perspective." *Journal of Economic* Perspectives—Volume 21, Number 1—Winter 2007—Pages 3–24.

Piketty Thomas, Emmanuel Saez and Stefanie Stantcheva. 2014. "Optimal Taxation of Top Labor Incomes: A Tale of Three Elasticities". *American Economic Journal: Economic Policy* 2014, 6(1): 230–271.

Piketty Thomas, Emmanuel Saez, Stefanie Stantcheva. 2011. "Taxing the 1%: Why the top tax rate could be over 80%." VOX CEPR's Policy Portal, December.

Pinto, Nick. 2015. "The Bail Trap." *New York Times*. August 13.

Pipes, Sally. 2014. Obamacare Increases Large Employers' Health Costs. *Forbes*. May 19.

Plotnick Robert D. 1993. "Changes in Poverty, Income Inequality, and the Standard of Living in the United States during the Reagan Year." *International Journal of Health Services*, Vol 23, Issue 2, pp. 347 – 358, April 1.

Pollack Harold A. 2015. "Saving SSDI." *The Atlantic*, August 31.

Poterba, J. M. 1997. 'Demographic Structure and the Political Economy of Public Education', *Journal of Policy Analysis and Management* 16, 48–66.

Preston Julia. 2016. "Deluged Immigration Courts., Where Cases Stall for Years, Begin to Buckle." *New York Times*, December 1.

Procon. "The Leading Source for Pros & Cons of Controversial Issues." http://socialsecurity.procon.org/. (Accessed November 24, 2016).

Pros Noodle. 2015. "More Than Half of College Faculty Are Adjuncts: Should You Care? *Forbes*, May 28.

Public Policy Institute of California. 2008. "Immigrants and Crime." June. http://www.ppic.org/content/pubs/jtf/JTF_ImmigrantsCrimeJTF.pdf.

Putnam Robert D. 2007. "E Pluribus Unum: Diversity and Community in the 21st Century: The 2006 Johan Skytte Prize Lecture. *Scandinavian Political Studies* [Internet]. June 2007; 30:137-174.

Quillian, Lincoln. 1995. "Prejudice as a Response to Perceived Group Threat: Population Composition and Anti-immigrant and Racial Prejudice in Europe", *American Sociological Review* 60, 586–611.

-------. 1996. 'Group Threat and Regional Change in Attitudes towards African Americans', *American Journal of Sociology* 102, 816–60.

Rabuy Bernadette and Daniel Kopf. 2016. "Detaining the Poor: How money bail perpetuates an endless cycle of poverty and jail time." May 10, *Prison Policy Initiative*. https://www.prisonpolicy.org/reports/incomejails.html.

Rampell Catherine. 2017. Trump's health insurance proposal would start a race to the bottom. *Washington Post*. March 2.

Ramsey Donovan X. 2015. "Are You Smarter Than a Cop?" *Gawker*, March 10.

Ranjana Natarajan. 2014. "Racial profiling has destroyed public trust in police. Cops are exploiting our weak laws against it." *Washington Post*, December 15.

Ready, Justin T. and Jacob T. N. Young. 2015. "The impact of on-officer video cameras on police–citizen contacts: findings from a controlled experiment in Mesa, AZ." *Journal of Experimental Criminology*, September, Volume 11, Issue 3, pp 445–458. DOI: 10.1007/s11292-015-9237-8.

Reaves Brian A. Local Police Departments, 2013: Personnel, Policies, and Practices. *Bureau of Justice Statistics*, May 2015, NCJ 248677. https://www.bjs.gov/content/pub/pdf/lpd13ppp.pdf.

Reno Virginia and David John. "Reforming Social Security Option: Reduce Benefits for Higher Earners." AARP Public Policy Institute. http://www.aarp.org/content/dam/aarp/research/public_policy_institute/econ_sec/2012/option-reduce-benefits-for-higher-earners-AARP-ppi-econ-sec.pdf. (Accessed May 18, 2017).

Repard Pauline. 2015. "Report: Less force, fewer complaints with SDPD cameras." *San Diego Union Tribune*, March 18.

Reznik Gayle L. Dave Shoffner, and David A. Weaver. 2006. "Coping with the Demographic Challenge: Fewer Children and Living Longer." Social Security Bulletin, Vol. 66, No. 4, 2005/2006. Available at SSRN: https://ssrn.com/abstract=994283

Richburg Keith B. 1993. "Somalia Battle Killed 12 Americans, Wounded 78". *Washington Post*, October 5.

Ridgely M. Susan, John Engberg, Michael D. Greenberg, Susan Turner, Christine DeMartini, Jacob W. Dembosky. 2007. "Justice, Treatment, and Cost: An Evaluation of the Fiscal Impact of Allegheny County Mental Health Court." *RAND Corporation*, http://www.rand.org/content/dam/rand/pubs/technical_reports/2007/RAND_TR439.pdf.

Rinke Andreas. 2015. "Germany's Merkel says U.N. Security Council must be reformed" *Reuters*, September 26.

Robert Carroll. 2009. "The Economic Cost of High Tax Rates". *Tax Foundation*, July 29.

Rodriguez Michelle Natividad and Beth Avery. 2017. "Ban the Box." National Employment Law Project (NELP). May 2017. http://www.nelp.org/content/uploads/Ban-the-Box-Fair-Chance-State-and-Local-Guide.pdf.

Rodriguez Michelle Natividad and Maurice Emsellem. 2011. 65 Million "Need Not Apply: The Case for Reforming Criminal Background Checks for Employment. The *National Employment Law Project March*. http://www.nelp.org/content/uploads/2015/03/65_Million_Need_Not_Apply.pdf.

Ross, Alice. 2017. "NHS hospitals to charge overseas patients for non-urgent care". *The Guardian*, February 5.

Roy, Avik. 2012. Will Buying Health Insurance Across State Lines Reduce Costs? *Forbes*. May 11.

Rubin Alissa. 2016. "Fighting for the 'Soul of France,' More Towns Ban a Bathing Suit: The Burkini." *New York Times*, August 17.

Rudman WJ, John S Eberhardt, William Pierce, and Susan Hart-Hester. 2009. Healthcare Fraud and Abuse. *Perspectives in Health Information Management* / AHIMA, American Health Information Management Association. 2009;6(Fall):1g.

Ryan Camille L. and Julie Siebens. 2012. "Educational Attainment in the United States: 2009." *United States Census Bureau*, February. https://www.census.gov/prod/2012pubs/p20-566.pdf.

Saez Emmanuel and Gabriel Zucman. 2016. "Wealth Inequality in The United States Since 1913: Evidence from Capitalized Income Tax Data." *Quarterly Journal of Economics* 2016; 131 (2): 519-578. https://doi.org/10.1093/qje/qjw004.

Saez Emmanuel. 2013. "Striking it Richer: The Evolution of Top Incomes in the United States." Updated with 2012 preliminary estimates. *UC Berkeley*, September 3.

Sandbrook Jeremy. 2016. "The 10 Most Corrupt World Leaders of Recent History". *Integritas360*, July 20.

Sanger-Katz, Margot. 2015. The Problem with G.O.P. Plans to Sell Health Insurance Across State Lines. August 31.

-------. 2016. Even Insured Can Face Crushing Medical Debt, Study Finds. *New York Times*, January 5.

Schaefer Brett and Janice Smith. 2006. "The U.S. Should Support Japan's Call to Revise the UN Scale of Assessments". *The Heritage Foundation*, March 18.

Schneider Greg and Renae Merle. 2004. "Reagan's Defense Buildup Bridged Military Eras; Huge Budgets Brought Life Back to Industry". *Washington Post*, June 9.

Schuman, Howard, Charlotte Steeh, Lawrence D. Bobo, Maria Krysan. 1997. *Racial attitudes in America: Trends and interpretations*. Cambridge, MA: Harvard University Press.

Schwartz Robert B., and Francis Keppel. 2011. "Pathways to Prosperity Project." *Harvard Graduate School of Education*, February.

Schwirtz Michael, Michael Winerip and Robert Gebeloff. 2016. The Scourge of Racial Bias in New York State's Prisons. *New York Times*, December 3.

Sears, David O. 1988. Symbolic racism. In P. Katz & D. Taylor (Eds.), *Eliminating racism: Profiles in controversy* (pp. 53–84). New York: Plenum Press

Seddon Max. 2016. "Russia withdraws from International Criminal Court". *Financial Times*, November 16.

Senate Committee Report. 2012. "For Profit Higher Education: The Failure to Safeguard the Federal Investment and Ensure Student Success." Prepared By The Committee On Health, Education, Labor, And Pensions United States Senate, Volume 1 of 4—Parts I–III, July 30. https://www.gpo.gov/fdsys/pkg/CPRT-112SPRT74931/pdf/CPRT-112SPRT74931.pdf.

Shatto, John D. and M. Kent Clemens. 2015. Projected Medicare Expenditures under an Illustrative Scenario with Alternative Payment Updates to Medicare Providers. *Centers for Medicare & Medicaid Services, Office of The Actuary.* July 22. https://www.cms.gov/Research-Statistics-Data-and-Systems/Statistics-Trends-and-Reports/ReportsTrustFunds/Downloads/2015TRAlternativeScenario.pdf.

Sieff Kevin. 2016. "Members of A U.N. Peacekeeping Force in The Central African Republic Allegedly Turned to Sexual Predation, Betraying Their Duty to Protect". *Washington Post,* February 27.

Sims Calvin. 1997. "In Fujimori's Peru, Economy Grows as a Democracy Is Left to Wither". *New York Times,* April 6.

Sito-Sucic Daria and Katana Gordana. 2015. "Drop Srebrenica Genocide Resolution, Bosnian Serb Leader Urges U.N". *Reuters,* June 29.

Sloan Allan. 2010. "Let's talk turkey about privatizing Social Security." *Washington Post,* November 25.

Social Security Administration. 2014. "The 2014 Annual Report of The Board of Trustees of The Federal Old-Age and Survivors Insurance and Federal Disability Insurance Trust Funds." July 28. https://www.ssa.gov/oact/tr/2014/tr2014.pdf.

--------. 2017. "Monthly Statistical Snapshot." Released May 2017, https://www.ssa.gov/policy/docs/quickfacts/stat_snapshot/.

Social Security Trustee Report. 2015. "The 2015 Annual Report of The Board of Trustees of The Federal Old-Age and Survivors Insurance and Federal Disability Insurance Trust Funds." July 22. https://www.ssa.gov/oact/tr/2015/tr2015.pdf.

Social Security. "A Summary of the 2016 Annual Reports." https://www.ssa.gov/oact/TRSUM/index.html. (Accessed October 22, 2016).

-------. "Contribution and Benefit Base." https://www.ssa.gov/oact/cola/cbb.html. (Accessed May 18, 2016).

--------. 2016. "Annual Statistical Report on the Social Security Disability Insurance Program, 2015." October. https://www.ssa.gov/policy/docs/statcomps/di_asr/2015/di_asr15.pdf.

Soroka, Stuart N., John Helliwell and Richard Johnston. 2007. 'Measuring and Modeling Interpersonal Trust', in Kay, F. M. & Johnston, R., eds, *Social Capital, Diversity and the Welfare State.* Vancouver: UBC Press.

Southern Poverty Law Center. "917 hate groups are currently operating in the US." https://www.splcenter.org/hate-map. (Accessed May 30, 2017).

Sparshott Jeffrey. 2015. "Congratulations, Class of 2015. You're the Most Indebted Ever (For Now)." *Wall Street Journal,* May 8.

Spencer Richard. 2015. "UN at 70: Five greatest successes and failures". *The Telegraph,* September 15.

Stacey Kiran and Farhan Bokhari. 2017. "Pakistan Vows Nuclear Retaliation If India Attacks". *Financial Times,* January 19.

Staff Crimesider. 2017. "Officer Charged with Shooting Autistic Man's Unarmed Caregiver." *CBS News,* April 12.

State of New Jersey. 2016. "Attorney General Issues Directive to Guide Prosecutors and Police in Implementing Historic Bail Reform That Will Keep Dan-

gerous Criminals in Jail and Eliminate Unfair Monetary-Based Bail System."
October 13. http://www.nj.gov/oag/newsreleases16/pr20161013b.html.

Steuerle Eugene and Caleb Quakenbush. 2012 "Social Security and Medicare
Taxes and Benefits over a Lifetime." 2012 Update. *Urban Institute.*

--------. 2013. "Social Security and Medicare Taxes and Benefits over a Lifetime." 2013 Update. *Urban Institute*, November.

-------- 2015 "Social Security and Medicare Taxes and Benefits over a Lifetime." 2015 Update. *Urban Institute.*

Steuerle Eugene. "Column: Recent Social Security Reform Doesn't Fix Unfair
Spousal Benefits." PBS, November 5, 2015.

Stewart Catrina. 2011. "Russia accuses NATO of 'expanding' UN Libya resolution". *The Independent*, July 4.

Stiglitz Joseph E. 2014. "Reforming Taxation to Promote Growth and Equity".
Roosevelt Institute, May 28.

Stone Christopher, Todd Foglesong and Christine M. Cole. 2009. "Policing Los
Angeles Under a Consent Decree: The Dynamics of Change at the LAPD."
May, *Program in Criminal Justice Policy and Management, Harvard Kennedy
School.* http://assets.lapdonline.org/assets/pdf/Harvard-
LAPD%20Study.pdf.

Stouffer Samuel A. 1949. *The American soldier.* December 1, M A/A H Publishing.

Student loan Hero. 2017. A Look at the Shocking Student Loan Debt Statistics
for 2017. Last updated, May 17.

Study. "Requirements to Be a Corrections Officer."
http://study.com/requirements_to_be_a_corrections_officer.html. (Accessed May 17, 2017).

Sun Ivan Y., Brian K. Payne. 2004. Racial Differences in Resolving Conflicts: A
Comparison between Black and White Police Officers. *Crime & Delinquency*,
Vol 50, Issue 4, pp. 516 – 541. October 1.

Syrios Andrew. 2015. "The Good Ol' Days: When Tax Rates Were 90 Percent".
Mises Institute, November 24.

Tami Luhby. 2013. "Social Security: Many pay more in taxes than they'll get
back." *CNN*, April 14.

Taub Amanda. 2016. "A lesson From Brexit: On immigration feeling Trump
Facts." *New York Times*, June 26.

The Bronx Freedom Fund. "Poverty Is Not a Crime, But Every Day Thousands
Of New Yorkers Await Trial In City Jails Because They Cannot Afford Bail,
Which Is Often As Low As $250." http://www.thebronxfreedomfund.org/.

The Congressional Joint Economic Committee. 2016. "2015 Year in Review:
Kansas". January.
https://www.jec.senate.gov/public/_cache/files/428867de-a26f-49ef-9cbf-
2530f28c88c7/kansas.pdf.

The Economist. 2012. "Higher education: Not what it used to be." *The Economist, Print Edition, United States.* December 1.

-------. 2013. "The origins of the financial crisis. Crash Course." September 7.

-------. 2014. "How sustainable is Malaysian healthcare? April 11.

------- 2015. "Ethnic minorities in France: An edgy inquiry." April 4. http://www.economist.com/news/europe/21647638-taboo-studying-immigrant-families-performance-fraying-edgy-inquiry.

The Pew Charitable Trusts. One in 31 U.S. Adults are Behind Bars, on Parole or Probation. http://www.pewtrusts.org/en/about/news-room/press-releases/0001/01/01/one-in-31-us-adults-are-behind-bars-on-parole-or-probation.

The Rialto Police Department. 2013. "The Rialto Police Department's Body-Worn Video Camera Experiment: Operation Candid Camera." April 29, https://ccjs.umd.edu/sites/ccjs.umd.edu/files/Wearable_Cameras_Capitol_Hill_Final_Presentation_Jerry_Lee_Symposium_2013.pdf.

The Sentencing Project. "Americans with Criminal Record." http://www.sentencingproject.org/wp-content/uploads/2015/11/Americans-with-Criminal-Records-Poverty-and-Opportunity-Profile.pdf. (Accessed May 14, 2017).

-------. 2014. Race and Punishment: Racial Perceptions of Crime and Support for Punitive Policies. The Sentencing Project. http://www.sentencingproject.org/wp-content/uploads/2015/11/Race-and-Punishment.pdf.

Thorpe, Kenneth E. 2016. "An Analysis of Senator Sanders Single Payer Plan." Emory University. January 27. https://www.healthcare-now.org/296831690-Kenneth-Thorpe-s-analysis-of-Bernie-Sanders-s-single-payer-proposal.pdf.

Torsoli Albertina. 2013. "France's Health-Care System Is Going Broke." *Bloomberg.* January 3.

Totten Jordan. 2014. "BRICS New Development Bank Threatens Hegemony of U.S. Dollar". *Forbes*, December 22.

Treisman Daniel. 2016. "Why Putin Took Crimea". *Foreign Affairs,* May/June Issue.

Turner Tracy M. and Brandon Blagg. 2017. The Short-term Effects of the Kansas Income Tax Cuts on Employment Growth. *Public Finance Review,* doi. 10.1177/1091142117699274.

Tuttle, Brad. 2016. "8 States Where Obamacare Rates Are Rising by at Least 30%." Times, Oct 18.

U.K. Department of Business Innovation and Skills. 2015. "Freezing the Student Loan Repayment Threshold: Equality Analysis" November. http://dera.ioe.ac.uk/23629/8/bis-15-635-freezing-student-loan-repayment-threshold-equality-analysis.pdf.

U.S. Chamber of Commerce Report. Available at http://www.usdoj.gov/usao/vaw/health_care_fraud/index.html

U.S. Department of Homeland Security. "Fiscal Year 2016 Entry/Exit Overstay Report." https://www.dhs.gov/sites/default/files/publications/Entry%20and%20Exit%20Overstay%20Report%2C%20Fiscal%20Year%202016.pdf. (Accessed May 23, 2017).

--------. 2016. "Entry/Exit Overstay Report: Fiscal Year 2015." January 19. https://www.dhs.gov/sites/default/files/publications/FY%2015%20DHS%20Entry%20and%20Exit%20Overstay%20Report.pdf.

--------. 2016. "Fiscal Year 2015 Entry/Exit Overstay Report." January 19, 2016.
   https://www.dhs.gov/sites/default/files/publications/FY%2015%20DHS%2
   0Entry%20and%20Exit%20Overstay%20Report.pdf.

U.S. Department of State. "The United States and the Founding of the United
   Nations, August 1941 - October 1945". *U.S. Department of State, Office of the
   Historian, Bureau of Public Affairs*. https://2001-
   2009.state.gov/r/pa/ho/pubs/fs/55407.htm (Accessed May 30, 2017).

Udende Patrick and Salau A.A. 2012. "National Youth Service Corps Scheme
   and the Quest for National Unity and Development: A Public Relations Perspective". University of Ilorin, Ilorin, Nigeria, Department of Mass Communication, January.

United Nations. "Kosovo: The Untold Story of a Diplomatic Breakthrough".
   http://www.un.org/en/events/tenstories/08/kosovo.shtml. (Accessed May
   30, 2017).

-------. "Sierra Leone: A success story in peacekeeping".
   http://www.un.org/en/peacekeeping/publications/yir/2005/PDFs/major_p
   k_operations.pdf. (Accessed May 30, 2017).

-------. "The United Nations in Burundi: Peacekeeping Mission Completes its
   Mandate". December 31, 2006.
   http://www.un.org/en/peacekeeping/missions/past/onub/photos.pdf. (Accessed May 30, 2017).

-------. 1999. "Reports of The Independent Inquiry into The Actions of The
   United Nations During The 1994 Genocide in Rwanda." December 15.
   http://www.securitycouncilreport.org/atf/cf/%7B65BFCF9B-6D27-4E9C-
   8CD3-CF6E4FF96FF9%7D/POC%20S19991257.pdf.

-------. 2016. "Syrian Tragedy 'Shames Us All', Secretary-General Tells Security
   Council, saying that Failure to End Conflict Should Haunt Entire Membership". *U.N. Security Council 7774th Meeting*, September 21.

--------. "Charter of the United Nations". http://www.un.org/en/charter-
   united-nations/. (Accessed May 30, 2017).

United States Senate. "2015 Medicare/Social Security Trustees' Report Analysis." Prepared by Senate Republican Finance Committee Staff. (Accessed
   May 15, 2017).

Urbina Ian and Sean D. Hamill. 2009. "Judge Pleads Guilty in Scheme to Jail
   Youths for Profit." *New York Times*, February 12.

US Department of Education. 2016. 12,000 Incarcerated Students to Enroll in
   Postsecondary Educational and Training Programs Through Education Department's New Second Chance Pell Pilot Program." June 24.

Vaughn Michael G, Christopher P. Salas-Wright, Matt DeLisi, and Brandy R.
   Maynard. 2014. "The immigrant paradox: immigrants are less antisocial
   than native-born Americans." *Social Psychiatry and Psychiatric Epidemiology*. 2014;49(7):1129-1137. doi:10.1007/s00127-013-0799-3.

Vigdor, J. L. 2004. 'Community Composition and Collective Action: Analyzing
   Initial Mail Response to the 2000 Census', *Review of Economics and Statistics*
   86, 303–12

VOA. "New York Police Reportedly Spy on American Muslims. 2011. *VOA*, September 06.

-------- 2009. "Nigerian Court Battle Tests Power of 'Godfathers- 2004-01-16". *VOA*, October 30.

-------- 2017. "UN Faces Unprecedented Number of Challenges Amid Proposed US Budget Cut". *VOA*, March 20.

von Mises Ludwig. 1962. "*The Ultimate Foundation of Economic Science*. Liberty Fund; 2nd edition, June 2006.

Wadhwa Vivek, AnnaLee Saxenian and Daniel Siciliano F. 2012. "America's New Immigrant Entrepreneurs: Then and Now." *Kauffman Foundation*, October.

Wadsworth Jonathan, Swati Dhingra, Gianmarco Ottaviano and John Van Reenen. "Brexit and the Impact of Immigration on the UK." *Center for Economic Performance. The London School of Economics and Political Science.* http://cep.lse.ac.uk/pubs/download/brexit05.pdf. (Accessed May 21, 2017).

Walshe Sadhbh. 2013. "America's Bail System: One Law for The Rich, Another for Poor." *The Guardian*, February14.

Wan Norhasniah Wan Husin. 2011."Nation-Building And 1malaysia Concept: Ethnic Relations Challenges in The Educational Field." *International Journal of Humanities and Social Science*. Vol. 1 No. 9, Special Issue – July.

Webber Tammy and Emily Swanson. 2016. "Americans happy at home, upset with federal government". AP-GFK, April.

Webber, Sheila S. & Lisa M. Donahue. 2001. 'Impact of Highly and Less Job-related Diversity on Work Group Cohesion and Performance: A Meta-analysis', *Journal of Management* 27(2), 141– 62. DOI: 10.1177/014920630102700202.

Weisburd David, Rosann Greenspan, Edwin E. Hamilton, Hubert Williams, and Kellie A. Bryant. 2000. "Police Attitudes Toward Abuse of Authority: Findings from a National Study." *US Department of Justice*. May, https://www.ncjrs.gov/pdffiles1/nij/181312.pdf.

Wesley Lowery. 2016. "Aren't more white people than black people killed by police? Yes, but no. *Washington Post*, July 11.

White Gillian B. 2015. "Education Gaps Don't Fully Explain Why Black Unemployment Is So High." *The Atlantic*, December 21.

Wike Richard. 2014. "In Europe, Sentiment Against Immigrants, Minorities Runs High." *Pew Research Center*, May 14.

Wilkinson M. James and Christopher D. O'Sullivan. 2004. "The Security Council and Iraq". *University of North Carolina*, February.

Williams Timothy. 2015. Chicago Police Rarely Punishes Officers for Complaints, Data Shows. New York Times, November 18.

Williams, Sean. 2016. Obamacare Premiums May Rise By 10% In 2017—Here's Why. *Newsweek*. August 14.

Wilson Valerie. 2015. "Black Unemployment Is Significantly Higher Than White Unemployment Regardless of Educational Attainment." *Economic Policy Institute*. December 17.

Winerip Michael and Michael Schwirtz. 2015. An Inmate dies and no one is punished." *New York Times*. December 3.

Winerip Michael, Michael Schwirtz, and Robert Gebeloff. 2016. For Blacks Facing Parole in New York State, Signs of a Broken System. New York Times, December 4.

Winship Scott. 2015. "How to Fix Disability Insurance." *National Review*, Spring.

Withnall Adam. 2016. "The Brutal Central African Dictator Whose Playboy Son Faces French Corruption Trial". *The Independent*, September 12.

Witte Griff. 2015. "In a kosher grocery store in Paris, terror takes a deadly toll." *Washington Post*, January 9.

-------. 2015. "What can US trigger-happy cops learn from Britain's gunless police? *The independent*, June12.

Wong Sue-Lin. 2016. "China Launches New AIIB Development Bank as Power Balance Shifts". *Reuters*, January 17.

Worth Robert F. 2013. "Saudi Arabia Rejects U.N. Security Council Seat in Protest Move". *New York Times*, October 18.

Zere Abraham T. 2017. "Eritrea is a prison state – no wonder so many are desperate to escape". *The Guardian*, last modified March 9.

Zezima Katie and Adam Goldman. 2016. "Ted Cruz calls for law enforcement to 'patrol and secure' Muslim neighborhoods." *Washington Post*, March 22.

Zidar Owen M. 2013. "Tax Cuts for Whom? Heterogeneous Effects of Income Tax Changes on Growth & Employment". *University of Chicago - Booth School of Business*, February.

Zong Jie and Jeanne Batalova. 2017. "Frequently Requested Statistics on Immigrants and Immigration in the United States." *Migration Policy Institute*, March 8.

Zorn Eric. 2016. "Kansas' Experiment in Conservative Economics Still A Bust". *Chicago Tribune*, May 17.

Zucman Gabriel. 2013. "The Missing Wealth of Nations: Are Europe and the U.S. net Debtors or net Creditors? *Quarterly Journal of Economics* 2013, 128:1321–1364.

------2014. "Taxing across Borders: Tracking Personal Wealth and Corporate Profits". *Journal of Economic Perspectives*—Volume 28, Number 4—2014—Pages 121–148.

Index